SAILING SEVEN SEAS

For Katrina and Nigel Taylor — splice the mainbrace

SAILING SEVEN SEAS

A History of the Canadian Pacific Line

PETER PIGOTT

DUNDURN PRESS

TORONTO

Editor: Allison Hirst
Design: Courtney Horner
Printer: Transcontinental

Library and Archives Canada Cataloguing in Publication

Pigott, Peter
    Sailing seven seas : a history of the Canadian
Pacific Line / by Peter Pigott.

Includes bibliographical references and index.
Issued also in an electronic format.
ISBN 1-55488-765-8.--ISBN 978-1-55488-765-1

    1. Canadian Pacific Steamships--History.
2. Shipping--Canada--History. 3. Ocean
liners--Canada--History. I. Title.

HE945.C3P54 2010   387.50971   C2010-902672-1

1   2   3   4   5   14   13   12   11   10

  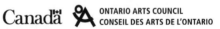

We acknowledge the support of the **Canada Council for the Arts** and the **Ontario Arts Council** for our publishing program. We also acknowledge the financial support of the **Government of Canada** through the **Canada Book Fund** and **Livres Canada Books**, and the **Government of Ontario** through the **Ontario Book Publishers Tax Credit program**, and the **Ontario Media Development Corporation**.

Care has been taken to trace the ownership of copyright material used in this book. The author and the publisher welcome any information enabling them to rectify any references or credits in subsequent editions.

J. Kirk Howard, President

Printed and bound in Canada.
www.dundurn.com

Dundurn Press	Gazelle Book Services Limited	Dundurn Press
3 Church Street, Suite 500	White Cross Mills	2250 Military Road
Toronto, Ontario, Canada	High Town, Lancaster, England	Tonawanda, NY
M5E 1M2	LA1 4XS	U.S.A. 14150

CONTENTS

PREFACE

I am no seaman, and this will come as no surprise to those who know me. Having translated my passion for aircraft into more than a dozen books, it was with some amazement on my part that I became captivated by the story of a shipping line. I grew up enjoying Gilbert and Sullivan's *HMS Pinafore* and the authors C.S. Forester and Nicholas Monsarrat — subsequently discovering that Monsarrat had written here in Ottawa while working for the British Information Office. That was the sum total of all I knew about the sea, having been born too late to take passage on the great ships — the whistles on a foggy day, deck chairs, shipboard romances, the clack of shuffleboard, and dressing for dinner. I suppose, like Dr. Johnson, I held that going to sea was like going to prison — with the chance of being drowned. So how I came about writing *Sailing Seven Seas* deserves some explanation.

It had been a particularly horrendous flight on an airline which shall be unnamed. Crammed into a metal tube, confined for hours to a seat that would not recline, my face three inches from the person ahead, I subsisted for what seemed an interminable length of time on recycled air and stale pretzels, the last flung at me by a single harried, overworked flight attendant. In my self-pity, I reflected then that a century before, ships' passengers must have certainly been better off — when, as a travel slogan said, "getting there was half the fun." In the name of speed and progress, the human race had sacrificed gracious travel and civility. We had consigned to the same dust heap of history (and almost at the same time), both railroads and the great ships.

As a Canadian, I was drawn to explore our own experiences with transoceanic shipping. The result is this book, which attempts to sketch what occurred under the red-and-white-checkered flag — the distinctive marker of Canadian Pacific's ships — between 1883 and 2005. As I did with Canadian Pacific's airline, I chose to write about the company's men, women, and machines. There are no balance sheets, menus, or lists of shipboard entertainment. *Sailing Seven Seas* is about people — stewardesses and captains — and the ships they knew — the "Princesses," "Empresses," and "Beavers." Perhaps some who have served on CP ships will feel that there is not enough information about his or her favourite Empress or VLCC (Very Large Crude Carriers). I can only say that I, too, wish there were more and confess that (for an aviation author) there is much that I do not know.

It is evident that, for an industry that has remade itself so dramatically, CP has made every attempt to forget its past and has spared few resources to preserving its history. I discovered that little archival evidence existed, either in Canada or Britain, on the Canadian Pacific shipping line and have thus based this book on well-known standard works. Readers with a nautical interest are warned that they will find little here that is new. Other authors have described the company from the passenger's point of view — the cruise itineraries, the 17 kinds of cold buffet, the choice of dance bands et cetera, but that will not be the case here.

As the purely commercial aspects would make no sense in isolation, I have set the narrative against the general background of Anglo-Canadian history. To write a history of Canadian Pacific's ships on the scale of George Musk's would require the work and passion of a lifetime and this book makes no pretensions to be anything of the kind.

To compensate for the dearth of archival material available, I decided to go straight to the source. Through the help of Andrew Linington, the editor of the NUMAST (National Union of Marine, Aviation and Shipping Transport Officers) *Telegraph*, I was able to publicize the need for first-hand accounts, and former captains, shore staff, stewardesses, and pursers were overwhelmingly co-operative. Two amongst the many who wrote in must especially be thanked. Geoffrey Wright, employed by CP Ships from 1970–1984, found me the prolific Captain Peter John Roberts, who was well-known in CP as an aviator, as well. There is no doubt in my mind that he could have written this book without my help. Pat Adair joined his first CP vessel as a cadet in May 1960 and served as a chief officer until being made redundant in May 1986. He sent me his private collection of photographs and through the years his encouragement with this work was indispensable.

It is a pleasure to acknowledge the help of so many others who responded to the ad: Captain Brian Scott of Whangarie, New Zealand; George Monk, who worked for the Marconi Company on the *Beaverbrae* during the war; John Dunn, master of the *Beaverpine*, who won the gold cane at Montreal in 1969–70; Captain Geoff Wright, Trinity House Deep Sea Pilot No. 3183; Captain J.H. Arton; Mike Gray of Victoria, British Columbia, who just missed the Empress days but served on the *T.G. Shaughnessy*, *N.R. Crump*, and *CP Trader*; John MacPhail; Terry Foskett, who was a purser on all three Empresses from 1961 to 1969; nursing sister Margaret Cuming (née Knox); and Derek Jones, who served on all post-war Empresses. For many former CP employees, this is family history, as they either married stewardesses or, like retired chief engineer Edmond Owen-Humphreys, whose parents had met while working on the *Montrose II* in the 1920s, were born to the Canadian Pacific.

Thanks also to Jo-Anne Colby at the Canadian Pacific Railway Archives at Windsor Station, who allowed me to peruse the collections. All information on the *Empress of Asia* has been reproduced through the kind permission of the *Empress of Asia* Research Group (EARG). To remedy my ignorance with all things nautical, and CP Ships in particular, the company's head of communications, Elizabeth Canna, arranged a journey on the MV *Canmar Pride*, from Montreal to Antwerp. Its master was the company's longest-serving captain, the now retired John Simcox. Patient with my ignorance, he was courteous, encouraging, and took great pride in demonstrating how to keep the crockery from falling off the table during a storm by pouring a jug of water over the tablecloth. He also arranged lifeboat drills to give me the authentic flavour of life at sea. I am grateful, too, to Chief Officer Harsh Kumar Johari, Third Officer Bopanna Mandana, and Chief Engineer Pradeep Kumar Pillai of the *Canmar Pride*'s crew. Although employed by Anglo-Eastern Ship Management, they represent the best traditions of Canadian Pacific seamen.

Years ago, when I was posted to the Canadian Mission to the United Nations, I trekked across Manhattan to the fabled piers on the west side of the island where ocean liners had once routinely docked, and where, in the winter of 1942, between piers 88 and 90, the greatest of them all, the *Normandie*, had burned and capsized. Those sheds that were not boarded up were being used as garages for the city buses and the scene was of peeling paint, Styrofoam cups, and derelicts. Not even the most rabid steamship enthusiast could have conjured up the ghosts of the great liners. I imagine that it is a scene played out in Southampton, Rotterdam, and Cherbourg. For the great ships live on now only in memorabilia — in faded tickets, old postcards, excursion sheets, stateroom baggage stubs, and family photo albums, and in the imaginations of those like myself who never knew them. As with the *Titanic* and *Lusitania*, a few have been immortalized in books and movies, for all the wrong reasons. The others have passed into history. Although he was writing about the sailing ships that they had replaced, the poet John Masefield had it right:

> These splendid ships, each with her grace, her glory,
> Her memory of old song or comrade's story,
> Still in my mind the image of life's need,
> Beauty in hardest action, beauty indeed …
> They are my country's line, her great art done …
> They mark our passage as a race of men,
> Earth will not see such ships as those again.
>
> — excerpt from "Ships"

Introduction

It is sometimes forgotten that Samuel Cunard, who began transatlantic travel by steam, was born in Halifax, Nova Scotia. The son of a Loyalist who wanted his mail delivered in less than the six weeks that it took for sailing ships to cross from Britain, Cunard saw steam's potential early. So did other Canadians, and the second steamship to cross the Atlantic was Canadian-made. Built at Trois Rivières, Quebec, in 1831, the *Royal William* was towed to Montreal for the installation of its machinery and steamed out of port destined for London on August 5, 1833, arriving there on September 16. The 25-day voyage was hardly an improvement over sailing ships — the salt had to be cleaned out of its copper boilers every four days — but because the *Royal William* was the first steamship to carry passengers, it could be said that all transatlantic commercial non-sailing ships have evolved from it.

The cholera epidemic in Montreal later that year killed off any immediate commerce, and the Canadian shipowners were quick to get rid of the steamship in Europe and return to sail. But in 1840, Cunard, one of the owners of the *Royal William*, began the British and North American Steam Packet Company (fortunately shortened to Cunard) with his own steamship, *Britannia*, and obtained a subsidized mail contract from the British government. Two years later, when Charles Dickens came to Canada on a book tour, he wrote that his cabin onboard the *Britannia* was "a preposterous box" and that the ship's dining room reminded him of a "hearse with windows." But the steamship did cut the crossing time to two weeks, and although Cunard himself never condoned it, the shattering of transatlantic speed records would be a consistent theme for the next hundred years.

At the mercy of British mail subsidies, Cunard left Canada for the more lucrative Boston/New York run. And who could blame him? With the St. Lawrence ice-bound for much of the winter and known for sudden, dangerous fog, and the port of Montreal besieged by huge ice ramparts, the Canadian shipping "season" was limited to between the months of April and December. And until the St. Lawrence & Atlantic Railroad connected it with the nearest ice-free port, located in Portland, Maine, the financial capital of British North America was effectively cut off from Europe each winter.

In 1840, to stimulate transatlantic business, the port commissioners took to awarding a trophy to the captain of the first ocean-going vessel to reach their city in the new year. A top hat was given as the first prize, and, as tastes changed, it was replaced in 1880 by the gold-headed cane that is still awarded today. Through the years the cane has varied in shape according to the fashion. Sometimes straight and sometimes curved, several were ordered by the commissioners to give the captain a choice. Although Canadian Coast Guard icebreakers have kept the channel clear of ice since 1965 and the port of Montreal is open for business throughout the year, the award ceremony is still held for the first ship to "pass the harbour clock." Today, a hardwood cane, 31 inches in length and finished in dark brown varnish, is presented. The 14-carat-gold head is crowned with a relief Canadian coat of arms coloured with inlaid enamel.

The more prestigious, faster transatlantic ships, however, would always go to the United States, where the potential for profit was higher. This intensified the rivalry between American and Canadian ports, especially New York and Montreal. In 1862, the average length of passage by steamers to cover the 2,662 nautical miles between Halifax and Liverpool was 13 days. As slow as it seems today, it was a definite improvement on sailing vessels, which for the same runs took 36 days from Britain and 50 days from some European ports. By 1881, the average Atlantic crossing to Halifax had been shortened to nine days — two more than to an American port. The perils involved in racing across the Atlantic at full steam were well known, with the treacherous icefields and, before the use of technology such as radar, the danger of collision with rocks and other ships in the fog.

There were added disadvantages to shipping to Canada. Montreal was prone to cholera epidemics. In 1832, 4,000 out of the city's population of 36,000 died, and there were outbreaks again in 1834, 1849, 1853, and 1854, with immigrants — rightly or wrongly — blamed for the contagion. Ships were ordered to lie off St. Helen's Island in quarantine, and sheds were later built at Point St. Charles to accommodate the sick and dying. Opening in 1785, Saint John, New Brunswick, was the oldest quarantine station in North America, but from 1832 to 1937 the station at Grosse Île in the St. Lawrence became the frontline defence for the entry into Canada of European immigrants via the Port of Quebec.

Angel Island (San Francisco), Manly (Sydney, Australia), Staten Island Quarantine Station (New York), and Partridge Island, Albert Head, and William Head in British Columbia, like Grosse Île, have seen probably the saddest events in human history, as shiploads of immigrants overcame incredible odds to get to the land of their dreams, only to die within sight of it. Desperate for manpower, colonial governments would zealously guard against the scourges of ship fever (typhus), smallpox, and cholera by imposing 40 days of isolation at one of the stations.

Competing with the American ports also meant faster trips, which used more coal, leaving less room for cargo — a situation that was hardly competitive.

For these reasons, shipping companies like the Inman Line, which took over the British mail contract in 1867, were content to go only as far as Halifax, the mail for the interior of Canada being sent on via the railway. But all of this was balanced by the happy situation that the Dominion of Canada was geographically closer to Europe than the United States, cutting 400 miles off a voyage — an advantage that Canadian Pacific capitalized on with slogans such as "Only Three to Four Days of Open Sea" and "Thirty-nine percent less ocean" saying it all. The solution was to sail between Liverpool and Quebec City when the St. Lawrence was open for navigation in the summer, or up to Saint John, New Brunswick, when it was not.

To break the country out of its isolation, the Canadian government initially negotiated a seven-year contract with the British firm of McKean, McLarty & Lamont for monthly steamship service between Liverpool and Montreal, and on May 13, 1853, their *Genova* arrived in Montreal, making history as the first regular transatlantic steamship to use the port. But when they could not sustain the service, the following year Ottawa was approached by local shipowners, brothers Hugh and Andrew Allan, and in 1855 the Atlantic mail contract was awarded to their Montreal Ocean Steamship Company, better known as the Allan Line. With the Allan Line a precursor to the Canadian Pacific, the histories of both companies are inextricably linked.

The Allan family's connection with Canada began on June 5, 1819, when the 169-ton brigantine *Jean* sailed from Greenock, Scotland, for Quebec City, with Captain Sandy Allan as master. He had made his money transporting British troops to the Peninsula War but this was his first venture across the Atlantic. With few maps or lighthouses, navigation into the Gulf of St. Lawrence and the approaches to Quebec had little improved since James Cook guided General Wolfe's fleet up it 60 years before, but Allan saw the potential in discharging immigrants in Canada and returning with lumber and cattle. In 1822, he began a regular service from the Clyde to the St. Lawrence with full-rigged ships, the first christened *Canada*. His son Hugh had learnt to read and write — so legend had it — while sweeping out the schoolroom back in Ayrshire, Scotland. In 1826 he immigrated to Canada, soon becoming a partner in a Montreal shipping company, Millar, Edmonstone & Allan.

With the support of his brothers, Hugh Allan had parlayed his business acumen into financing the Montreal Ocean Steam Ship Company, better known as the Allan Line, by 1853. While his competitors' paddle-wheel steamers floundered on the ice-jammed St. Lawrence, Allan invested in the earliest single-screw steamships, and within a year his 1,750-ton *Canadian* dramatically reduced the crossing time to 12 days. Then, as his father had done, he earned the gratitude of the British government by using his "immigrant tubs," as they were called, to carry troops, this time from Britain to the Crimea. Rewarded with the imperial mail contract in 1855 for fortnightly sailings between Liverpool and Montreal from April to October, and monthly sailings between Liverpool and Portland, Maine, in the winter, Allan was well-situated to build a transcontinental railway across Canada, for he understood that whoever did so would monopolize the sea routes on both coasts. By 1869, his ships were already bringing British passengers bound for the Far East over to Montreal, where they connected via Chicago with the railroad for San Francisco.

Sir John A. Macdonald, the country's first prime minister, made funds available to steamship companies and their local European agents to induce immigrants to take passage to Canada — sometimes above the protests of foreign governments. He enticed the European landless with what Canada had in plenty — land! Through the Dominion Land Act of 1872, Macdonald promised up to 160 acres without charge to any immigrant who would build a homestead in the Canadian West. Even before the Canadian government posted its first immigration officers to Europe with the slogan that Canada wanted "men of good muscle who were willing to hustle," authorizing them to grant assisted ocean passages to all who took advantage of the act, Allan's agents were already distributing pamphlets titled "Practical Hints and Directions to Intending Emigrants" in many overcrowded British cities.

For the Allan Line and their contemporaries, European passenger agents ranged from bank managers, local clergy, orphanage managers, and the registrars of births, marriages, and deaths. Convincing the recently bereaved and/or dispossessed of the advantages of taking a ship to Canada, where land was free, must have served as a safety valve for social problems.

Had the "Pacific Scandal" not disgraced its founder, it would have been the Allan Line rather than the Canadian Pacific that would have gone down in history as having financed the transcontinental railway, and there might never have been a Canadian Pacific Railway — or shipping line. When, in 1871, on the promise that it would be joined to the rest of Canada by rail, British Columbia acceded into Confederation, railway promoters descended on an increasingly desperate government in Ottawa, waving schemes and courting politicians. It was understood that the contract to build the railway would be given to whoever had the strongest political representation in Ottawa. A general election was called in 1872 just as Allan had his Canadian Pacific Railway Company incorporated, ready to fund Macdonald's return to power. He and his backers poured more than $350,000 into the re-election campaigns of both Macdonald in Ontario and George-Étienne Cartier, who could bring in votes from Quebec.

At a time in Canadian history when politics were highly partisan, politicians poorly paid, and voters susceptible to bribes, this was not untoward. But despite the inducements expended, Cartier lost and Macdonald was very narrowly re-elected. As a result, when Parliament convened in April 1873, the Opposition called for a Royal Commission to investigate the extent of Allan's political contributions, and the Pacific Scandal was born. Vilified by the partisan press and history, and betrayed by his lawyer, John Abbott, who switched to advising the CPR and succeeding Macdonald as Canada's next prime minister, Allan retired from any further involvement in politics and concentrated on expanding his company's routes to South America. He remained friendly with Macdonald (who had done little to save him), and died on December 9, 1882, in Edinburgh.

The Fathers of Confederation were keenly aware that only a railway between Montreal and Vancouver could make possible the union of British North America. In the aftermath of the Pacific Scandal, on February 16, 1881, through an Act of Parliament, the Canadian Pacific Railway was given by the government of Canada $25 million, 25 million acres of land, and 710 miles of existing rail track. In return, it was to build and operate a railway from Montreal to the Pacific Coast and thus bring the province of British Columbia into Confederation. The board of the new company met the next day and elected George Stephen as its first president. His cousin, Donald Smith (like Allan and Macdonald, a Scottish immigrant), along with American engineer William Cornelius Van Horne, also sat on the board. Scrapping around for investment would dog the lives of all the directors, with Stephen and Smith often pledging their homes as collateral and meeting operating expenses from their personal bank accounts. But as railroad financiers, they had a knack for turning bankrupt railways around to sell at a profit.

With the launch of its first *Empress* in 1890, the CPR was a late entrant to oceanic shipping. Cunard was already half a century old, Hamburg-Amerikanische Packetfahrt-Actien-Gesellschaft (Hapag) and Norddeutscher Lloyd (NDL) had been founded in 1847 and 1857 respectively, Compagnie Generale Transatlantique in 1864, and White Star in 1871. The CP line would go through several incarnations, beginning in 1883 with the Canadian Pacific Railway Steamship Services, created to assist the Canadian Pacific Railway to move its passengers onward over water, whether it be on the Great Lakes or the Pacific Ocean. With its ships now plying the Atlantic, by 1915 the company was renamed the Canadian Pacific Ocean Services. When its management moved to London in 1921, it was as Canadian Pacific Steamships, a name it retained until 1969 when it became CP Ships.

But the St. Lawrence was off the beaten track, and the ships that came to Halifax, Quebec, and Montreal carried few of the rich and glamorous passengers that graced the Cunard and White Star lines. But unlike the Canadian Pacific, neither of these legendary companies could have flourished without massive infusions of government money. By the late 19th century, no longer just a means of transport, ocean liners had evolved into national status symbols and flag-bearers, second only for a country to acquiring a colonial empire.

Britannic, *Île de France*, and *Vaterland* — their very names said it all. The building of larger, more luxurious and faster ships also kept whole regions in Scotland, Germany, and France employed, with the winning of the Blue Riband, presented to the ship crossing the Atlantic in regular service with the record highest speed, a matter of national honour.

The Canadian Pacific was never in this fortunate position, but the company's hold on transport and important resources in the country gave it other advantages. Its ships brought European immigrants to a Canadian port, where CPR trains transported them to the Prairies. There they were sold CPR land upon which they grew wheat that the CPR had developed — which was then harvested and exported to Europe on CPR trains and ships. If its directors saw the company as the catalyst to Confederation, in reality it was a well-oiled, profit-making machine, and to this day there are many Canadians who feel that the Canadian Pacific stole the country. Of those immigrants, a CPR director was supposed to have said, "Take their money while they still have it."

The Hudson's Bay Company — so ancient that in parts of Canada its initials are known as "Here Before Christ" — may have been equally unscrupulous as to how it gouged its wealth out of the First Nations, but somehow it has attained canonization and become enshrined into our national mythology. Not so the CPR. There is the historic anti-CPR joke: a Prairie farmer comes home one afternoon to find that a hailstorm has destroyed his crop, the farmhouse has been struck by lightning, and his wife has run off with the hired hand. He raises his eyes to heaven, shakes his fist angrily, and yells, "Goddamn the CPR!"

No one likes a landlord, and as the country's biggest, the CPR was viewed by politicians, businessmen, and citizens alike as a corporate free-loader that retained its highhandedness and arrogance until very recently.

And in the popularity stakes, its shipping line faired little better. For the name and beaver logo notwithstanding, it had been founded by Scots and Americans (like Van Horne), its ships were built on the Clyde in Scotland and for the most part registered in Britain and crewed mainly by British seamen — it was 1936 when the first Canadian-born master, Captain R.G. Perry, took the commodore's chair. Only two of the Canadian Pacific's ships sunk in the Second World War — the *Empress of Asia* and the *Princess Marguerite* — appear on the Merchant Navy Memorial at Sackville Landing, Halifax, because they were the only two registered in Canada. The company was managed from London and its principal stockholders were, until recently, British.

All of this caused the prime minister, Mackenzie King, to remark that when he talked to CP's directors, he always felt as if he was talking to Number 10 Downing Street. King's Liberal government so distrusted private enterprise to run the country's transportation system that to counterbalance it they created the Canadian National Railway (CNR), with its own trains, ships, and airline. As a result, no matter who was elected, the coherent policy was to keep both the CPR and the CNR transportation empires in delicate balance, each serving as a financial yardstick for and political check of the other. The hope was that neither would succeed in monopolizing transport in Canada.

But whatever Ottawa might hold, with its ships named after Hudson Bay forts (*Fort Rouge* and *Fort Kamloops*), the First Nations (*Kyuquot*, *Kootenay*, and *Nootka*), and small Canadian towns (*Mattawa* and *Metagama*), by carrying immigrants, wartime child evacuees, troops in both world wars, war brides, and Hungarian refugees to the world, the ships that flew the checkered flag *were* Canada. As the sinking of the CP's *Empress of Ireland* and the sacrifice of the *Beaverford* in the Second World War proved, Canadian Pacific ships would never bask in the publicity or romance enjoyed by the ships of the White Star and Cunard lines, either in war or peace. But in the 75 years of the CP line's existence, they did define Canada and Britain's maritime history.

If the two world wars devastated the Canadian Pacific Line, the advent of mass air travel in the 1960s killed off the passenger side of the business completely. Who could have guessed that the nemesis of those leviathans would be, not icebergs, U-boats, or the Luftwaffe, but jet airliners made in Seattle and Long Beach? But when their twilight came and the last of the Empresses were sold off, the old company adapted. Its directors, now Calgary-based, continued to take enormous risks, diversifying away from carrying passengers by ship and rail, and into the business of oil, gas, mining, forestry, and real estate. As CP Ships, the company successfully embraced the container revolution, and 100 years after it was chartered, focused entirely on container shipping.

When the Canadian Pacific conglomerate dissolved in October 2001 and, with the four other divisions, CP Ships was spun out onto its own, the shipping line aggressively "rode the wave" of expanding global trade.

As it had once acquired rival shipping lines like Allan and Dempster, it took over other shipping companies: Canada Maritime, Cast (1995), Lykes Lines and Contship Containerlines (1997), ANZDL (1998), TMM Lines (1999), and the Italia Line (2002). Then, two years later, CP Ships ran aground. It became a takeover target itself, and on July 29, 2005, its directors confirmed that they were negotiating with a buyer regarding the potential sale of the company. By the end of the year, to strengthen its container shipping division, Germany's TUI AG, the parent of Hapag-Lloyd, had acquired it for a purchase price of $2.4 billion. At a special meeting of shareholders in Toronto on December 14, 2005, the sale was approved and company shares ceased trading on the Toronto Stock Exchange. The disappearance of the company followed when the new owners decided that as Hapag-Lloyd was the stronger brand, the name CP Ships would gradually be dropped.

There are still ships with powerful engines and sumptuous fittings on the world's oceans, their passengers enjoying conveniences and luxuries that would have been unimaginable to those who crossed on the Empresses. But with the exception of Cunard's two Queens, these are cruise ships — floating vacation resorts and casinos at sea — surely a degradation of the whole maritime tradition. Slab-shaped, gaudily decorated, their decks crowded with geriatric celebrants, they do not bring immigrants to Pier 21 or troops to distant battlefields. Today they are out of fashion, the remaining few in drydock or waiting to be scrapped somewhere in the world. But for nearly 200 years, the great steamships dominated our imaginations and social structures, making technological, and in two wars military, history.

CHAPTER 1

From Rail to Sea

… acquire, own, hold, charter, work and run steam and other vessels upon any navigable water which the Canadian Pacific Railway (CPR) may reach or connect with.

— Statutes of Canada, 44 Victoria, Chapter 1

Within two years of its birth on February 16, 1881, the Canadian Pacific Railway Company had entered the shipping business and in the decades to come would diversify into running hotels, telegraph services, insurance companies, abattoirs, foundries, mining companies, trucking, an airline, and, its critics alleged, at times the government of Canada itself. But after the transcontinental railway, until after the Second World War, shipping would be the CPR's fundamental asset, the company proclaiming itself "The World's Greatest Travel System," its philosophy that of "seamless" transportation by rail and water on five continents.

It had been pointed out to prime minister John A. Macdonald that it made good economic sense for the railway go through either Detroit or Sault Ste. Marie to Minnesota and connect with existing lines in Winnipeg, but the prime minister and his party were adamant: it was to be an all-Canadian route — away from the Yankees, from Montreal up over the north shore of Lake Superior to the Prairies. Thus, in the summer of 1883, CPR engineers found themselves blasting their way through the seemingly impenetrable Canadian Shield with Van Horne's three locally built dynamite factories supplying their entire output to the construction crews. To ferry men, rails, and explosives to the wonderfully named construction sites of Little Pic, Big Pic, Gravel River, Jack Fish, and Maggot River, the CPR bought a tiny steamboat, *Champion Number 2*, in Quebec City and had it brought to Port Arthur, Ontario.

Historically, this was the first ship that the company would own (although there is some evidence in 1882 the CPR bought a small wooden screw ship, the *Georgian*, to carry construction camp workers and supplies), a stop-gap measure until its three freight/passenger ships were ready. For the then astronomical sum of $300,000 each, these ships, the *Alberta*, *Algoma*, and *Athabasca*, were constructed at Aiken & Mansell, Glasgow, on the banks of the Clyde River in Scotland. Each had special bulkheads amidships so that they could be halved and transported overland.

William Henry Beatty, a partner in the North-West Transportation Company (which ran ships on the Great Lakes) was hired as manager of the Canadian Pacific Lake Transportation Services. After what is recorded as a "perilous crossing," the three ships arrived in Montreal. There they were disassembled and towed in parts by tug through the canals to Buffalo, New York, where they were reassembled and then launched from Owen Sound, Ontario, the port calling itself "The Gateway to the West." Each ship was 263 feet long with 38-foot beam and could carry up to 2,000 tons of freight and 374 passengers. The first on the Great Lakes to carry the Plimsoll mark, recently adopted by the British Board of Trade and made compulsory by an Act of Parliament, consisted of a diamond with a horizontal line through it indicating the safe depth to which a ship could be loaded. The trio would also be the first on the Great Lakes to later be equipped with electric lights.

Service began with the *Algoma* from Owen Sound to Port Arthur, connecting with CPR rail service to Winnipeg. If anything proved the desperate need for some form of transport to the Prairies, it was this first voyage. On Sunday May 11, 1884, the *Algoma* sailed, crowded with 1,100 passengers, mainly immigrants from England, Scotland, and Sweden. The three CPR ships would initiate a thrice-weekly service, always timed in conjunction with connecting Toronto and Winnipeg trains. Even once the transcontinental railway had been completed, because the rail grades on the Algoma district were too severe for the engine power then available, the three were kept in service for heavy cargoes.

The only mishap took place on November 7, 1885, the date of the railway's greatest triumph, the driving in of "The Last Spike," when the *Algoma*, blown aground off Isle Royale (Greenstone Island) on Lake Superior, struck a reef and broke in two. The crew and passengers clung to the wreckage for two days. In David Laurence Jones's *Tales of the CPR*, a survivor recalls the courage of the ship's Captain Moore, who, "hurt as he was, said 'Men, let us unite in prayer,' and there with death flapping its wings over us, knelt down in the snow and water and prayed with us." The distress signals were seen by the *Athabasca*, but of the 56 onboard, only 14 were saved — the sole time that the Great Lakes service would lose any lives.

The *Algoma*'s engine and boilers were recovered in 1886 and put into its replacement, the *Manitoba*, which this time was built at Polson's Iron Works, in Owen Sound. Through the next 61 years of service, as part of the Great Lakes Transit Company, it would become a familiar sight and in 1924 was adapted to accommodate automobiles onboard. In 1908, the *Assiniboia* and the *Keewatin*, both built at Fairfields, Govan, Scotland, joined the CPR fleet and for 28 years they, too, carried thousands of passengers between Port McNicoll (which replaced Owen Sound) and Fort William. As to the original ships, the *Alberta* and *Athabasca* were withdrawn from passenger service in 1916, only to be recalled in 1938 to run a freight service between Port McNicoll, Ontario, and Chicago and Milwaukee. The two continued in Canadian Pacific service until 1947, when they were towed through the Chicago Drainage Canal to the Mississippi River and sold to a Florida company to begin a new lease of life as "banana boats" on the Gulf of Mexico.

The *Manitoba* was retired in 1949 and sold for scrap in Hamilton, Ontario, and the *Keewatin* carried passengers until November 1966, when its retirement ended 83 years of service by CP on the Great Lakes. Fortunately, the ship was not demolished and is today partially restored as a museum ship at Saugatuck (Douglas), Michigan. Its sister ship, the freight-carrying *Assiniboia*, was the very last of the CPR's ships on the Great Lakes, completing its last voyage on November 26, 1967. Overshadowed in Canada's history by the CPR's oceanic fleet, its Great Lakes ships also played their part, arriving just in time to cope with the ever-increasing flood of immigrants from Europe making for the Prairies. For between the beginning of the 19th century and the First World War, Canada experienced the largest wave of immigration in its history, when nearly four million immigrants sailed up the St. Lawrence to settle in North America.

Even before the railway was completed, in July 1884, the prime minister proposed to George Stephen that he consider a government-subsidized steamship service on the Pacific Coast that would connect with the transcontinental railway. Always a superb manipulator, Macdonald let it slip that a Japanese shipping company, the "Mitsu Bishi," had made overtures to the Canadian government to do just this and mentioned that some form of collaboration with them was possible. Mindful of his experiences in the shipping business in 1863 when the North American Steamship Company (of which he had been a board member) sank without a trace for lack of investment, Stephen initially demurred. At the time he was more concerned about restoring the CPR's low credit rating and completion of the railway than about a fleet of ocean-going ships.

Raising the finances to construct what was then the longest railway in the world should have been enough of a task for any man, but Stephen knew how desperate the situation was for the Canadian Pacific. The CPR had been listed on the New York Stock Exchange — the first non-American company to be so — yet private financing and the public had been wary of the whole scheme. By 1883, while railway construction was progressing rapidly, the $25 million given by the Dominion to build the railway had run out and CPR was close to bankruptcy. In response, on January 31, 1884, the government passed the Railway Relief Bill, providing a further $22,500,000 in loans to the CPR. As a result, five years ahead of schedule, the transcontinental railway was completed, and on November 7, 1885, at Salmon Arm, British Columbia, Donald Smith drove in the last spike. Reflecting the desperation of the times, Smith, Stephen, and Van Horne later named the station where the last spike went in "Craigellachie," the name of the rock in Banffshire, Scotland, where the clan mustered to gain strength and redouble their efforts against their enemies.

At the driving ceremony Smith would be standing in for his cousin, then in London negotiating with Barings Bank on a bond issue. It was here that Stephen received a letter from Macdonald, who had learnt that the British postmaster general was going to terminate the Peninsula & Orient mail contract to the Far East and was about to ask for tenders for a route to Japan — via Vancouver. With this privileged information, he advised Stephen to quickly call on the British Post Office and follow this up with a visit to the Colonial Office and even the London Chamber of Commerce. The CPR president was advised to lobby the British government for a contract to carry the mail between London and the Far East, via Canada. Macdonald: "You should tender so low that there might be no mistake about it, and I dare say that we can persuade Parliament to give you a subsidy." He even advised Stephen to get the Admiralty "onboard" by offering to build ships to naval specifications so that in times of war they could be used as armed merchant cruisers. Macdonald was good on his word and the CPR got a subsidy of $5 million to complete the line and buy the ships.

Stephen needed little encouragement. Like Allan, he was infected with an imperial zealousness and saw, he wrote Macdonald, "a service stretching from Liverpool to Hong Kong." Both the British and Canadian governments had to be made to subsidize a steamship service across the oceans on either side of Canada, for unless those trains could be filled with passengers and freight, the CPR would be just so much metal. Each mode of transport was to feed its payload, whether it be mail, silk, tea, or immigrants, into the other, the connection ensuring that the company would see a profit from both modes of transport. He proposed that a new company, the Canadian Pacific Ocean Steamship Services (CPOSS), would furnish the Imperial government with a fortnightly steamer service between Hong Kong and Vancouver for £100,000 annually for ten years.

Stephen's lobbying for a shipping line on both coasts of Canada might have been thought hopeless. For one thing, the port of Vancouver was barely that on paper as the railway would not arrive there for another two years. The established shipping route from the Orient made for Portland, Oregon, which already had rail connections to the American East Coast. Because of this, New York tea merchants like Frazer & Co (who were also the CPR agent in Hong Kong) were unconvinced as to viability of the Canadian route.

The first scheduled steamship service between North America and the Far East had begun in 1867 when the San Francisco-based Orient Occidental Line chartered White Star ships to do so. This company had a firm relationship with the Union Pacific and Southern Pacific Railways to bring in tea, silk, rice (and some opium), and more importantly, ever-growing numbers of Chinese labourers needed for railway construction. The Chinese steerage trade was so important to the United States economy that in August 1888, a special committee was appointed in the Senate to investigate what effect Canadian competition would have and what retaliation to take. On the other side of the world, the Peninsula & Orient Steam Navigation Company (P&O) had the monopoly on the London–Far East route and the Suez Canal had just opened, allowing Britain to reach her colonies in Asia and Australia quicker. In Canada, the Allan Line had a virtual monopoly on the Montreal to Liverpool service.

Against all of these interests, the case for the Canadian Pacific shipping line looked bleak. However, the logic of Stephen and Van Horne's arguments was appealing — and irrefutable. Giving evidence at the Senate enquiry, Van Horne used figures tabulated by consular officials in China to prove that, if anything, competition between the Canadian Pacific and the Oriental Occidental had caused trans-Pacific traffic to double — all at the expense of the Suez Canal. As to the French-engineered canal, Van Horne admitted that it was remarkable, a feat of almost impossible engineering (and having pushed a railway across Canada, he could speak with some authority on such things). But to get to Suez, those P&O ships still had to navigate through the Mediterranean Sea. There they were exposed to countries that were, as former enemies of Britain, untrustworthy if not hostile. Meanwhile, CPR agents in the Far East were busy mobilizing opinion in favour of the Canadian route, and the Chancellor of the Exchequer, Lord Salisbury, suddenly found himself bombarded with telegrams demanding action on the issue. Finally, shipping into Portland was not without its perils either. Vessels ran the risk of going aground on the three sandbars across the mouth of the Columbia River and not only did this increase the insurance rates but to tow them off cost considerably more than towing charges into Port Moody, British Columbia.

Even as the CPR president made the rounds in London in 1885, the newspapers were full of Major General Charles Gordon being besieged in Khartoum, and the subsequent Sudanese campaign would demonstrate how tenuous a Suez link really was. A steamship service between Liverpool and Montreal, on the other hand, that connected with the CPR to Vancouver and then on to Australasia, was not only safer and politically more reliable but it had the potential to be faster. It would be, and here Stephen could be counted on to win votes, an "all-red route," wholly British, firmly knitting the Empire together, almost girdling the world. However, he knew what really would clinch the deal among the business community was that the freight rates from the Far East to New York were lower (because of the insurance) than via the Suez Canal.

That same month, on July 26, two days before the first scheduled CPR train pulled out of Montreal to cross the continent to British Columbia, the *W.B. Flint* arrived at Royal Roads off Victoria. The little American barque had been chartered by the CPOSS to transport a cargo of tea from Yokohama, Japan. The three-masted *W.B. Flint* was surprisingly small — 178.4 feet long and 835 gross tonnage. Built in Maine in 1885, it later sailed in the nitrate trade and was still active in the 1920s bringing salmon from Alaska to Puget Sound. In 1923, the *Flint* hit a submerged object and was holed. Laid up off Puget Sound, it was burned in 1937 for its metal.

Commanded by Captain H. Pearsons, the *W.B. Flint* had made a slow 35-day voyage across the Pacific, for while the ship had been kept at full sail, the winds had been light. The next day it was towed into Port Moody by the tug *Alexander*. The cargo of 17,430 half-chests of tea was unloaded, translating into 30 carloads, which were rushed by the CPR to Toronto. On sale in Montreal on August 7 and New York on August 9, the consignment's whole journey from Japan had taken a record 47 days! It was proof that the cross-Canada "all red" route worked. The success of the *W.B. Flint* and the speed of the transhipment influenced the senior partner of Frazer & Co, Everett Frazer, who inspected Port Moody to declare that he was very pleased with the facilities and that no more of his company's tea would be sent to Portland. But rather than sail, he thought a steam service would prove more regular and that the Canadian Pacific might even be able to take away some of the Chinese silk trade that then went through San Francisco.

The company was thinking along the same lines — the *W.B. Flint* had only been a stop-gap measure, too slow and too small to take the traffic away from San Francisco. On February 11, 1887, the Canadian Pacific obtained its first three ocean-going ships, justifying this at its annual meeting in May, the directors reporting that, "Although the railway has been open only for the last five months, no less than seven cargoes of tea and other Chinese and Japanese commodities were brought to our line during that time by sailing ships ... indicating the expectations of the Directors as to a large and profitable trans-Pacific trade will be fully realised upon the establishment of a regular line of steamships."

Cautious as ever, the directors chartered three old iron-hulled steamships from the Guion Line, former Cunarders that had been given as part payment to the shipbuilders John Elder & Co for the construction of new ones. Only 365 feet long and 42 feet wide, too small for the expanding Atlantic trade, they had been returned to the shipyard to be overhauled. As the Guion Line was on the verge of bankruptcy, the trio was then offered to the Canadian Pacific. At an average of 3,000 gross tonnages (gt), the *Abyssinia, Batavia,* and *Parthia* were the first Cunard liners to have a straight, slightly raking stem or bow, as opposed to the clipper bows of their predecessors. They were also the first to have bathrooms (one on each side,) and the last liners on the Atlantic to be fitted with simple-expansion engines.

Low in the water, the three pitched heavily in the high seas of the North Pacific but as former immigrant ships they could carry 50 passengers comfortably in first class and 500 in the cramped conditions of steerage. Whatever their limitations, they were steam-powered and served their purpose — to ply the Hong Kong–Yokohama–Vancouver route (with a side trip to San Francisco) until the company decided to build its own ships. On its first voyage, the *Abyssinia* left Hong Kong on May 17, 1887, stopped at Yokohama on May 31, and arrived at Vancouver — Port Moody was no longer used — on June 13, a fortnight after leaving Asia, a considerable improvement over the *W.B. Flint*.

The mayor, the city's band, and hundreds of citizens met the *Abyssinia* at the new CPR wharf, for besides a cargo of tea for the New York market, it carried mail, newspapers, and passengers, mainly Chinese labourers in transit to the United States. It was proof enough that London could now liaison with and reinforce its Far Eastern possessions through Canada quickly and safely. As to Vancouver, hardly more than the terminus of a railroad line and the edge of the continent as far as Montreal and London were concerned, the CPR invested heavily in it — the railway's telegraph to Montreal had begun operation the year before and the first of the company's great hotels, the Hotel Vancouver, had just opened its doors.

The three chartered steamers averaged 600 passengers a voyage — also taking American flour from Portland, Oregon, and British cotton goods from Montreal. The three would remain in operation until the company's own Empresses replaced them in 1891, the year that the poor *Abyssinia* was destroyed by fire while at sea. It had resumed service for the Guion Line from Liverpool to New York, and in December 1891 was abandoned after catching fire five days out of New York, en route to Liverpool. Its companions, the *Batavia* and *Parthia*, had long, useful lives: the latter became part of the Alaska Steamship Company's fleet and was broken up in Japan in 1956 — after 86 years of service. There is a builder's hull model of the SS *Abyssinia*, unrigged, wood, scale 1:48, in the Merseyside Maritime Museum, Liverpool.

Within two years of Craigellachie, with a rail connection through Maine to Saint John, New Brunswick, the CPR truly became a "coast-to-coast" system, and in July 1887, from its offices at Place d'Armes in Montreal's commercial area, and renamed the Canadian Pacific Steam Ship Line (CPSL), the company modified its original tender — it offered to bring the great port of Shanghai into the route, including it within the contract of the land carriage across Canada.

Stephen's dream was fulfilled on July 15, 1889. For a monthly mail service between Hong Kong and Vancouver (onward through Canada to Britain) both the Imperial and Canadian governments offered the CPR handsome subsidies: £45,000 from London and £15,000 from Ottawa (which also threw in an offer of £25,000 for a fortnightly service). Signed on May 14, 1890, the agreement called for a complete monthly service — 684 hours from April to November and 732 hours December to March, between Halifax and Hong Kong. As it was a mail contract, the British government specified that the ships used had to attain a trial speed of 17 knots and a sea speed of 16 knots. The Admiralty was given the legal powers to specify the design, equipment, and how the ships were to be used. Citing Russian expansion, London wanted to tie its Pacific colonies closer to it and, as Macdonald had predicted, a provision of the contract was that the CPR fit its ships with gun platforms so that in times of war they could serve as armed merchant cruisers.

By then both Stephen and Smith had retired and been rewarded with peerages, the former becoming Baron Mount Stephen, the first Canadian to be so honoured. Smith would be made Lord Strathcona, and in April 1896, asked by the new prime minister, Sir Wilfrid Laurier, to be Canada's second high commissioner to London, a post he served at until he died in office in January 1914. The former homes of Stephen, Allan, and Beatty lay within the Square Mile — an area of Montreal bounded by McGill University on the east, Guy Street on the west, Dorchester Street on the south, and Pine Avenue on the north, which contained the most elegant mansions in Canada and was populated by those who effectively (the politicians in Ottawa notwithstanding) ran the country. Their houses still exist — perhaps the only monuments to the trio that remain. Stephen's is on 1440 Drummond Street and beautifully maintained as a private club. Allan's gothic mansion "Ravenscrag," built on the slopes of Mount Royal so he could see his ships coming into the harbour, is part of the Allan Memorial Institute of Psychiatry in McGill University. (Allan is also remembered for the Allan Cup that the family donated to amateur hockey.) Beatty's home on Pine Avenue was also bought by McGill to be the Centre for Nursing and now of Mental Disorders.

The British government had offered Smith a burial site in Westminister Abbey but, characteristic of the man, he refused and was buried in Highgate Cemetery, London — although he could not prevent two grateful nations from erecting a stained glass window to his memory in Westminister Abbey. It would be another Canadian High Commissioner, the Honorable Peter Larkin, who in 1924 would buy the imposing building owned by the Union Club, opposite the Canadian Pacific offices, now the present-day Canada House.

CHAPTER 2

The First Empresses

In memory of GEORGE A. ROCKET, late Petty Officer R.N., who was killed by falling into the dock at Kowloon November 4th 1891 when serving as a seaman on board the RMS *Empress of China*

In memory of John HIBBERT, for 16 years Boiler Maker of RMS *Empress of China* who departed this life 6th October 1906, aged 52 years

In remembrance of William NICHOLSON, late Boilermaker of RMS *Empress of India*, who died at Hong Kong on the 26th January 1911. Erected by his shipmates as a token of esteem

Sacred to the memory of Charles WATKINS, who died in Hong Kong 31st March 1901, aged 22 [?] years. As a token of esteem and regret by his shipmates RMS *Empress of China*

In remembrance of James SMITH, 2nd Engineer of RMS *Empress of Japan*, who died at Hong Kong 15th April 1911, aged 40 years

— gravestones in the old colonial cemetery
of Happy Valley, Hong Kong

More than seamen's gravestones, the inscriptions above are the only remaining memorials to the very first Canadian Pacific Empresses. Business on the Pacific had been so profitable that in 1889 the railway placed an order at Fairfields for its own ocean liners. Founded by John Elder in 1867, the year that Confederation came to Canada, and located in Govan, a Glasgow suburb on the Clyde, Fairfields would become Canadian Pacific's first choice in shipbuilders. With six shipbuilding berths and a fitting-out basin at its western end, Elder's first transatlantic ship was launched in 1868 and an in-house engine and boiler works completed in 1874. William Pearce, one of Elder's partners, took it over in 1886 and formed the Fairfield Shipbuilding and Engineering Company, Ltd. The company had the good fortune to be just in time for the shipbuilding boom at the turn of the century. The company was directed by Dr. Francis Elgar and Bryce Douglas, the best naval architect and marine engineers in Edwardian England. From 1879 to 1884, the pair were responsible for the fastest steamers on the Atlantic, the Guion's *Arizona*, *Alaska*, and *Oregon*, and the Cunarders *Etruria* and *Umbria* — and the design of the first Empresses was heavily influenced by their masterpiece, the graceful, yacht-like *City of Rome*.

Shipowners gave their business to certain shipyards — for instance, all of the White Star's ships were built at Harland & Wolff, Belfast, and like the Allan Line before it, the Canadian Pacific, from its very first passenger ship to the last, it would be to the Scottish shipbuilding industry on the Clyde. At the beginning of the 20th century, the shipyards of the Clydebank, Birkenhead, Dumbarton, Whiteinch, and Jarrow were as busy with the building of great ships for the Canadian Pacific as those in Osaka and Nagasaki, Japan, in the 1960s and Okpo, South Korea, in 2000. With Scots so prominent both in the Canadian Pacific and in Ottawa, the reasons were self-evident, but historically, the origins could be traced to the Allan family. Over the years, this would earn the CPR the enmity of later generations of Canadians and the local shipbuilding industry, but the relationship must be put in the perspective of the times.

The kinship between the Clyde shipbuilders and the CPR would always be a close one, the companies even sharing directors. Other Scottish yards like Barclay Curle, John Brown, and even C.S. Swan & Hunter, Newcastle, were sometimes given Canadian Pacific contracts, but Fairfields built 21 ships for the company. It was what the company's investors, most of whom were British, wanted. Between 1883 and 1971, the company placed orders in the British yards for a total of 26 liners, 15 cargo ships, 19 coastal ships, 5 Great Lakes ships, 2 Bay of Fundy ships, and 6 tugs — a grand total of 639,240 gross tonnage. The Clyde shipyards continue today, albeit in shrunken form, with Elder's Fairfields part of the BAE Ministry of Defence shipyard.

Smith and Stephen's successor in the Canadian Pacific was the third titan, the American engineer, William Cornelius Van Horne, who fully supported the integrated ship/rail system. Van Horne sent Thomas G. Shaughnessy and William Henry Beatty to oversee the design of the new ships. It was a farsighted choice. The politically well-connected Beatty had run his own Great Lakes shipping company until it was bought out by the Canadian Pacific, and brought with him his Toronto banking connections. Besides marrying into the wealthy Gooderham's distilling family in Toronto, Beatty was probably the most influential business lawyer in Canada for more than 50 years, from 1865 to 1907. The Canadian Pacific might have been run from Montreal, but Beatty, who had financed the building of the Lachine Canal, was its window of influence in Toronto. He called himself a "true blue Conservative" but refused to run for office, preferring to shape business through the Toronto Board of Trade, which he controlled with Walter Nesbitt. The North-West Transportation Company was only one of Beatty's companies (he was also president of the Bank of Toronto, the Canada Permanent Mortgage Corporation, and Confederation Life) but perhaps, as a good yachtsman, he enjoyed it the most.

On these trips, Beatty would take along his son Edward, who would one day sit in Van Horne's chair. American like Van Horne, Shaughnessy had been personally lured over by him in 1881 from their previous common employer, the Milwaukee Railroad, and on his return from England, Van Horne would send him to the Far East for four months to set up the company's business in China and Japan. When Van Horne retired in 1899, Shaughnessy, to no one's surprise, would serve as the next president of the Canadian Pacific.

But even as the keel of the first was being laid in November 1889, the question arose as to what to name them. As with other modes of transport, the proper naming of ships is as essential to their success as their form of propulsion. The Victorian engineer Isambard Kingdom Brunel understood this and reassured his company's investors by baptizing his creations *Great Eastern* and *Mammoth*. When they became disillusioned with the losses that the *Mammoth* incurred, Brunel renamed it *Great Britain*, the patriotic appeal always a good one. As fleets grew, one could usually tell the company by the ship's name.

The Allan Line favoured names ending with *an* and *ian* and most of the Beaver Line ships' names began with *Mont*. All Cunard's vessels were given names ending in *ia* with vaguely classical connections (*Aquitania*, for example, was a former province of the Roman empire in the Bay of Biscay). White Star's descriptive names ended in *ic* and were blatantly devised to impress — the three ill-fated sisters, *Titanic*, *Olympic*, and *Gigantic* (the last later changed to *Britannic*) being the most famous. Although the Canadian Pacific classed their ships according to "Empress," "Duchess," and "Beaver," as in *Empress of India*, *Duchess of Atholl*, and *Beaverford*, they were frequently renamed, either to reflect a change in ownership, the times, or their status within the company.

For example, when the Allan Line ship *Alsatian* became part of the Canadian Pacific fleet in 1915, it was crowned the *Empress of France*. A technological wonder when launched in 1906, the *Empress of Britain* was by 1924 outdated and reduced in status as the *Montroyal* before being scrapped in 1930. Her lounge survives in the Norwegian School for Hotel Management in Stavenger, Norway, giving historians an idea what her sister ship, the ill-fated *Empress of Ireland*, must have looked like.

After the Second World War, because of its depleted fleet, two Duchess-class ships, *Bedford* and *Richmond*, were elevated to "Empress" status, as *France II* and *Canada II* respectively. Ship names were also changed during the war: after the Japanese attack on Pearl Harbor, it was no longer politically expedient for the company to have an *Empress of Japan* and the liner was more suitably re-baptized as the *Empress of Scotland*. In the Swinging Sixties, when the company redesigned its image, the "woodsy" names of *Beaverpine* and *Beaveroak* were dropped in favour of *CP Ambassador* and *CP Explorer*. To get even more confusing, the *Princess of Nanaimo* (1950–63), *Princess of Acadia I* (1963–71), and *Princess of Nanaimo* were the same ship.

As to the first Empresses, Kersey felt that they should be named *Manchuria*, *Mongolia*, and *Tiara*, with possibly *Formosa* and *Corea* kept in reserve. Van Horne thought otherwise: why not name them after the great Chinese dynasties: *Tai Cho*, *Tai Ming*, and *Tai Ching*? But with China then in turmoil and about to cast off its imperial burden, Kersey objected to this and put forth names of Chinese rivers and towns. It was R.B. Angus, an up-and-coming director that suggested the names *Empress of India*, *Empress of Japan*, and *Empress of China*. Van Horne agreed: the names reflected the two ideals that he wanted the public to associate with all his ships, trains, and hotels. The public could expect the highest form of service from them and the names should fit in with the imperial dream — then at its height.

Accordingly, they were named after Queen Victoria (the Empress of India), Tz'u-hsi (the Empress Dowager of China), and Shoken (the Empress of Japan). Like the checkered flag, it was a master stroke. The Americans called their ships after presidents and Cunard chose to name theirs after British queens — but every potential customer knew that an empress outranked both. As for R.B. Angus, he was commemorated when the CPR's vast Montreal railway yards were named in his honour.

The three ships were designed by Professor J.H. Biles, one of the most celebrated naval architects at the time, and their machinery by Bryce Douglas, in collaboration with the company's own engineer, James Fowler. At a cost of $1,157,000 each, these were the first Empresses of an illustrious line. Before oil, all ships were steam-powered and thus coal-fired. In the *Empress of Asia*, the steam was produced in ten cylindrical "Scotch" boilers. Each boiler was filled with water that was heated by furnaces that passed fire through tubes that ran through the boiler. When the hot gases had been expended, the exhaust was vented through the ship's three smokestacks. Six of the boilers were double-ended and four were single-ended. Each end contained three furnaces, giving the ship a total of 64 furnaces. Trimmers delivered coal through chutes and wheelbarrows to firemen who cared for the furnaces. It was the firemen's responsibility to maintain the fires in the furnaces. A slice bar was used to turn the coal to ensure a thorough burn and ash had to be removed from the fires regularly.

The boilers, producing a pressure of 190 parts per square inch (psi), were capable of consuming 300 tons of coal a day — a typical round-trip voyage to the Far East from Vancouver, which would take approximately six weeks, consumed over 10,000 tons of coal. The engines consisted of four Parsons turbines (a type designed by the British engineer Charles Parsons). The turbines were connected to the boilers and the steam passed first through the high-pressure turbine, then the intermediate-pressure turbine, and finally into the two low-pressure turbines. Each turbine was directly coupled to a nine-foot propeller that turned at the same speed as the turbine. The *Empress of Asia*'s engines were rated at 18,500 horsepower. Additional turbines were fitted to the low-pressure shafts to provide astern propulsion. When the used steam exited the last turbines it passed into the condenser, where it was returned to water by contacting cooling pipes circulating cold seawater. The newly formed water from the condenser was returned to the boiler and the warmed seawater was discharged over the side.

Whatever the amenities in the glittering palaces far above, stoking the furnaces under the boilers was done with shovels, tongs, slice bars, and wheelbarrows by men whose bodies were dehydrated and burnt with exposure to the open furnaces. The engines required a large crew of engineers and greasers who repaired and maintained them, and as late as 1941, the engine department of the coal-burning *Empress of Asia* totalled 152 men. Labouring in hot, filthy, deafening conditions — made worse when the ship pitched and rolled — to shovel the 400 tons of coal a day that a great liner needed to keep running, the "black gang," as they were called, did this with the certain knowledge that if the ship was ever "holed" (damaged by an iceberg, a collision, or torpedoed), they would never make it up on deck to be saved.

It was no wonder they were known to be an aggressive, brutal caste, given to hard fighting and harder drinking — and treasured by the company. No one apart from them ever saw the inside of a stoke-hold of a coal-burning ship, and there are few photos of one or its occupants. As a result, the remainder of the crew and all passengers regarded these beings from the underworld with superstitious awe and the black gang retained their reputation well into the war years. In September 1942, when the same *Empress of Asia*, battle-scarred and packed with Allied troops from the Greek campaign, docked in New York, its two-month voyage around the Cape of Good Hope had been made longer because the ship's engine room crew had staged a "slow down" strike along the way. An officer told the *New York Times* that the black gang was made up of "a lot of Liverpool rats," and that he would like nothing better than to go down to the engine room with a tommy gun "and start shooting from the doorway." Twenty sailors had tended the fires after the firemen "mutinied." — "If we were flying the White Ensign instead of the Red Duster," the officer added, "those rats would have been shot." One of those naval personnel who had stoked the fires was Prince Philip, son of the king of Greece and future Duke of Edinburgh. He was presented with his trimmer's certificate by the company at the end of the voyage.

Although the first Empresses (5,905 gt) were of an overall length of 485 feet (more than 100 feet longer than the *Abyssinia*) with a width of 51 feet, they were half the size of the largest ships then on the Atlantic, which in 1889 registered at 10,600 gross tonnage. They made 18 knots on trial and 16 at sea and were the first twin-screw steamers on the Pacific with two independent, triple-expansion engines, each driving a separate propeller. With lines reminiscent of the *City of Rome*, two funnels, raked masts, all-white hulls and superstructure, the three were handsome ships that could carry 160 first-class passengers, 40 in second class, and 700 in steerage.

The upper decks housed the first-class staterooms in "outside" rooms and most had three berths — the special suites advertised were four large cabins on the promenade deck. Each was extensively fitted with electrical comforts like lighting and refrigeration, and the luxurious staterooms even had bedsteads and sofas instead of bunks. The three Empresses became synonymous with speed, and could make the crossing from Yokohama to Race Rocks, British Columbia, in ten days, 13 hours. Each was also distinguished by its own figurehead — a sleek figurehead of Her Majesty Queen Victoria graced the *Empress of India*. The other two had dragons; the *Empress of China*'s Chinese dragon was made in Kowloon, and is the only one which has survived. Lady Alice Stanley, the daughter-in-law of Lord Stanley, the governor general (who later donated the Stanley Cup to hockey), launched the *Empress of Japan* on December 13, 1890.

Each of the ships took their maiden voyages from Britain to Vancouver via the Suez Canal, and to cut costs, carried passengers, the whole trip costing $600 — it would be the first world cruise (almost) of the line. Under the command of Captain O.P. Marshall, the *Empress of India* departed Liverpool on February 8, 1891, and sailed via Gibraltar, Marseilles, Naples, the Suez Canal (where everyone disembarked to see the Pyramids), Colombo (where the crew played cricket), Singapore (where four waterspouts were seen), and across the Pacific (during which a battle was witnessed between a whale and a killer whale). On April 29, a gun was fired at Mission Point, Vancouver, announcing the arrival of the *Empress* and, as the ship rounded Brockton Point, the waiting municipal band struck up a tune.

To greet the 131 passengers onboard (and 355 Chinese in steerage) at the pier was Van Horne and the mayor of Vancouver. That night a grand banquet and ball was held at the Hotel Vancouver and Marshall was presented with an illuminated scroll, later given to the city's archives. More importantly, the 27 bags of mail unloaded would arrive in London 15 days later. Called through the years, with some justification, "Marshall's Private Yacht," the *Empress of India* was also the first Canadian Pacific ship to carry British royalty. On October 1, 1901, the Duke and Duchess of York (later King George V and Queen Mary) visited British Columbia and crossed on the *Empress* from Vancouver to Victoria. The royal party returned to Vancouver on it on October 3, with the duke so impressed by the ship and its master that His Royal Highness made Marshall an Elder Brother of Trinity House.

The largest and fastest ships on the Pacific, their reputation for luxury and speed attracted the well-to-do and shippers of merchandise that needed to be transported quickly. In 1890, the three chartered ships brought 279 saloon (first-class) passengers to either Victoria or Vancouver. In 1892, the first year that all three Empresses were in service, the figure had risen to 993. In 1897, Van Horne could boast that his ships had cornered 60 percent of the first-class travel on the Pacific. Besides the wealthy, colonial officials, and missionaries, the three ships also took American troops to the Philippines, British troops to quell the Boxer Rebellion in China, and, in steerage, millions of Chinese labourers destined for the United States and Canada.

Recurring plagues brought from the Far East meant that the Empresses were forbidden to carry Chinese passengers in steerage several times. With the effects of the exclusion acts both in Canada and the United States and the doubling of the head tax imposed upon the Chinese from $50 to $100, the steerage passengers, until then predominantly Chinese, gradually changed to immigrants from India in the early 1900s. The peak for the latter was 1908, when 700 Indians were landed on a single Canadian Pacific ship.

And it wasn't only passengers. The CPR transported raw silk cocoons from the Orient to Vancouver and onward by rail to silk mills in New York and New Jersey. Raw silk had to be transported with all speed, and since the Empresses were the fastest, shipments valued at millions of dollars were soon commonplace. In 1902, within a 40-day period, they landed four silk cargoes in Vancouver valued at $5,941,000.

In 1910, the company concluded that the three Empresses no longer had the capacity for the burgeoning Pacific traffic — the Philippine government wanted Manila to be part of its route, and ordered two larger vessels. Built by Fairfield's, the *Empress of Asia* (16,908 gt) and the *Empress of Russia* (16,810 gt) were both launched in 1912 within a month of each other. On their maiden voyages a year later they were sent from Liverpool to Hong Kong by diverse routes — the *Empress of Russia* via

Suez, the *Empress of Asia* via Cape Town. In the wars to come, the pair was destined for busy military service as armed merchant cruisers and trooping. Few ships would serve a line as faithfully as the pair — and the only fault that either had was a disconcerting weakness for splashing the officers on the bridge when their bows cut deep into a wave. That and the fact that neither was ever converted to burn oil were the only criticisms of the fine ships.

Meticulously maintained and annually overhauled in Hong Kong, from 1891 onward, the first Empresses established a regular mail and passenger run between Hong Kong, Shanghai, Nagasaki, Kobe, and Yokohama and Victoria and Vancouver, bringing mail across Canada and onward to London within a record 26 days after it had left Japan. Like their predecessors, they had an alarming tendency to roll and pitch in rough seas so that all were fitted with bilge keels in 1901. Each also had their share of mishaps. The *Empress of Japan* collided with the steamer *Abby Palmer* in 1900 and all three ran down junks at sometime, but only the *Empress of Japan* rammed a whale. The Chinese cruiser *Quang-Kai* blundered into the *Empress of India* in August 1903, without loss of life.

Nothing, however, matched the *Empress of China*'s run of bad luck. On the ship's second trip from Yokohama to Vancouver in 1891 the *Empress* encountered a gale so severe that all movables on deck were carried away, a metal lifeboat was crumpled, and water poured through the stokehole. When it finally arrived at Vancouver, smallpox was discovered onboard and the ship was put into quarantine at Albert Head. Three years later, in August 1894, an incompetent local pilot stranded her on Woosung Spit for nine days. Then, in June 1901, when plague broke out in steerage, the *Empress of China* was held at Nagasaki for ten days. Six years later, it sank at the company's dock in Vancouver. Water poured in through a condenser discharge while it was being loaded with coal, and S.C. Binns, the purser, recalled that it took hours to block the opening and close the valve. Then, with the help of every fire engine in Vancouver, the water was pumped out of the hold and the ship refloated. The damaged cargo had to be taken off, and carpets, furniture, and electrical equipment replaced. But that was nothing compared with what was to come.

The *Empress of China*'s misfortunes would in the end be the death of it. On July 26, 1911, en route to Yokohama, the ship was making for the entrance of Tokyo Bay in the middle of a typhoon. If this wasn't bad enough, the next day a heavy fog covered it. Binns remembered that the fog had been made worse because of the heavy smoke caused by the locals onshore who burned seaweed to make iodine. Not hearing any signals from the shore (the lighthouse at Shiramaya was out of commission), the master guessed that he had a lot of sea room to manoeuvre ... when the ship ran aground on Mera Reef. The steering gear was wrecked and, as water poured in through the bottom, the steerage passengers panicked, forcing the ships' officers to restore order at gunpoint. For those above the waterline, there was no terror, and they enjoyed breakfast as Japanese fishing boats converged on the scene.

The 185 passengers and all in steerage were safely evacuated with the mail, but helpless on the reef the *Empress*, already past its prime, was mercilessly pounded by the surf and began to break up. The rocks it was on were pumice stone and the ship ground its way into them, making itself a cradle. It was refloated in 1911 but was in such poor condition that the underwriters sold it for scrap in Yokohama for $65,500. There were rumours that much of the *Empress* was worked into two Japanese ships, especially the much-prized engines and boilers. A court of inquiry fully exonerated the master on the grounds that he could not have properly ascertained his position in the fog.

Besides overseeing the development of CP's premier ships, Van Horne was responsible for introducing a corporate identity. In a pre-electronic age, the use of semaphore, the flags that a ship flew, told everything about it. There were flags identifying its nationality, intentions, cargo, and even the health of its passengers. But pre-eminent and flown from the ship's tallest mast as it entered port, was its house flag. This was the shipowner's coat of arms and corporate identity, telling of the company's origins. For example, the Peninsula & Oriental's house flag was composed of the colours of the royal families of Spain and Portugal, the area where the company began operations. A red and white chessboard pattern had already been in use with the CPR, evolving from the way that land on either side of the railroad track had been allocated between the government and railway in alternate blocks — on a map this was coloured red and white.

Van Horne chose the pattern as the shipping line's flag — legend is that he enjoyed a good game of poker, and like a winning hand of cards, the red and white flag would be recognizable anywhere — whether or not the wind was blowing. Another story is that, as he was an accomplished gardener and roses were his speciality, the red and white design was inspired by his flowers. As Frank Bowen described in his *History of the Canadian Pacific Line*, years later, Van Horne himself would admit to Mr. McDuff, assistant to the chairman of the CPR, "Yes, I designed the house flag, partly to differ from any in use and partly that it might be easily recognized when hanging loose. It has no historic or heraldic significance. Somebody has suggested that it meant 'three of a kind' but that would not be a big enough hand for the CPR for which a 'straight flush' only would be appropriate." Whatever the origin, the design has proved timeless and continues to be flown by CP Ships today. Along with the red-and-white-checkered House Flag, Canadian Pacific ships also flew the Red Ensign of the Merchant Navy and, later, when they carried the Royal Mail, besides earning the right to use the prefix *RMS* (for Royal Mail Ship) before their names, they flew the Mail pennant.

Later, the checkered pattern would also be added to the ships' funnels. In the era of "four stacker" steamships, the number and size of a ships' funnels had assumed an importance out of all proportion. Maritime smokestacks provide a draft for the furnaces and dispel smoke and soot and, understandably, the taller they were, the more soot they kept off the passengers on the promenade deck — the ship's doctor's main job was removing specks of soot from passengers' eyes. Apart from that, the number and size of the smokestacks caused maritime architects to disdain them (for all the structural problems and guy ropes that they entailed).

But as the first object to be sighted when a ship came into view, smokestacks were a publicity agent's dream. They were giant billboards in triplicate that could be used to demonstrate corporate identity, and shipping lines became known by the colour of their funnels — buff and black top (White Star) or buff with green and white bands (Holland America). The distinctive red of the Cunard funnels came from the rust-proofing mixture that Sam Cunard invented. He had observed that to prevent rust, the crews of Nova Scotia coastal steamers blended butter-milk with red ochre and smeared that on their ships' funnels. Initially the CPR's ships' funnels were simply buff coloured, and then topped off with a black stripe (a sensible idea in the days of coal smoke), with the familiar checker pattern added in 1946.

The choice of what to paint the hulls of the Canadian Pacific ships was made in 1892. Before the launch of the latest acquisition, to gain as much publicity as possible, shipping lines sent models out to travel agents and their ticket offices for display in their shop windows. H. Maitland Kersey, the chief liaison between the builders of the first Empresses and the Canadian Pacific, had three ship's models constructed for this pur-pose. As nothing had been specified, each of their hulls were painted a different colour — black, ivory-white, and French grey — and sent off to the CPS offices. A discussion with a Royal Navy admiral who when stationed in Hong Kong had experience in ship maintenance, resolved the issue. Ivory-white hulls would be the easiest to sustain in a tropical climate, the admiral maintained. Kersey immediately lobbied Van Horne and Shaughnessy for white as the standard colour of the hulls and by the time the first model with the black hull came to the Canadian Pacific Steamships office in Montreal in the winter of 1893, staff noted that it had been repainted white.

Van Horne was also responsible for beginning the CPR's public-ity campaign and while all shipping lines published posters, brochures, and pamphlets in many languages, to him we owe the school of distinc-tive ships posters, maps of routes, ships models, and photographs that have come to epitomize the Canadian Pacific today. He understood the values of the emerging middle class, the new customers, with his slo-gan, "All Sensible People Travel the CPR." And with a gift for the snappy phrase, he also coined, "Wise Men of the East go West on the CPR," and "Said the Prince to the Duke: How High We live on the CPR." He even personally sketched some of the posters used across Europe. Van

Horne went a bit too far, however, when he coined the slogan describing the Rockies as "1,001 Switzerlands Rolled into One." The Swiss government was not amused and threatened the CPR with legal action if it were not removed.

Van Horne died in 1915 at his home on Sherbrooke Street in Montreal. His house, which he had described as "fat and bulgy like myself," was demolished in 1973. The great engineer is only commemorated by the Montreal street that bears his name and a private girl's school he founded in Montreal at 507 Guy Street (now at 525 Mount Pleasant Avenue), which continues to thrive today.

CHAPTER 3

Braving the Atlantic

Canada is doing business on a back street.... We must put her on
a thoroughfare.
— attributed to W.C. Van Horne in *From Telegraph to Titan*

Van Horne's ambition was to expand the CPR fleet twofold: within
Canada and on the Atlantic. With its mountainous terrain, the
first highways of British Columba were its rivers and lakes and many
of the earliest settlers had travelled on the Columbia River using riv-
erboats and sternwheelers — shallow draft vessels that needed as little
as 22 inches of water, their boilers powered by wood. Sicamous was
on the main CPR line between Revelstoke and Salmon Arm, and to
expand into the growing Kelowna/Penticton area, the CPR first built
a branch line from it to Okanagan Lake and then its own shipyard
at Okanagan Landing. On May 22, 1893, its first sternwheeler, the

Aberdeen (554 gt), was launched for services to Penticton. When the local Columbia and Kootenay Steam Navigation Company was purchased in 1897, the railway was operating its own shipyards and a fleet of picturesque sternwheelers on Okanagan Lake, Arrow Lakes, Slocan Lake, and Kootenay Lake.

The first were built in Toronto and brought over by train in thousands of parts, but later boats were made in British Columbia and launched at the Okanagan Landing. While most sternwheelers were hardworking boats with basic comforts, a few, like the *Bonnington*, *Nasookin*, and *Sicamous*, had ornate smoking and dining rooms that would not have been out of place on the Mississippi River. Their working lives varied, too: the CPR sternwheeler, the 800-ton *Moyie* (835 gt) ran on Kootenay Lake from 1898 until 1956, but others like the larger *Bonnington* (1,700 gt) had a much shorter career, running from 1911 to 1931. Until displaced by automobiles, trucks, and float planes, the sternwheelers were a lifeline to isolated communities, carrying prospectors, Mounties, loggers, and settlers, providing not only transport of passengers and goods in and out but communications, postal, and banking facilities, as well. After steadily losing money to trucks through the 1960s, the CPR steamboats ended service in 1977.

The British Columbia Pacific Coast had seen a steamer as early as 1836 when the Hudson's Bay Company had operated its tiny *Beaver*. In 1882, the CPR contracted with Master J. Irving of the Canadian Pacific Navigation Company to carry freight and passengers from New Westminister to Yale, British Columbia, in the building of the railway. Then, in 1901, to take advantage of the Gold Rush, the CPR bought the Canadian Pacific Navigation Company outright and started the British Columbia Coastal Steamship Services (BCCSS), placing it under the management of the legendary Master J.W. Troup, then the superintendent of the B.C. Lake and River Steamers. He reorganized the fleet of inherited screw steamers and paddlewheelers, put them on scheduled services to carry prospectors and freight north from Victoria to northern British Columbia ports and Alaska, and in 1897 bought two ships, the *Tartar* (4,339 gt) and the *Athenian* (4,240 gt), from the British-owned Union Line, both with triple-expansion engines.

The next logical move after the completion of the railway to Vancouver was to run a ferry service to Victoria and in 1903 the CPR bought out the local ferry company to do so, later expanding its routes to Seattle with what was to become the famous "triangle service." The first of its Princess coastal ships, the *Princess Victoria* (1,943 gt) was launched from Swan Hunter and Wigham Richardson Ltd., Great Britain, on November 18, 1902, and sailed across the Atlantic, around the Horn to Victoria, where it arrived in May of 1903. Perhaps because of the new engines, originally designed for the Swedish navy (which gave it speeds in excess of 20 knots), the *Victoria* encountered initial prejudice and was dubbed "Troup's Folly." But it was so fast, and could make Victoria–Vancouver–Victoria–Seattle–Victoria within a day, and along with its sister Princesses, would become a familiar sight on the Pacific until 1950.

Typical of the class was the *Princess Charlotte* (3,925 gt), built on the Clyde and launched in 1908 for the Vancouver–Victoria service. Refitted in 1926, the *Charlotte* would be laid up in 1949 and sold for use in the Mediterranean. The *Princess May* (1,697 gt) was the first BCCSS coastal steamer to be equipped with a wireless telegraph — and a good thing, too. On August 5, 1910, when on the Skagway–Juneau run, because of a fog, it ran aground in the Lynn Canal at Sentinel Island. All 148 passengers were taken off safely but the ship stayed perched on the rocks for a month. If the vistas afforded by the Lynn Canal were not spectacular enough, the precariously balanced *Princess May* made for some wonderful photos. Eventually it was pulled off and towed to Esquimalt for repairs. Eight years later, in almost exactly the same place, its sister coastal steamer, *Princess Sophia* (2,320 gt), would do the same, but with tragic consequences.

Finally, to supplement its rail network in the Maritimes, in 1912 the CPR also ran steamers on the Bay of Fundy. In order to get their passengers to and from Halifax faster than was possible over the Intercontinental Railway, Canadian Pacific took over six ships from the Dominion Atlantic Railway in 1911. Four of them were called after members of the royal family — Princes George, Arthur, Albert, and Rupert. By the 1930s, all were scrapped and replaced by their own ships, notable of which were *Princess Helene* and *Princess of Arcadia*, which entered Saint John–Digby service in 1963.

Donald Smith (1820–1914) was a leading figure in the creation of the Canadian Pacific Railway. It was a fellow Scotsman, Prime Minister Sir John A. Macdonald, who proposed to Smith and George Stephen that they consider a government-subsidized steamship service to connect with the transcontinental railway. When Smith retired, he was the first Canadian to be honoured with a peerage, and would be made Lord Strathcona. In April 1896, he was asked by the new prime minister, Sir Wilfrid Laurier, to be Canada's second High Commissioner to London.

Sir William Cornelius Van Horne (1843–1915) was a hard-driving American engineer and president of the CPR from to 1888 to 1899. He fully supported the integrated ship/rail system and named the first ships "Empresses." He also chose the red-and-white-checkerboard pattern as the company's corporate colours. Photo *circa* 1900.

Above: The SS *Empress of China* was named for Tz'u-hsi, the Empress Dowager of China. The three white Empresses were the first twin-screw vessels on the Pacific. Gun platforms were built into them and 4.7-inch guns were supplied by the Admiralty so they could be converted quickly into armed merchant cruisers. Vancouver, British Columbia, 1904.

Right: Coaling the *Empress of Britain*, 1908. This was the only way to load coal into the great ships. Unseen by the passengers, "the black gang" — dehydrated and black with exposure to the open furnaces — stoked the furnaces under the boilers. They worked with the certain knowledge that if a ship was "holed" by an iceberg or a torpedo, there was no escape for them.

The Canadian Pacific sternwheeler SS *Bonnington*, with its ornate smoking and dining rooms, would not have been out of place on the Mississippi River. 1912.

The ill-fated SS *Empress of Ireland*. Early in the morning of May 29, 1914, the great ship disappeared beneath the St. Lawrence, taking with it 1,012 lives — 134 of whom were children — after being struck by the Norwegian collier *Storstad* in a heavy fog.

The Canadian Pacific passenger ship *Princess Sophia, circa* 1912. The *Sophia* sank on October 25, 1918, after grounding on Vanderbilt Reef in the Lynn Canal near Juneau, Alaska. With the loss of all 343 aboard, the wreck of the *Princess Sophia* is the worst maritime accident in the history of British Columbia and Alaska.

A convoy carrying Canadian Expeditionary Forces to Britain, October 8, 1914. Ten Canadian Pacific ships were part of the 30-ship convoy that transported horses, artillery, motor vehicles, nearly 30,000 men, and Canada's first and only aircraft to the Great War. The popular expectation was that all would be back home by Christmas.

Airplanes escort the *Empress of Britain* out of Halifax Harbour, Nova Scotia, June 15, 1939.

The SS *Empress of Canada* at Vancouver, British Columbia, 1927.

The Royal Mail Ship *Metagama* of the Canadian Pacific Steam Ships Line, near Quebec City, in June 1927. Before radar, collisions at sea were frequent. The *Metagama* survived the First World War only to collide with SS *Baron Vernon* on the Clyde in 1923 and with SS *Clara Camus* off Cape Race in 1924. Three years after this photo was taken, the *Metagama* was laid up to be broken up at Firth of Forth.

Canadian Pacific Railway bronze memorial to the many who lost their lives during the First World War in the service of the CPR. Windsor Station, Montreal, 1922.

The SS *Empress of Canada*, Queen of the Pacific, arrives in Vancouver, British Columbia, on her maiden voyage, June 24, 1922.

The *Beaverdale* was launched at Newcastle on September 28, 1927. In May 1933, rail track was laid on the deck of the ship to carry the "Royal Scot" — a fast British steam locomotive — and eight cars. The train toured Canada and the United States for eight months before returning home the same way. In May 1940, the *Beaverdale* crew helped with the evacuation of British soldiers stranded on the beach at Dunkirk. The ship was sunk by the German submarine *U-48* on April 1, 1941.

The Right Honourable William Lyon Mackenzie King and Sir George McLaren Brown being greeted by the Honourable Peter Larkin aboard the SS *Montcalm* en route to the Imperial Conference in London. Liverpool, England, September 29, 1923.

Second-class baggage onboard the SS *Empress of Britain*.

Van Horne's next step was to fill the remaining gap in the sea/rail route between Hong Kong and Liverpool — the busy Atlantic, where the railway had been dependant on the Allan and the Elder Dempster lines for their traffic. Because there was no shortage of rivals here for the mail contract, all shipowners understood that on the Atlantic only the fastest, biggest ships would do. Stephen may have dismissed Allan's ships as "those cattle boats," but at the turn of the century, his rival's 17 vessels dominated the Canada–Britain route and had set transatlantic records: their *Buenos Ayrean* had been the first steel ship on the North Atlantic and in another historic "first" in 1901, the *Sardinian* had carried Marconi and his equipment from Britain to set up the first radio station at St. John's, Newfoundland.

Aware of the Canadian Pacific's growing interest, in 1905 the Allan Line invested heavily in their *Victorian* (10,629 gt) and *Virginian* (10,757 gt), the first triple-screw, steam turbine liners in service in the North Atlantic. The Elder Dempster Line carried immigrants to Montreal from Liverpool in its "Beaver" ships. In 1874, the Beaver Line ship *Caspian* had brought the first cargo of refrigerated (chilled) meat to Liverpool from Canada, and another first had come in 1901 when their ship, *Lake Champlain*, left Liverpool after being fitted with the first radio to be used in a merchant ship. But as the Elder Dempster's concentration really was on the African trade, it was never a serious rival to the CPR, unlike the Allan Line.

Competition from the Allan Line did nothing to deter Van Horne, who was already planning an Atlantic service for the Canadian Pacific and had reserved the names *Empress of Austria* and *Empress of Germany* for its first liners. The Atlantic trade was all about speed — a quality that the former telegrapher and railway engineer understood. With the investment, the CPR's directors concluded that a Liverpool–Montreal service that connected through Canada with the Orient would be quicker, with less fuel used than going through the Mediterranean and Suez.

Then, in July 1886, the Canadian government called for tenders for a transatlantic mail service for ships at not less than 6,500 tons that could steam at between 15 to 18 knots. This was difficult enough for the fastest Allan Line ships to achieve but the London shipping company Anderson

& Anderson went one better by tendering for ships that could steam at 20 knots. Said to be acting for the Canadian Pacific Railway, they cabled Prime Minister Macdonald that they were sure of a contract from Stephen. He had other ideas and complained to Van Horne that he thought the Andersons were floating their scheme on the London Stock Exchange. The government then jumped on the bandwagon and took up the slogan "Twenty Knots to Canada." In the furor, the members of Parliament from Quebec insisted that the ships also call at a French port on every voyage — something that the Allan Line refused to consider outright.

For its part, the British government imposed its own conditions. Firmly entrenched in the imperial consciousness, the P&O retained it's monopoly to carry passengers and mail from Britain to the Far East. The great European shipping lines might be private, but their governments subsidized them in the form of outright loans (or guarantees on loans for the building of new liners) or contracts for the transport of mail and government cargo or per-passenger payments for the carriage of immigrants. The British government was already paying huge subsidies to help the Cunard Line compete with the American White Star Line. Although registered in Britain, White Star was owned by J. Pierpont Morgan who at that moment in time could, dollar for dollar, probably have competed with the British government itself.

For the British, it wasn't only the Americans that they had to compete with on the Atlantic. Aggressively expanding German lines like Hamburg-Amerika and the North German Lloyd were to be feared — and with good reason. It is forgotten today that until the First World War, Germany dominated transatlantic ocean traffic and that in 1898 the North German Lloyd line carried 30 percent of all passengers who arrived in New York. In 1897, the first of its fast ships, the *Kaiser Wilhelm der Grosse*, had the audacity to take the Blue Riband from Cunard! And besides the Germans, there was also the Holland-Amerika Line out of Rotterdam and the very elegant Compagnie Générale Transatlantique (CGT) of France, better known as the French Line.

Subsidizing national shipping lines was for much more than national prestige — as mass transit movers the liners were ideal troop carriers, and hundreds of soldiers and horses could be accommodated in steerage. The main reason that the French government so encouraged the French Line was the scandalous circumstances during the Crimean War, when French troops had travelled on foreign (British) ships to the Crimea. Military planners also appreciated the speed of liners. In 1902, when London pumped a huge government subsidy into Cunard so that it could order the *Lusitania* and *Mauretania*, the Admiralty specified that both ships be equipped with gun platforms. As the U-boat captains would one day claim in their defence, in time of war, the big passenger ships were legitimate targets.

If obtaining a subsidy from the British for a London–Montreal mail service was out of the question, the Canadian Pacific's directors knew that going to Ottawa for financial incentives was a waste of time. Much of the Canadian public held that the CPR had gotten a free ride off the previous Conservative governments, and in 1896, when the Liberals under Sir Wilfrid Laurier came to power, they were determined to break the Canadian Pacific's monopoly on transport on land and sea. To ensure that there was competition, the Laurier government went so far as to pour millions of the taxpayers' dollars into propping up the CPR's rivals, like the failing Grand Trunk Railway and the Canadian Northern. Far from enjoying government encouragement, for all of its existence whether as railway, steamship line, or airline, the Canadian Pacific would have to go it alone.

Fortunately, the CPR's new president, Sir Thomas G. Shaughnessy, had no need of subsidies. In 1903, the railway was wealthy enough to buy up 14 ships that the Elder Dempster Line, also known as the "Beaver" line, used on the Atlantic. Valued by Lloyd's at £1,120,000, Sir Alfred Jones, the head of Elder Dempster, realized a small profit by selling them to Canadian Pacific for £1,150,000. The twin-screw ships had accommodation for 100 passengers in first class, 80 in second class, and 500 in third class, and with them the company could begin a bi-weekly service between Montreal and London with a weekly service from Montreal to Bristol and Liverpool. On the other side of the country, an Australian service between Sydney and Victoria had started, with James Huddart as Canadian Pacific traffic agent with the first sailing from Sydney on May 18, 1893. The Union Steamship Company of New Zealand bought the company outright, and in 1911 it was incorporated as the Canadian–Australian Royal Mail Line.

In truth, Canadian Pacific now had to look to its laurels. The Cunard Line returned to Canada in 1903, first with its own ships and then in 1911 buying the Thompson and later the Anchor and Donaldson lines to compete for traffic between the Clyde and Canada. There were discussions between the CPR and Cunard to form a joint company on the North Atlantic route — a move that would certainly give both enough leverage over the German companies — but nothing came of it. Canadian Pacific's disadvantage was that it did not have the monopoly on the St. Lawrence, nor did it have any direct connection with American ports. What it did exploit in advertising was that by the sheltered St. Lawrence its ships plied a shorter route across the Atlantic. They also promised a high standard of service in accommodation, food, and amenities onboard.

When Andrew Allan, the son of the founder and now the chairman of the line, died in 1901, he was succeeded by Nathaniel Dunlop. The Allan fleet was in need of expensive renovation — its last sailing ship, the full rigged *Glenmorag*, had been disposed of as late as 1896; its ship, the *Huronian*, had disappeared without trace on its way from Liverpool to Saint John in March 1902; and there was no money to finance the building of more modern vessels. In 1909, at his advanced age of 80, Dunlop was ready to retire home to Glasgow, and there were rumours that he was preparing to sell out to the White Star. On July 6, lawyers for the Royal Trust Company acting on behalf of "clients whose names were not disclosed," offered to acquire the capital stock of the Allan Line Steamship Company Limited at a price of £1,609,000. And in addition, they were willing to pay £100,000 for "the goodwill of the agencies on both sides of the Atlantic." Of the 60,639 shares in the line, the Royal Trust bought 57,637, holding them in trust, with the Allan family continuing in managerial positions in Montreal.

Shaughnessy allowed the public to speculate that it was the Grand Trunk Railway that had bought the Allan Line and, although it became public knowledge in 1915, details of its official transfer to the Canadian Pacific did not become public until January 28, 1931, when the annual report showed that the Allan Line's deposits of $8.5 million were transferred from reserve to the CPR replacement fund. Some historians claim that Shaughnessy obtained the historic company through guile, others that the founder's descendants were pleased to sell — perhaps the truth lies in between. The sale was kept secret until officially announced in the House of Commons on October 1, 1915, when, following a meeting in Montreal of both boards, a new company was formed — Canadian Pacific Ocean Services — which took over both fleets.

The gross tonnage of the Allan Line was thought to be 155,000 tons and that of the CPR about 239,000 tons. On July 16, 1917, Allan's house flag was lowered for the last time, so ending a significant chapter in Canada's maritime history. In belated recognition for their places in Canada's maritime history, in 2004, both Hugh Allan and Samuel Cunard were commemorated with their own postage stamps.

On the date of the purchase, the company also chose to announce the separation of the management of Canadian Pacific's ocean-going fleet from the railway, hotels, and all other company branches. Logically seen as extensions of the railway, the CPR's internal and coastal ships were kept with it. While ownership and control of the 39 ships of approximately 400,000 gross tonnage (including seven under construction) would still be exercised by the Canadian Pacific Railway from the headquarters at Windsor Station, their management would be vested in the Board of Directors of the Canadian Pacific Ocean Services (CPOS) at 8 Waterloo Place, London. All the former Allan offices at Cockspur Street, Leadenhall Street, Glasgow, Dundee, and Londonderry were taken over and the Liverpool office in James Street closed in favour of the Canadian Pacific office in the Liver Building.

Cockspur Street was a particular prize. On Trafalgar Square, near Whitehall, Westminister, and the city, it was at the heart of the Empire, and the Grand Trunk Railway already had an office there. Canadian Pacific realized that the location made it an ideal venue for selling Canada and emigration to it to the British public — to the chagrin of the Canadian High Commission, which had to do the same from cramped offices on Victoria Street. In 1910, the CPR even resorted to the use of a "cinematograph" at its Trafalgar Square office, running movies that extolled the scenery of the country and the availability of farmland to all who applied. Although the company has since moved out of this classic (but what must have been increasingly crowded) building, still to be seen today are the CANADIAN PACIFIC RAILWAY letters engraved high above on its front facade.

With the purchase of the Beaver and Allan's passenger and cargo ships, the railway now had a substantial, fully operational fleet on the Atlantic. Because Quebec and Montreal were the summer terminals for the Canadian Pacific, the peninsula of Father Point (Point-au-Pere), near the Quebec town of Rimouski, took on a special significance. As the first and last point of contact for ships in Canada, one of the earliest lighthouses, wireless station, and government airport in Canada would be built here, for Father Point was where the pilot embarked or disembarked and mailbags were exchanged. More significantly for the immigrants, it was where the government immigration officers got on.

Masters and company directors dreaded their ships being stranded in quarantine if health inspectors discovered cases of smallpox or typhus in steerage. Those among them who were unfortunate were sent to Grosse Île, one of the islands forming the Île-aux-Grues archipelago bounded by Île d'Orléans and Île-aux-Coudres. Built to cope with the thousands who died here of typhus after escaping the Irish Potato Famine, the quarantine station for the port of Quebec from 1832 to 1937 at Grosse Île would play a major role in the protection of public health in Canada.

From 1904, after sailing from London, the Canadian Pacific ships *Montrose, Montreal, Mount Temple,* and *Montfort* stopped at Antwerp — the Dutch and German ports were reserved for their national lines — to pick up immigrants from all over Central Europe. History has recorded so much about the privileged few who enjoyed the amenities of the great Edwardian floating palaces, that their fellow voyagers in steerage remain forgotten. Steerage and third class meant crowded surroundings, bland food, and a place where one made one's own amusements — in short, exactly as the poor would have experienced ashore! Fares for immigrants were kept heavily subsidized and for the short timespan it took to get across the Atlantic, conditions were tolerable. Strangely enough, while a democratic mingling did occur during church services (as on shore), it was the invention of the cinema that allowed for the first daily mixing of the classes. But it would take two world wars before the one-class ships appeared.

Until the 1950s, one barrier that would never disappear onboard was class. Excited passengers soon discovered upon boarding that they were not allowed to explore wherever they chose — especially not the living quarters of another social strata. First-class decks and stairways were off-limits to those who had not paid for the privilege of using them. Mirroring the Edwardian society, where everyone knew their place, the patricians were high above the waterline, far from those in steerage. At the very top of the scale, both physically and socially, were those who could afford the staterooms with beds instead of bunks.

As they were escaping poverty, conditions for the immigrants in steerage had never been high, but the CPR ensured that these were improved with the new Empresses. By 1903, the disease-incubating dormitories had largely disappeared on all transatlantic ships and they were equipped with electric heating, hot and cold salt water on tap, and four-berth emigrant cabins came with spring mattresses. Those in third class were even served meals at a table. The German lines were famous for giving away blankets to those in steerage — it prevented the emigrants from bringing their own less-than-trustworthy bedding — but CPR's proud boast was that every emigrant-passenger was also supplied, without charge, with their own utensils to begin their new lives.

Along with Quebec and Montreal, in January 1881 Halifax was declared an official port of entry for immigrants to Canada. Until 1917, when it was destroyed in the Halifax explosion, all arrivals were processed at the north end, not far from the North Street Railway Station. Unlike the German lines and the Canadian Pacific, the British lines disdained carrying immigrants from Central Europe because of the filthy condition they were in. As fleas and lice from steerage travelled quite democratically through the classes, many ships had to be fumigated in port. Led by the German lines, shipping companies gradually realized that it made good economic sense to provide sanitary conditions in steerage.

Like the Allan Line, the Canadian Pacific Railway also opened European commercial/immigration offices, ran trade shows, and

CANADIAN PACIFIC — THE EASY WAY TO CANADA

The Canadian Pacific have successfully placed many hundreds of immigrants in the past, and the services of a large staff of colonization experts are available to look after the individual requirements of every settler, thus ensuring satisfaction. These specially reduced fares are considerably lower than the newly announced Reduced Third Class Ocean Fare of £10, applicable irrespective of occupation to persons of British nationality going out from residence in the United Kingdom to settle in Canada.

Fares from British ports to Canadian Pacific Centres are according to the following schedule:

Halifax, Nova Scotia	£2
Saint John, NB	£2
Quebec	£2
Montreal	£3
Toronto	£3 10 sh
Winnipeg	£4 10 sh
Saskatoon	£5
Regina	£5
Moose Jaw	£5
Edmonton	£5 10 sh
Calgary	£5 10 sh
Vancouver	£8

Special Rates are given to:

Families — Married men of farming experience and their wives and children.

British Farm Trainees — Men under 35 who have passed through the Ministry of Labour Training Course in the United Kingdom.

Domestic Servants — Women between 18 and 48 years with some household experience going to assured employment.

Nominated Passengers — Passengers for whom arrangements have been made by relatives or others authorized to do so in Canada.

Boys — Boys from 14 to 18 and children under 19 going out for arranged placement to be trained as farmers in Canada are provided with free passage.

THE WAY TO TRAVEL — Approved settlers have choice of sailings from Glasgow, Liverpool, Southampton and Belfast. Canadian Pacific have weekly sailings from all these ports with Third Class accommodation giving utmost comfort for families.

RECEPTION IN CANADA — Specially trained experienced men will meet all steamers and trains to assist settlers on their arrival, and arrange train journeys to final destination.

TRAVEL CANADIAN PACIFIC — ONE SERVICE, OCEAN AND RAIL

published advertisements, all extolling the wonders of Canada and its need for hardworking immigrants. The Prairies were not filling up as quickly as the railway hoped and, as humorist Stephen Leacock observed, there were years when plagues of grasshoppers would devour everything except the rails. Worse was the competition for prospective settlers from the shipping companies and railway lines in the United States. But what the CPR did have in plenty was land, and to attract the immigrants to buy it up, passages across the Atlantic were kept artificially low.

While the immigration drive was successful in Britain and Ireland — Canada was after all the breadbasket of the Empire — in 1913, when the company sought to tap into the Austro-Hungarian market, it overreached itself. It renamed two of its Elder Dempster ships, *Lake Champlain* and *Lake Erie*, the *Ruthenia* and the *Tyrolia* respectively and opened an "immigration facilitation" office in Vienna. The two carried Austrian subjects from Trieste to Montreal but not in numbers sufficient to make a profit. Worse, this angered the German shipping lines who felt that they should have the monopoly on all Austrian immigrant traffic. Viennese police arrested the staff at the CPR office on the trumped-up charge that the company had bribed 600,000 Austrians of military age to emigrate, and the case went to court. The company fortunately closed down the route just as the war broke out. During the First World War, the *Ruthenia* was converted to a dummy battleship, and HMS *King George V* later to a naval oiler. In 1929 it was taken out to Singapore for use as an oil hulk. Captured there by the Japanese in 1942, the ship was renamed *Choran Maru*. It survived the war intact, but in 1949 was towed to Dalmuir and scrapped, not far from where it had been built.

The lowest among the immigrant classes, in the very nethermost regions of the great ship, were the "assisted passages." The British shipped their convicts to Australia but the "assisted passages" were mainly sent to Canada. These were the unwanted of urban crowded Britain — destitute children, displaced families, and unemployed domestics who were put onboard the empty lumber and cattle ships returning to Canada, their passage paid for by charitable organizations, reformatories, churches, industrial schools, and emigration groups. It was a matter of convenience: the Allan Line ships brought cattle to Glasgow, so it made good economic sense to fill the same holds on the return voyage with "assisted passages." In 1910, when the cattle were unloaded, the *Sicilian* (6,224 gt) was flushed down with hoses and then bunks were built in the stalls with hay, called "donkey's breakfasts," with six persons to each. Seven decades later, the children who took that very ship still recalled the rats that shared their accommodation, the tubs of greasy food, and "thirteen and half days of sea-tossing."

The official immigration records and the ship's passenger lists are sparse as to who or how many they were, and few names, sex, numbers, or ages of "assisted passages" were recorded — only the Canadian destination to pass them on to. In a single year, 1913, these were just a few that the CPOS and former Allan ships landed in Canada. Unless otherwise noted, all were taken to the port of Quebec with its quarantine facilities (NB is Saint John, New Brunswick; H is Halifax).

Ship Arrivals 1913

March 1(H)	*Hesperian*	Children's group Knowlton, Quebec (School Farm)
March 17 (H)	*Canada*	Home Boys to Hamilton
March 29/30	*Corinthian*	Children's group to Peterborough/ Toronto (Dr. Barnardo's)
March 31(H)	*Scotian*	Children's group to Brockville
April (?)	*Megantic*	Mrs. Francis's party (domestics); Boys' League
April 12	*Corsican*	Mrs. Birt's party
April 18 (H)	*Virginian*	Children's group to Belleville
April 26	*Teutonic*	Mrs. Francis's party (domestics); Marquette party (?); O.B. Smith party (?); Mr. Pender's party (children)
April 27 (?)	*Lake Manitoba*	Party of Boys under Mr. Fagan for Toronto
May 7 (?)	*Victorian*	Home Children from Church of England, Waifs & Strays Society
May 7 (?)	*Victorian*	Miss Lightbourne's party (domestics); Children's Group Children's Aid Society
May 7 (?)	*Royal Edward*	Mrs. Joyce's party; Miss Lightbourne's party (domestics)
May 9	*Empress of Britain*	Mrs. Joyce's party; O.B. Smith party (?); Black's party
May 12	*Corsican*	Catholic party
May 12	*Corsican*	Mrs. Radford's party (domestics)
May 15	*Virginian*	O.B. Smith party (families); Mrs. Radford's party (domestics)
May 15	*Virginian*	Children's group; Waifs & Strays Society

May 26	*Tunisian*	Farrell party (families); Ontario Government party (families); Children's group Waifs & Strays Society
May 27	*Teutonic*	Mrs. Francis's party (domestics); Boys' League Farm group; Marquette party (?)
May 31	*Victorian*	Boys and Girls from Refugee Home Chatham, Manchester
May 31	*Victorian*	O.B. Smith party (?)
June 2	*Grampian*	Children's group to Brockville (Quarrier)
June 6	*Empress of Britain*	Salvation Army party (families); Mrs. Joyce's party (domestics)
June 9	*Corsican*	Children's groups going to Knowlton, Ottawa, and Sherbrooke
June 9 (H)	*Mongolian*	Orphans to Middlemore Home
June 9	*Corsican*	Mrs. Radford's party (domestics); Children's groups, Birk's Party and Roman Catholic Emigration Society Party and Protestant party
June 25	*Corinthian*	Ontario Government party (families); Children's group, Dr. Barnardo's for Peterborough, Toronto
June 27	*Victorian*	Mrs. MacArthur's party (domestics); Children's group Waifs & Strays Society Church of England London to Sherbrooke
July 8	*Corsican*	CPR party (families); Children's group

July 8	*Royal Edward*	Mrs. Joyce's party; British Women's Emigration Association (domestics); Hone & Rivet party (families); Miss Lightbourne's party (domestics); Abbot party (?); Roth party (?)
July 12 (NB)	*Orthia*	Mr. Garson's Farm
August 1	*Corsican*	Children's group to Ottawa
August 1	*Empress of Britain*	Mrs. Joyce's party; Hone & Rivet party (?)
August 1	*Corsican*	Nicol party (?); Mrs. Radford's party (domestics); Children's group (St. George's Home)
August 14	*Tunisian*	Children's group to Stratford (Mcpherson Homes)
August 14	*Tunisian*	Mrs. McArthur's party (domestics)
August 18	*Pretorian*	Children's group to Winnipeg
August 28	*Corsican*	Hone & Rivet party (?); Mrs. Radford's party (domestics); Children's group; Naval party
August 29	*Empress of Britain*	Mrs. Joyce's party; Salvation Army party (families?)
September 3	*Virginian*	Children's group to Stratford
September 6	*Hesperian*	Ontario Government party (?); Children's group (Mr. Costar's party) [Cossar]
September 25	*Corsican*	Mrs. Radford's party (domestics); Mrs. MacArthur's party (domestics); Children's group
September 26	*Empress of Britain*	Dowell party (domestics); Joyce party; Hone & Rivet party (?)

September 28	*Canada*	Mrs. Francis's party (domestics); Marquette party (?); Smith party (?); Joyce party
October 5	*Corinthian*	Home Boys to Peterborough/ Toronto
October 24	*Corsican*	Home Boys Roman Catholic to Ottawa (Catholic Emigration Association)
October 24	*Corsican*	Mrs. Radford's party (domestics); Catholic Women's Immigration Society (domestics); Mrs. MacArthur's party (domestics); Catholic League party (?); Mrs. McCantry's party (?)
October 25	*Empress of Britain*	Miss Black's party (?); Mrs. Joyce's party
October 27	*Corsican*	Roman Catholic Party of Children to Ottawa

*Note: In the early years, the report for the port of Quebec was the only one given.
Source: Government of Canada *Sessional Papers*, Government Immigration Reports (GIR), and passenger list records.

CHAPTER 4

The Era of the Great Ships

By 1912, as the largest movable objects that man had ever created, the great ships had evolved into floating metropolises. Rudyard Kipling thought that the *Mauretania* was a monstrous nine-decked city going out to sea and everyone chuckled along with actress Beatrice Lillie who, on boarding such a ship, quipped, "Say, when does this place get to New York?" With all that black metal plate bolted together they looked so solid, is it any wonder that they were thought unsinkable?

The new century saw the great ships in their heyday. No longer the unsafe vessels that took Canadian timber and cattle to Europe and returned with the same holds crammed with immigrants, they had gained from the advances in industrial design and power that had occurred during the late Victorian era. Electricity was first introduced on Cunard ships in 1886 in the form of bells to summon stewards, and the bridge was connected with the engine room by telephone.

Until then, a boy was stationed with the master and conveyed his instructions by running down flights of stairs to the engine room — a situation with obvious hazards. By 1900, there was electric lighting throughout every liner, with heating and hot water soon to follow. The first elevator to be installed on a ship was on the Hamburg Amerika Line's *Amerika* in 1905, its operation closely watched by those who said that it would jam every time the ship rolled. By the time the *Mauretania* was launched two years later, elevators had become essential on all new ships. At a time when much of the world didn't have them, by 1910 flush toilets were installed on all large liners and no longer were chamber pots emptied over the side. But water for showering and bathing, even in first class, remained salt with special soaps that had been designed to lather in it.

Before refrigeration, fresh food lasted the first and second day out but after that everything was tinned or salted, with pork appearing with monotonous regularity, as for some reason now lost, Victorians thought it conquered seasickness. At first in the basic form of an "ice room," refrigeration made a considerable difference to ship design and passenger comfort. Until electrically powered refrigeration first appeared on the Montreal–Liverpool route on the Allan Line's *Bavarian* in 1899, passenger ships had always carried a few cows and dozens of hens for fresh milk and eggs, and cattle and poultry men were an integral part of the crew.

In the first family of Empresses, the dining room was forward on the upper deck, with large windows. There were two main tables and small tables against the walls. Only the master had a chair and, as was the custom, the benches along the tables were kept as far away as possible from their edge so that the diners could escape quickly and be seasick. Just as airlines would six decades later, shipping lines competed for passengers by advertising more comforts — especially better food. It was this competition that demanded they produce great cuisine on the high seas and food in great variety and quantity played a huge part in the voyages — despite seasickness (or perhaps because of it). In 1912, the German lines even went to the extreme by employing the hotelier Cesar Ritz and the great chef Auguste Escoffier to plan the catering on their ships.

But Canadian Pacific's chefs were not far behind. The years of running dining cars on their trains and dining rooms at the hotels in Banff, Jasper, and all large Canadian cities had given the company the culinary expertise needed. The following description from the Chung Collection website gives an idea of the dining experience:

> An ocean voyage on the Canadian Pacific Empress Class of liners was a supreme travel experience for the affluent traveler. Nowhere was this experience more evident than in the first class dining-room. Food was prepared by the best of chefs and served by attentive, expert waiters. The menus catered to every whim and an extensive variety of choice was offered. One passenger, clearly impressed by the service, counted 117 items on the breakfast menu of the *Empress of Britain* and this was the simplest meal of the day!

Cuisine standards fell in the war years (ironically, when the company carried its greatest number of passengers — soldiers, POWs, and refugees) and the quality (though not the quantity) of the fare served on Canadian Pacific ships deteriorated as the war drew on. Items such as stodgy Victoria Pudding, made mainly with raisins, and the tapioca dessert remembered as "fish eyes in glue," were not well received. As meat, sugar, and coffee became increasingly scarce in 1943–45, after long voyages, passengers and crew looked forward to calling in at Capetown, Sydney, or New York where there were no such shortages.

> First Class passengers could take their meals in the opulent dining-rooms of the Empress Class or be served privately in their cabins. Between meals, waiters might come around with bouillon in cold weather, and ice cream when the weather was hot and, of course, a multitude of reviving drinks was never far away — the *Empress of Britain* offered 13 different kinds of champagne! All Empress Class ships carried a distinctive

line of china and silverware. Minton of England, W.H.
Grindley, and North Staffordshire all manufactured fine
dinnerware in the Empress pattern showing a vase of
multi-coloured flowers with birds all in an Asian motif
on a white body.

The menu for each meal was printed exclusively for the day and
there was a different one for each of the three classes. There were even
menus printed for special tables and occasions — sometimes they
included the selection of music to be played by the ship's orchestra at
the sitting — and the menus became a souvenir of the meal. All of this
was done by the ship's own printers who also issued a ship's newspaper,
the *Empress Daily News*, which was distributed free of charge onboard.
If that wasn't enough, there were the ships' own song books for sing-
a-longs, the contents varying according to class. When the round-the-
world cruises began, whole libraries of "shore sheets" were published,
telling of the delights of Siam, tropical fruits of Java, Javanese batik, the
perils of Cairo, Shanghai, and Gibraltar, and even information sheets to
pass around your family and friends as to where, when, and how you
could be reached at each of the ship's ports of call.

A constant from Sam Cunard's day was that every new ship that
joined the North Atlantic run boasted a higher standard of luxury and
comfort for its passengers than its predecessors. Increasingly resembling
hotels at sea, the liners attracted those privileged people who expected
ever-grander public rooms, to eat even finer food, and to enjoy such
modern conveniences as private bathrooms with hot and cold running
water, electric lights, and heat. By continuously increasing the size and
number of facilities on the ship, it seemed that designers were working at
inventing the illusion that the traveller had never left dry land.

Movie stars Douglas Fairbanks and Mary Pickford were among the
many celebrities on the inaugural voyage of the greatest, most luxurious
Canadian Pacific liner of them all, the *Empress of Britain II*. On June
2, 1931, when it arrived at Wolfe's Cove, Fairbanks was asked by the
press what he thought of the ship. He founds two faults with it, he said:
the voyage was too short because of the many attractions that the ship

offered, and second, these same attractions robbed one of the sense of being on an ocean voyage.

Then and until the very last Empress sailed from Canada for Liverpool in 1971, the passenger was supreme. "The transition from humble cargo ship to a passenger ship comes as something of a culture shock," remembers Peter Roberts, who joined the *Empress of Canada II* as 4th Officer in 1952. "Once you have got over the structure of the ship, its masses of passage ways, elegant public spaces, promenade decks, watertight doors, cavernous engine rooms and people, a whole new set of rules have to be observed."

According to Roberts, a strict hierarchy was mantained onboard a passenger ship, spreading from the captain, who was "virtually master of all he surveyed," down. Juniors held the senior officers in awe, and since most of them had seen service in the Second World War, they were heroes in Robert's eyes. New entrants who had not served as cadets with the company were generally assigned to passenger ships to learn the "Canadian Pacific Way."

"I think that there were two distinct types of seaman: those that chose the carefree, wandering, somewhat laid back life on a cargo ship crewed only by men, and those that can accept the life on a passenger ship, which is necessarily more formal, a strict dress code where there is a uniform for every occasion, and considerably more discipline," Robert observed. "Many of the senior officers at that time were in the Royal Naval Reserve and they brought with them a touch of the Navy. Saluting was not uncommon."

Roberts explained that a deck officer was expected to know all about "driving a boat," and would have obtained his Masters Foreign Going Certificate. He would be skilled in navigation by sextant, compass, and chronometer, and know how to avoid collisions, He was trained in ship construction, damage control, firefighting, first aid, meteorology, signals, maritime law, marine insurance, and thoroughly conversant with the Merchant Shipping Acts. He continued:

> You knew how to load and discharge any type of cargo,
> filthy, smelly, very heavy, fragile, dangerous, bullion,

bulk oil or grain etc., coal, pig iron, steam locomotives, scrap metal, wool, timber, oranges, cattle and explosives ... you name it. And have a sufficient knowledge of geography to know where to take it.... You've experienced tropical storms, ice bergs, shifting cargo, leaks and fires, crew troubles, rescue missions, stowaways, extreme cold and heat, injuries and occasional deaths ... been subjected to injections [and] vaccinations to protect you against strange tropical diseases.

One thing these seamen had not been taught, however, was how to deal with passengers. "It was paramount that you didn't upset a passenger," Roberts noted. "After all, this was your cargo and the source of your livelihood." Regular passengers had their favourite captains and would only travel on his ship. And it was not unknown for even well-respected captains to lose their jobs because they had upset a valued passenger: "You could chat your way out of many things on your ship, bend it, delay it, catch fire to it, get lost, but a letter to the President of the Company from a disgruntled customer was fatal."

Much has been written about Captain Edward John Smith, master on the *Titanic*, and his faults have been magnified since that fateful night: at 62 he was "too old," he was "too amiable," or he was "too soft-spoken." But he was a society captain, chosen by White Star for his ability to entertain the passengers, rather than an aloof martinet. The perfect master of a ship probably never existed in any line, but Canadian Pacific had its share of the best. To command a company ocean liner, coastal steamer, or bulk carrier required a very special individual. Coping equally well with the elements, the crew, and the passengers, the masters had been chosen by the directors not only to get their substantial investment (whether it be a Stikine River sternwheeler at 277 tons or the *Empress of Britain II* at 42,500 tons) from A to B, but to do so in such a manner as to make it look easy. The great Canadian Pacific masters, such as R.G. Latta, R.N., Stuart VC. DSO, Samuel Robinson, and J.P. "Dobbie" Dobson, were revered by crew and passengers alike, and rightly so. Many others were relatively unknown — Chief Officer H. Pybus, one of the outstanding figures in the company's early history, or Captain L.D. Douglas, who would rise to be general superintendent of Canadian Pacific Steamships, for example.

Most were like Captain "Dick" Hickey, who in 1942 was appointed marine superintendent for Canadian Pacific Steamships. The son of Captain P.J. Hickey, an Irish Newfoundlander, Hickey had gone to sea at 13 — and was referred to as "Young Dick Hickey" by those who knew him for decades after. A "quarterdeck boy" on the Alaska runs, within the next ten years he had won his master's ticket. In 1916, he joined the *Monteagle* on the Pacific as a fourth officer and then managed to get on the *Empress of Japan*, where he came to Captain Hopcroft's attention. He rose through various berths on the *Asia, Russia, France,* and finally came to the *Empress of Canada* as a staff captain.

The only misfortune that the shipping companies could not shield their passengers from was that perennial curse of all mariners — seasickness — now compounded by the vibration of the ship's engines. On the *Britannia*, Charles Dickens would record in his diary, "Not sick, but going to be." And a century later, little had improved when, in *Brideshead Revisted*, Evelyn Waugh has Mr. and Mrs. Charles Ryder endure a miserable crossing of the Atlantic. As the crockery begins to slide, Mrs. Ryder remarks, "Either I am a little drunk or it's getting rough." In the era of sail, the privileged had cabins at the rear of the ship, but now that the solution was to escape the vibration of the engines, the best cabins were located as far away from them and as high as possible in the superstructure. For those in steerage, though, there was no escape.

Decades before the Canadian Pacific opened theirs in 1912, the White Star Line, Cunard, and P&O had operated staff recruitment offices in Southampton for what would be described as "hospitality personnel." The effect that competition for passengers had on the expansion and sex of the ship's crew was proportionate to the number and wealth of the passengers. When Sam Cunard put his first ship to sea in 1840, the only person that the eight passengers could turn to for comfort was an untrained ship's surgeon. In 1903, the Empresses carried 50 stewards, pursers, and

A Day on the *Duchess of York*

Morning: The assistants and kitchen-boys were up at 05:30, and fifteen minutes later would be coming up the companion ways like commuters from the underground. The first chore was to give the stewards their breakfast. Then breakfast for a thousand people and lighting the charcoal grilles. The two sittings for breakfast put the pressure on three sections, two in the still-room preparing thousands of rounds of toast, waffles, griddle cakes, eggs and gallons of coffee, hot milk and tea; the third section prepared the fried eggs and grilled bacon and omelettes. After breakfast the assistants formed into a cleaning squad to thoroughly clean the kitchen with boiling soapy water. If there was to be a captain's inspection (we had two a week) we were kept very busy until 10:30 hours. We returned to the kitchen at 11:00 hours having washed and changed and were now ready for the next onslaught — lunch, the soup section having already sent the beef tea to the promenade deck. A very extensive a la carte menu was offered to the Cabin passengers including a large cold buffet table. A reduced menu was offered the Tourist class and table d'hote to the Third Class. The bedroom stewards did all the carving on the hotplate and the cold buffet; the bellboys acted as runners to replenish the buffet.

Afternoon: Lunch would be over by 14:00 hours and it was then customary for the chef to allocate any food that had been left over for the waiters, the kitchen staff having made their own arrangements. The chef then left the kitchen leaving the senior kitchen staff to act out a time honoured perk. Many of the senior stewards, who made substantial tips, paid to be 'looked after,' a fee having been agreed between the parties concerned. The grill cook would barter steaks with the larder chef for seafood salads or with the entree cook for special entrees, the vegetable cook provided vegetables for all three. Although this may appear to have been a sordid exercise … it was a way of supplementing poor pay and it maintained an *entente cordiale* between restaurant and kitchen.

Evening: After lunch the assistants and kitchen boys prepared for dinner at 19:30 hours. In the larder they would prepare hundreds [of] cocktail canapes for early evening cocktail parties. The vegetable section might have hundreds of potatoes to turn, crates of beans to string, peas to shell, but there was always a fantastic spirit. The senior cooks were recalled at 16:00 hours, when there was a hectic run-up to dinner. When we had finished our dinner at about 21:45 hours, the senior staff departed and the assistants formed into three gangs, washing, scrubbing and squeegeeing the kitchen. We then reported to the vegetable preparing room to put three-quarters of a ton of potatoes through the machines. The chef usually looked in to be treated with the greatest respect, especially at 23:00 hours, when he would say, "The rest of the day is your own — and don't forget there is an hour on the clock." (This when we were sailing east.)

Nighttime: The night before the ship docked we would work through the night, following the tradition that you never took a dirty ship into port. We washed every square-inch of the paintwork, burnished the stove tops until they gleamed as new, pickled and polished every piece of copper equipment; next morning we collected our cards.

Source: John Crowley's (1930s) *Hotel, Catering and Institutional Management Journal.*

catering staff — and 68 deck and engineering staff. Soon such trades as shop attendants, musicians, printers, baggage handlers, elevator engineers and operators, barkeepers, and stenographers outnumbered the crew. By the 1930s, the Empresses had 380 staff who catered only to the passengers and 250 for the running of the ship.

When Dickens had sailed on the *Britannia*, he and the ship's doctor had distracted themselves from the motion caused by a stormy passage by playing endless card games. The ship's surgeon was an ancient profession, owing more to the bloody cruelty of naval warfare than the comfort of passengers. While the crew was kept away from the passengers, only the captain and the doctor were encouraged to socialize. As Thomas E. Appleton noted in his book *Ravenscrag: The Allan Royal Mail Line*,

> The social pattern tended to revolve around the doctor … an officer of importance … he could order medical comforts for the relief of emigrants and dispense his sympathy in the best bedside manner to the more interesting ladies in the first class. Most seagoing surgeons were fresh from university, unmarried and a source of great interest to mothers and daughters.

Atlantic crossings were too short for major medical traumas to develop — except perhaps for hypochondria among the pampered — but as ships ventured on round-the-world cruises, as the Canadian Pacific did between the wars, a fully staffed and equipped dispensary became essential. In the 1930s, the *Empress of Britain* fielded a surgeon, two nurses, and a dentist. Prior to joining the *Empress of Britain* in 1957 as Ship's Nurse, Margaret Knox had been a district nurse and midwife in Scotland:

> The medical staff consisted of the doctor, the dispenser, the hospital attendant and the nurse. The hospital had a treatment room also used by the doctor as a consulting room, 2 wards and an isolation area of 3 wards separate from the main hospital. The doctor did his rounds each morning accompanied by the nurse — there always seemed to be a list of cabins where a visit was requested. And not just the passengers: there were 450 officers and crew too. Passengers who were seasick were the responsibility of the stewards. Another duty of the nurse was to stand at the gangway with the doctor on embarkation watching the passengers boarding for any signs of disablement, advanced pregnancy, spots … anything that might cause problems during the voyage, but particularly infections.

A Canadian Pacific officer in the 1950s recalled, "We seemed to have a pretty high turn over in surgeons, whether it was because they joined a ship to practice or to avoid a practice ashore. On occasions I used to offer a prayer to God to keep me healthy, but in the main they were pretty good chaps and sometimes brought about some miraculous cures." He remembered a doctor in the 1960s who had had to treat a hemorrhaging patient, so he blood tested everyone onboard until he found a compatible group. "The Doctor kept the patient alive with transfused blood from a couple of donors until this airlifted supply was dropped to us." An RCAF Maritime Lancaster dropped the blood supply, which was recovered by a lifeboat. On arrival at Quebec, the ship was met by an RCAF officer who wanted his parachute back.

Ships, even Canadian Pacific ones, were meant to be English country houses at sea and, until broken down by the Second World War, the British class system was rigidly enforced. Brochures warned that servants were not entitled to sit at meals in the dining room. For staff, it was no different than working in a hotel. Canadian Pacific stewardesses who sailed in the 1930s recalled that "you had to be very subservient to passengers." For example, they had dinner in the passengers' dining room after they'd eaten — at different tables but the same food. And no staff was ever allowed to use the swimming pool. Even among the crew themselves there was a strictly observed hierarchy. John MacPhail, a steward onboard the Empresses in the 1950s, remembered:

> You had to work many years in the company to become a waiter in the First Class saloon or in the Smoking Rooms and Lounges. Except for forays into Montreal where the ship was docked for four to five days, people mixed only among their own group — the deck, engineering, and catering departments kept to themselves. Of course, the deck department didn't think that the rest of the crew were proper seamen.

Under the terms of the Berlin Conventions of 1903 and 1906, all large ocean liners were required to install wireless telegraph equipment

— especially if visiting North American ports. The first merchant ship ever fitted with wireless (radio) was the Elder Dempster's (later Canadian Pacific's) *Lake Champlain* (7,392 tons) in 1901. But the first passengers to owe their lives to a "Marconi" operator (as radio operators were called) were those on the White Star's *Republic*. Lost in a Nantucket fog on January 23, 1909, the ship was rammed by the Italian liner *Florida*. All power went out, but by using batteries, the *Republic*'s radio operator sent out a "CQD" signal — ("SOS" had not come into being yet) and the *Florida* returned and safely took all the passengers off.

After that, shipowners hired radio operators (invariably called "Sparks" — because the primitive equipment sparked) directly from the Marconi Company. Soon, every Canadian Pacific ship was equipped with Marconi equipment, which had a 984-foot wavelength and a standard range of 250 miles. They also used "callsigns," for example *Montcalm* was MLZ, *Empress of Britain* was MPB, *Empress of Ireland* was MPL, and *Empress of India* was MPI. Masters came to rely on the operators for weather reports and iceberg warnings, the passengers for the latest Wall Street prices and connecting travel arrangements. In May 1907, the Meteorological Service of the Dominion of Canada began sending, by telegraph, time signals from the Observatory at Saint John, new Brunswick, to the Marconi Wireless Station at Camperdown, where they were automatically transmitted to ships at sea. The *Empress of Ireland*, out of Liverpool and bound for Saint John via Halifax, on April 23, 1908, reported reception of the very distinct 10:00 a.m. wireless time signal while 160 miles southeast of Halifax. The navigating officer could now check the ship's chronometers by wireless.

The great shipping lines spent the early years of the twentieth century trying to outdo one another in the size and luxury of their ocean liners. The White Star Line was in the process of having the three sisters built: *Titanic*, *Britannic*, and *Olympic*. Cunard met White Star with its own behemoths, the *Mauretania* and *Lusitania*. What 50 years earlier had been transport for mail, immigrants, and soldiers were now national

A Murder Mystery on the High Seas

Oh Miss Le Neve, oh Miss Le Neve, Is it true that you are sittin' On the lap of Dr. Crippen, In your boy's clothes, On the *Montrose*, Miss Le Neve?

— popular song, 1910, London, England

The Canadian Pacific ship *Montrose* (5,431 tons) entered the history books on July 7, 1910, when a radio message sent from it led to the arrest of the murderer Dr. Hawley Harvey Crippen. If the use of the new technology was not newsworthy enough, the story behind it had all the ingredients of an Edwardian melodrama — Crippen was a mild-mannered American chemist (he did not have a medical degree) in London, married to the wealthy, extroverted Belle. When he had the misfortune to fall in love with his secretary, the meek Miss Ethel Le Neve, he poisoned Belle, dismembered her body, and buried the parts in the cellar of the family home. The lovebirds escaped the attention of the police but not Belle's social circle — Miss Le Neve having made the foolish mistake of wearing Belle's jewellery in public.

Crippen told the police that his wife had left for America, and before Belle's friends could persuade Scotland Yard to break into his home, fled to "foreign parts" with Le Neve, boarding the *Montrose* at Antwerp. With the grisly discovery in the cellar coming so soon after the still unsolved Jack the Ripper killings, the tabloid press, vaudeville halls, and politicians played the murder up. Taking a second-class cabin, with Ethel disguised as a boy, the pair posed as father and son and attempted to keep to themselves. But during the voyage, Ethel attracted the attention of the other passengers when "he" saved a little Belgian child from falling overboard.

It might still have worked had not the *Montrose*'s master, Harry Kendall, noticed that the boy's hips swayed "unnaturally" and that his hair under the floppy cap was too soft. Also, his pants were held up by a large safety pin. Kendall confirmed his suspicions by studying the pairs' photos in a copy of the last newspaper bought before leaving Liverpool and then had the Marconi operator alert London as to the identities of the "father and son" onboard.

The new Home Secretary, a young Winston Churchill, realized that this case could do his political career no harm and ordered Scotland Yard's Inspector Walter C. Dew to Canada on Cunard's *Laurentic*. The *Montrose* made its way across the Atlantic, Kendall ensuring that its passengers were kept blissfully unaware of the drama around them. But the press kept the story on the front page in Britain and Canada: Would the *Laurentic* pass the *Montrose* and allow Dew to intercept the Crippens? Or would they escape into the wilderness of Canada?

The *Laurentic* did outrace the *Montrose* and waiting for the CPOS ship at Father Point, wearing pilots' uniforms (so as not to arouse suspicions), was Inspector Dew and two Canadian policemen. They came aboard and arrested Crippen, who was said to have cursed Kendall: "You will suffer for this treachery, sir!" Miss Le Neve, on the other hand, seemed quite relieved. The suspects were returned to London, where, after a sensational trial, Le Neve was declared innocent and Crippen was found guilty. He was executed on November 23, 1910 — becoming the first criminal to be caught by ship-to-shore communications.

Churchill sent Kendall a cheque for £250 — which the captain had framed. Crippen's nemesis, the *Laurentic*, was converted to an armed merchant cruiser during the war, and on January 25, 1917, after hitting two mines, sank off the coast of Donegal in less than an hour. Its sinking was the largest loss of life ever in a mining of a ship: of the 475 onboard, only 121 survived. Kendall would go on to face the worst disaster in Canadian maritime history, as master of the doomed *Empress of Ireland*. Later, he left Canadian Pacific to join the Royal Navy and command the HMS *Calgarian*, only to have it torpedoed under him. He died in 1965 at the ripe old age of 91.

status symbols and reflections of the ambitions of a country. While all of these ships were for the United States ports, to lure passengers for their Liverpool–Quebec City route, Canadian Pacific ordered two luxury liners of its own. With growing Austro-German belligerence, the new Empresses were named not after Germany and Austria (as Van Horne had intended) but the countries from where most of the immigrants originated. The *Empress of Britain* and *Empress of Ireland* were twin-screw ships of 14,000 tons each and designed to carry 1,550 passengers at an average speed of 20 knots.

Because they were in competition for passengers with the New York–bound ships, the company spared no expense, with each Empress costing £375,000. Both had complete libraries, a café, and an atrium that was on two levels. There was leather upholstery in the dining room and the ornate ceilings were shamelessly copied from regal country houses. In 1910, the first movie to be shown onboard any CPOS ship took place on the *Britain*. The twins also rivalled each other in speed, but the *Britain* was faster, completing her first trip across in six days, 17 hours. In all, the two ships were masterpieces to Edwardian taste and technology.

The sinking of the White Star's *Titanic* in 1912 was a tragedy that affected the maritime industry deeply. A little-known fact is that, of the 1,320 passengers onboard the *Titanic* on its fateful last voyage, 130 of them had been bound for Canada — mainly in middle class and steerage. They were proof of the competition on the Atlantic faced by the Canadian Pacific. Of the Canadians onboard, 82 died and 48 survived. Many were from Winnipeg where there are streets named after them. Fortunately for Canadian aviation, a young lady named Ethel Fortune survived. On returning home, she married her fiancé, Crawford Gordon, and their eldest son, Crawford Gordon, Jr., would become head of A.V. Roe and be instrumental in building the Avro Arrow, possibly the greatest aircraft that Canada would ever produce.

Just as aircraft manufacturers and airlines do today, the significance of a speed record being broken on a maiden voyage assumed significance out of all proportion. In 1898, Morgan Robertson's novel *Futility, the Wreck of the Titan* presciently told of a liner called the *Titan* that in racing across the Atlantic on its maiden voyage rams another ship in two, then hits an iceberg and sinks. Some of the CPOS's ships, such as the *Mount Temple*, received the *Titanic*'s desperate SOSs but were too far away to do anything. But at the inquest, the company's masters were considered so knowledgeable about icebergs in the Atlantic that they were called upon to give evidence.

Because of the northerly route that they habitually took, the Canadian Pacific captains knew that if given a choice, it was safer to ram an iceberg head on rather than sideswipe it. In 1927, the *Montcalm* struck an iceberg in the Strait of Belle Isle but was sufficiently undamaged to continue on her way to the Clyde for repairs. On Easter Monday 1928, heading out of Saint John, the master of the *Montrose II* turned his ship to avoid an iceberg — only to come upon another directly behind it! Rather than put his ship between the two, he rammed the second head on. The forward bow crumpled, the hold was flooded, and a mass of ice fell onto the deck, killing two seamen — but the ship remained afloat and made it into Liverpool.

The effects on the Edwardian world of the *Titanic* sinking are comparable in contemporary society with the events that took place on September 11, 2001. It forced all seafaring nations and shipping companies to take extraordinary safety measures, the International Ice Patrol was formed, and lifeboat, fire, and evacuation drills were now rigorously enforced. Ships were festooned with "collapsibles," and radio operators worked in shifts so that there was always someone on duty. The two Empresses, for example, were equipped with more than enough lifeboats and life jackets for all their passengers and crew — each had 16 steel lifeboats and 20 Englehart "collapsibles." The hulls of both were divided into 11 sections sealed off by the bulkheads. This meant that when their doors were shut the ship was watertight and could float with two full compartments flooded. After the *Titanic* sinking, no one was taking any chances.

Although none of the CPOS's Empresses were sunk by an iceberg, they were not immune to what had befallen Robertson's *Titan* — collision with another ship. Before radar, there were several instances of collisions at sea. The *Empress of Canada* alone collided with Japanese *Kinsho Maru* in 1927 and the *Yetai Maru* in 1932. But none compared with what happened to the *Empress of Ireland*.

On the evening of May 28, 1914, the *Ireland* was steaming down the St. Lawrence with Harry Kendall, the same master from the Crippen capture, in command. Of the 1,477 passengers onboard, 167 were members of the Salvation Army who joined at Quebec. Seen off with their band playing the hymn "God Be with You Till We Meet Again," they were attending a congress in London.

The *Empress* had already done 95 crossings and had 16 steel lifeboats with an Englehart "collapsible" under each one. The day before, Kendall had an emergency drill performed and it had taken a record three minutes to shut each bulkhead door and less than one to swing out the lifeboats. The pilot was dropped at Father Point, the passengers retired to bed, and Kendall arrived on the bridge. At 1:38 a.m. he saw on his starboard bow the lights of the Norwegian collier *Storstad* coming upriver from Sydney, Nova Scotia, and had the *Empress* alter course. Then the collier disappeared into the fog. (Sudden fogs were a known hazard on the St. Lawrence — on July 27, 1912, the *Empress of Britain* had collided with and sunk the *Helvetia* in fog off Cape Madeleine.) Growing alarmed, Kendall put the *Empress* in full astern and gave three blasts of his whistle — the international signal that he was reversing. But there was no sign of the oncoming *Storstad*.

Fearing the worst, Kendall ordered his ship to stop dead in the water and gave two more blasts of the whistle. At 1:55 a.m., to his horror, he saw the collier appear out of the fog and make directly for him. He ordered full speed ahead to get out of its way but they had run out of time. The *Storstad* struck the *Empress* in its very centre, ripping it open. Kendall thought that, as it had impaled itself on his ship, the *Storstad* might just plug up the hole. He yelled for the master of the collier to put on full speed — but it was to no avail. Having gouged a tear across the *Empress*'s side, the *Storstad* continued on its way, disappearing into the fog.

Kendall attempted to beach the *Empress* in shallow water and ordered full speed toward the shore, two miles distant. But the 350-foot tear brought the river flooding in, extinguishing the dynamos. The ship lost all power. In the darkness of that first night out, passengers were unfamiliar with where they were sleeping, let alone where the lifeboats were, and those not still asleep panicked. The crew desperately attempted to close the electrically operated bulkhead doors manually but Kendall's order to head toward the shore only increased the flood of water pouring in and the ship began to list.

The Marconi operators sent out SOS signals as the lifeboats were lowered, but with the angle of the listing ship, only nine of the lifeboats were launched and the few passengers that made it onto the sloping deck chose instead to jump into the river. The *Eureka* and the *Lady Evelyn* were lying alongside the wharf at Father Point with steam up. Both put out on receiving the *Empress of Ireland*'s SOS. They picked up several hundred survivors, while the *Storstad*, which had turned back, found others, among them Kendall. "You sank my ship!" he is supposedly to have charged his rescuers. By 2:10 a.m. the *Empress of Ireland* had disappeared beneath the St. Lawrence, taking with it 1,012 lives — 134 of whom were children.

Unlike the *Titanic*, the *Empress* had sunk close to shore. Newspapers erroneously reported that passengers had dived off (depicted as comely young women) and swam ashore, and that the Canadian Pacific had at first attempted to refloat it. But (also unlike the *Titanic*) it had landed on the bottom on it side, forcing the company to abandon the plan. Instead, it had divers blow holes in the hull to retrieve the first-class mail, the purser's safe, and $150,000 in silver bullion (about $3 million today) — along with 250 bodies.

The sinking of the *Empress of Ireland* would be the worst maritime disaster in Canadian history. Unhappily, coming two years after the *Titanic* and a year before the *Lusitania*, it would fall between the cracks of history and be forgotten. Comparisons with the more famous ships were inevitable, with the newspapers even calling it "Another Titanic Disaster." But the *Ireland*'s passenger list had none of the railroad tycoons or "glitterati'" of the *Titanic*, and not having been torpedoed as the *Lusitania* was soon to be, the sinking was not newsworthy enough outside Canada. A fund set up in London by the Lord Mayor for the victims of the *Empress of Ireland* tragedy yielded barely £45,364 in Britain and $36,000 in Canada — sums which did not compare with the £430,780 that had been raised for the *Titanic* victims. And three months later, the First World War began, making mass murder commonplace. The *Empress of Ireland* disappeared into history — forgotten by all except the Salvation Army. The CPR erected three memorials: one at Father Point; another at the Archeveche de Rimouski Cemetery, Rimouski, for seven of those who lost their lives (including three unidentified victims); and a third at Mount Hermon Cemetery, Sillery, Quebec, for 39 unidentified victims.

The Board of Inquiry into the sinking convened at Quebec City on June 16, 1914, and was presided over by Lord Mersey, who had gained experience with the *Titanic* investigation and who would also preside over the sinking of the *Lusitania*. To nobody's surprise, the Chief Officer on the *Storstad* was found to be completely at fault for not waking the master in time. The Norwegian ship was sold to pay for some of the damages and would be torpedoed in 1917. Scuba divers located the wreck of the *Empress of Ireland* in 1964 and artifacts from it are on display at the Le Musée de la mer de Pointe-au-Père in Quebec. To prevent any further vandalism, on April 30, 1998, the Canadian government declared the remains of the *Empress of Ireland* a historic site. Grace Hanagan Martyn, the baby daughter of the Salvation Army Staff Commander, and the last survivor of the sinking, would die on May 15, 1995.

CHAPTER 5

War

On the eve of your departure from Canada I wish to congratulate you on having the privilege of taking part, with the other forces of the Crown, in fighting for the Honour of the King and Empire. You have nobly responded to the call of duty, and Canada will know how to appreciate the patriotic spirit that animates you. You leave these shores with the knowledge that all Canadian hearts beat for you, and that our prayers and best wishes will ever attend you. May God bless you and bring you back victorious.

— Arthur, Duke of Connaught, governor general of Canada

The First World War had a profound effect on the CPR and the company was involved with wartime duties from the very first day to the armistice and beyond. Arrangements for the transportation of the First

Contingent of the Canadian Army began on August 15, 1914, when Sir Sam Hughes, the minister of militia, met with the shipping companies. He told them that the government needed 20 ships to carry 25,000 men across the North Atlantic within a month. It took until September 11 for the details to be worked out and the contracts signed and by then the number of ships needed was increased to 30 with ten of these from the Canadian Pacific. All were prepared for their troopship role at Montreal and when ready were sent downriver to Quebec City, where the entire Canadian military force to be sent overseas was assembled at Valcartier.

The general assumption was that the soldiers would all be home after Christmas — victorious, of course — and the frenzy to get to Europe before the last shot was fired must have been palpable. The army began moving to the port of Quebec on the wet night of September 23/24, arriving at day-break drenched "but with morale high." At the wharf, it was, as one officer observed, complete chaos, adding, "I do not think one should be overly critical when it is remembered that an unmilitary nation had raised a force of nearly 30,000 fighting men in about six weeks, and was now sending it overseas." Barely three of the ships had been loaded according to the detailed plan drawn up by the director of supplies and transport when Hughes interfered, his erratic and contradictory orders causing the chaos to worsen.

The following is an example of what was being transported that September by the CPOS ships:

> *Corinthian* (formerly Allan Line): Passengers: Contingent HQ Staff, Heavy Battery and Ammunition Column, Div. Signals Comp., Motor Machine Gun personnel for total of 387. Cargo included small arms ammunition, grain, cheese, and lumber.
>
> *Scandinavian* (formerly Allan Line): Passengers: First Class 200; Second Class 200; Steerage 800 10th Battalion (Reserve) 4th CIB #1 General Hospital personnel for total 1,277. Cargo: ammunition and 21,109 sacks of flour.
>
> *Virginian* (formerly Allan Line): Passengers: 1,394 troops of 7th Btn (2nd Inf Bde) from British Columbia and

Div. Train, Railway Supply, and Hospital Staffs. Cargo:
Ammunition, medical stores, flour, and lumber.

Just before the sailing began, there was a portent of things to come: on September 22, a single German submarine *U-9* had torpedoed HMS *Aboukir*, *Hogue*, and *Cressy* in the North Sea in less than an hour, the British cruisers going down with the loss of 1,400 men. Whether this was kept secret from the troops is not known but the next day the embarkation began in earnest with the last ship loaded ready to sail at 5:00 p.m. October 1. Amazingly, the whole embarkation of horses, men, guns, and wagons had been completed in less than three days. Some ships had to load ballast for stability, and an extra ship had to be found to embark men, horses, and stores that had been left behind. The sum total of what was being taken by the 30 ships was: 1,547 officers, 29,070 men, 7,679 horses, 70 guns, 110 motor vehicles, 705 horsed vehicles, 82 bicycles, and the Burgess-Dunne, Canada's first (and only) military aircraft, lashed on the deck of the *Athenia* because there was no one who could dismantle it and it was too bulky to fit intact in the hold. Sharing the fate of most of the men and horses, the aircraft did not return home at Christmas — or ever.

As each ship was loaded, it went out into the river and anchored. The master was allowed to open his sealed orders, which directed him to proceed down the river and, after the pilot had been dropped at Father Point, to continue on to an anchorage in Gaspé Bay. German spies were thought to be everywhere and once the 30 ships were at their anchorages, they were ordered blacked out at night and wireless silence observed. On October 3, 1914, led by Royal Navy warships (an exception, as until 1917 all ships would be unescorted), the First Canadian Contingent left en masse for France, steaming out of Gaspé Bay in three lines, the first time that such a large contingent of troops had ever crossed the Atlantic.

On the way over, there was a U-boat scare — but otherwise it was a quiet crossing. Land's End was sighted and passed on the 14th, and then the ships, in a double line, ran in to Plymouth Harbour. The original destination had been Southampton, but rumours of German submarines off that port caused a last-minute change of plans. The Canadian armada moved upriver to Devonport, and by that same evening all were moored in pairs to buoys at the Hamoaze. Plymouth was completely unprepared for an invasion on so large a scale and it would be a week before the last transport, the *Tunisian*, with the 3rd Field Ambulance onboard, could land its troops who could then make for Salisbury Plain.

Arming merchantmen was not new — privateers had been used by Francis Drake and George Washington — as the practice released regular force officers for combatant duties. The British plans for DEMS (Defensively Equipped Merchant Ships) were ready long before 1914. In this role the *Empress of Britain* was sent early in the war to Admiral Stoddart's squadron in the south Atlantic where the fear was that German raiders would get among the important meat-carrying ships from the River Plate. Then it was sent to patrol the area between Finisterre and the Cape Verde Islands. As there were German colonies and naval units in the Pacific, the brand new Empresses, *Asia* and *Russia*, were requisitioned to patrol that ocean — the *Empress of Russia* rushing to Hong Kong as soon as war was declared.

Although the Royal Navy was to have had proper armament ready for the ship, all that could be found for the *Russia* were four antique 4.7-inch guns. These were manned with whoever could be found in Hong Kong — Royal Naval Reserve men, the crews from French gunboats, and Pathan sepoys. Later in the war, both ships were camouflaged in a bizarre "dazzle" scheme. The camouflage scheme was the creation of Norman Wilkinson, a British artist who in 1917 thought that a crazy design of black, white, and blue stripes would make Allied ships invisible to the enemy. The Admiralty, desperate for ways to combat U-boats, seized on the idea, and by 1918 most large ships were conspicuous in their "dazzle" colours. The *Russia* was transferred to the Indian Ocean and when the Australian cruiser HMAS *Sydney* caught and sank the German raider *Emden,* took onboard the survivors from the German cruiser. Sent on patrol in the Red Sea, it later joined *Asia* in the Atlantic where, because of their size, the pair was ideally suited to be troopships, carrying Chinese labour battalions and, after 1917, American troops to the front.

When the old *Empress of India* — the first to fly the checkered flag — arrived in Vancouver on August 14, 1914, having set a record for crossing the Pacific in 11 days and 18 hours, few suspected that it was also her last visit. Setting out on August 22 on her 238th trans-Pacific crossing, it made for Bombay, where its Canadian Pacific crew handed it over to the Indian Marine. It had been bought by the Maharajah of Gwalior for £85,000 as a hospital ship for Indian troops and renamed *Loyalty*, and over the next several years made 41 voyages between Europe and India, carrying more than 15,000 patients. In March 1919 it was sold to the local Scindia Steam Navigation Company where the former Empress made a few voyages from Bombay to Marseilles and London. Then, abandoned, it lay at anchor before being scrapped in 1923.

Ships belonging to the CPOS were also part of a bizarre project initiated by Winston Churchill, now First Lord of the Admiralty. To confuse the enemy, he had ten merchant ships disguised as battleships of the Grand Fleet. Fake plywood 12-inch guns and superstructures were built onto five Canadian Pacific ships — the old immigrant ship *Lake Champlain* became the HMS *King George V* and the former Allan Line *Montezuma* the *Iron Duke*. The scheme was dropped in 1915 when it was realized that as the "special squadron" of merchant ships could barely muster a speed of eight knots against the naval vessels' customary 20, even the most obtuse German spies would see through the deception.

The war brought together Master Kendall (now the company superintendent of shipping in London) and his former command, the *Montrose*. The *Montreal* and *Montrose* were in Antwerp when the conflict began, the latter's bunkers empty and the *Montreal*'s engines dismantled. The navy ordered both ships scuttled as the city fell to the Germans. But when refugees crowded onto them, Kendall refused to comply and, just ahead of the advancing enemy, ordered that the ships lie alongside each other. As much coal as possible was transferred to the *Montrose* to get its engines started and it towed the *Montreal* out. Both ships made it to safety but, typically, after all that, the Admiralty decided to scuttle the *Montrose* at the entrance to Dover Harbour. The holds were filled with cement and a tangle of gantries were built on the deck. But while it lay unattended in the harbour ready to be towed, a storm came up, and the cables holding the ship broke. Kendall's old command floated out into the channel — a menace in the crowded shipping lanes. Despite the enormous seas, a tug managed to get alongside the *Montrose* and land a volunteer crew. The crew on the tug began lighting flares and firing rockets to warn other ships, but then almost ran down the lifeboat which came to take the crew off the *Montrose*. Abandoned, the *Montrose* ran aground on the Goodwin Sands, where it remained long after the war.

A squadron of armed merchantmen enforced the blockade of German ports, especially the passage between the Shetlands and the Norwegian coast. Twenty ships representing nearly every shipping line in the Empire patrolled the waters from the Orkneys to the Arctic icefields throughout the war. The fleet was officially called the 10th Cruiser Squadron but was known in the navy as the "Muckle Fluggar Hussars" — the name taken from the most northerly point of the British Isles, Intercepting anyone that attempted to run the blockade around Germany was dangerous, cold, and arduous work for civilian crews but by October 1917, when the squadron was dispersed, it had intercepted 8,905 merchant ships, sent 1,816 into port under armed guard for examination, boarded 4,520 fishing vessels, and sunk a total of ten enemy merchantmen. Its own losses amounted to 12 ships and 1,000 lives but it was estimated that only 4 percent of the contraband escaped the attention of the "Muckle Hussars," the food blockade cited by historians as one of the main causes of Germany's surrender. It was frustrating, uncomfortable and thankless work — and would be entirely unknown to the general public.

The most famous of the "Muckle Hussars" was the Canadian Pacific (and former Allan Line) *Alsatian*. One of the first ships to get a wireless telegraphic direction finder, while in wartime service it flew the flags of three admirals, intercepted hundreds of ships, steamed nearly 300,000 miles, and burned 170,000 tons of coal. After being taken off the Orkney patrol and renamed the *Empress of France*, the ship was put on convoy service and went on to carry a number of distinguished passengers, including the Duke and Duchess of Connaught, Princess Patricia, and Canada's prime minister, Sir Robert Borden. The liner's end came late in the war. In March 1918, while convoying 30 ships across the Atlantic, the *Empress* was attacked by a U-boat. It may have survived one or two torpedoes but four were beyond even its powers of endurance and the old Allan liner sank with a loss of 49 lives.

As prime minister, Borden went to London several times by ship. In June 1915, in great secrecy, he took a train to New York and caught the White Star's *Adriatic*. The *Lusitania* had been sunk the month before, the U-boat scare was at its height, and possibly Borden thought taking a ship belonging to a neutral country from a neutral port was a good security measure. When the media and the Opposition discovered that the prime minister was unwilling to suffer the same dangers as so many thousands of Canadian soldiers, the outcry was such that on the next trip over in February 1917, he pointedly embarked on Canadian Pacific's *Calgarian* from Halifax. The voyage was fraught with danger from U-boat attacks but the *Calgarian* docked safely at Liverpool on February 21. A year later the *Calgarian* was torpedoed.

Ferrying troops, CPOS's ships found themselves in distant parts of the world throughout and even after the war. In May 1915, the *Empress of Britain*, now "Troop Transport No. 628," took Allied forces from France to the Middle East. In February 1916, along with the *Tunisian*, the *Empress* began ferrying Canadian and later American troops from North America to France, returning to Canada with prisoners of war. That same year, it took large numbers of the Imperial Army to the disastrous landing at Gallipoli and later on to Mesopotamia. The *Corsican* and the *Melita* brought Indian troops to and from France. After the armistice was signed, the *Pretorian* repatriated Belgian refugees and brought troops home, then went to Archangel with British forces to fight the Bolsheviks.

Because of their speed, none of the big ships in the class of the Empresses were caught by the enemy raiders, a fate that smaller ones, such as the 8,790-ton *Mount Temple*, could not avoid. The former Beaver Line ship was captured by the German surface raider *Moewe* on December 6, 1916, northwest of the western Azores. The crew put up a fight and four were killed before it surrendered. The Germans placed demolition charges below the ship's waterline and it was sunk. The last voyage of the *Mount Temple* is remembered for its cargo. In the summer of 1916, the American fossil collector Charles H. Sternberg was working in the Badlands of Alberta under contract to the British Museum of Natural History, London. In what is now Dinosaur Provincial Park, Alberta, his team had collected several dinosaur and other fossil specimens that were to be shipped to London in wooden crates. The first shipment was successfully transported on the SS *Milwaukee* but the second was on the Canadian Pacific ship. Sunk in 14,400 feet of water, 455 miles northwest of the Azores, there is speculation that the fossils will be salvaged. Ironically, the *Moewe* itself survived the war and was sold off to a British shipping company.

Two of the BCCSS Princess ships, the *Princess Margaret* and *Princess Irene* were being completed in Scotland when war broke out and both were requisitioned by the Admiralty as mine-layers. On May 27, 1915, the *Princess Irene*, loaded with mines for such an operation, exploded in Sheerness Harbour and sank with the loss of all crew, except for one man who was blown off the ship. The crew of the *Princess Margaret* continued its mine-laying duties and after the war the ship remained with the Admiralty, destined never to be part of the CPOS fleet.

Of the Canadian Pacific ships that continued to ply the Atlantic, the passenger lists of those in steerage varied very slightly. With Britain facing food shortages, the need to send those who were deemed part of the "surplus population" to Canada was now a patriotic necessity. G. Lebrun was a first-class pantryman on the *Sicilian* in 1915 when it transported several hundred children from the Barnardo Homes to Canada. At a stop in Le Havre to unload war supplies, the children began chatting with some British soldiers on the quay:

> They told the children that at nine o'clock a lot of German prisoners of war would come marching past. As the Germans came by the children started to sing "God Save the King." Then we put out to sea again. The carpenter made an imitation wooden gun to mount on the stern of the ship to frighten away the German submarines. Well, we buried two children on the way over. They died of pneumonia. Once we were in the St. Lawrence River, Captain Peters [had] a party. The children sang, a lady passenger played the piano and we served ice cream and cookies.

As in peacetime, merchant ships often carried Chinese labourers in steerage. During the First World War, 80,000 Chinese were transported to the front to serve in the labour battalions. Brought to Canada by Canadian Pacific ships, they passed through the William Head Quarantine station in batches of 8,000 at a time.

By the end of the war, the Allies were just beginning to cope with the U-boat menace and, although primitive when compared with the Second World War, a start was made in anti-submarine tactics. Aerial reconnaissance by airship and aircraft was limited in range to inshore patrols. In 1918, when the Allied Submarine Detection Committee approximated a science for tracking submarines by sound, the acronym "ASDIC" was given to it. The idea of regularly gathering ships together for their protection and proceeding in convoys was only attempted in the last year of the war. All of these measures came too late to help the Canadian Pacific, for it was in the final 18 months of the war that most of its ships were sunk.

> *Carthagian* sunk by mine on June 14, 1917, off Innistrahull.
>
> *Montezuma* torpedoed by *UC-41* on July 25, 1917, 64 miles northwest from Butt of Lewis.
>
> *Miniota* torpedoed by *U-62* August 31, 1917, off Start Point.
>
> *Ionian* narrowly missed a torpedo in the channel on March 24, 1917, but was sunk by mine on October 20, 1917, St. Gowan's Head.
>
> *Montcalm* torpedoed November 26, 1917, off southwest Ireland — later refloated to be used as a whaling ship in the Falklands. Finally broken up in Dalmuir, Scotland, in 1952.
>
> *Calgarian* torpedoed by *U-19* off Rathlin Island, March 1, 1918.
>
> *Pomeranian* torpedoed without warning nine miles from Portland Bill by *UC-77*, April 15, 1918, with a loss of 55 lives.
>
> *Lake Michigan* was torpedoed by *U-100* on April 16, 1918, 93 miles northwest of Eagle Island.

Medora torpedoed by *U-86* west-southwest of Mull of
Galloway, May 2, 1918.

Mongolian was torpedoed without warning near Filey
Brig with a loss of 36 lives, July 21, 1918.

Milwaukee torpedoed by *U-105* on August 31, 1918,
260 miles southwest of Fastnet.

Missanabie torpedoed off Gaunt's Rock, September 23,
1918, with a loss of 45 lives.

Montfort torpedoed by *U-55* on October 1, 1918, 170
miles west of Bishop Rock.

Not all casualties were enemy-related. The *Empress of Britain* was
dogged with bad luck, and on December 12, 1915, as it passed through
the Straits of Gibraltar, the sister ship of the *Ireland* collided with and
sank a small Greek freighter. And the former Elder Dempster ship,
Montreal, was rammed by the White Star's *Cedric* on January 29, 1918,
and sank 14 miles from the Bar, Liverpool.

G.D. Brophy, later CPR general agent for passengers (Montreal), was
onboard the *Metagama* when it sailed from Montreal on May 6, 1915, for
Liverpool. He later recalled (in 1943) that

> she was loaded with troops — the No. 3 (McGill
> University) Canadian Hospital Unit and the 21st
> Battalion (Queen's University) — both of which were to
> suffer terrific casualties in France. Our sole protection
> was one four pounder naval gun mounted astern — I
> wish depth charges had been invented then. The early
> part of the voyage was rough but the day that the news
> of the *Lusitania*'s sinking was received, the sea flattened
> out like a pond for the balance of the trip which added
> to our anxiety. The *Lusitania* had been 300 miles east
> of us when she was torpedoed. After that, the captain
> ordered a black out — no lights to be shown on the voy-
> age. All portholes darkened, no smoking, no matches
> to be lit on the deck. The blackout dampened the picnic

atmosphere that had prevailed among the university students. We were ordered by the Admiralty to forget Liverpool and stay away from the main shipping lanes, to lie off Land's End and wait for an escort of British destroyers. We sighted Land's End at sundown but no escort and the Canadian troops amused themselves by howling at the British crew, "Where's the blooming British Ny'vy?" and offering bets that the destroyers had lost their way. Finally, just before it got dark, four destroyers popped up like magic, so fast I don't think anyone saw where they came from. They escorted us into port, two on each side. The somewhat surprised Canadians changed their tune: "Well, I guess we've got a Ny'vy after all."

In the Pacific, the *Empress of Asia* was requisitioned by the Canadian government on April 13, 1918, and sailed for New York via Panama with 3,600 Chinese labourers, members of labour battalions. At New York, the crew on Chinese articles (of agreement) was signed off and a replacement crew from the *Empress of Japan* at Vancouver was rushed across the continent by rail, reaching New York on June 17, 1918. On June 20, the liner left for Liverpool — the first of six round trips from the eastern coast of the United States to Great Britain and France carrying American soldiers.

With the armistice, the *Asia* was enlisted to transport Canadian troops home, sailing from Liverpool on January 2, 1919, with over 1,300 military personnel onboard. But by January 25 it was back in Vancouver where, because of the urgent need for shipping on the Pacific, it was quickly refitted for peacetime duties at the Wallace yard in North Vancouver. The *Empress of Asia* re-entered the Trans-Pacific mercantile trade on February 27, 1919, bound for the Orient.

Even the last days of hostilities on the western front promised no respite for some Canadian Pacific ships. The *Empress of Japan* and the *Monteagle* were the only CPOS ships on the Pacific in 1918 and the company anxious to put them back to work asked Prime Minister Borden to remove them from military service. But with the Treaty of Brest-Litovsk, which kept the Russians in the war, the Allies launched a sorry expedition to Vladivostok to bolster the White Army. On October 11, 1918, packed with troops, horses, and mounted police that were Canada's contribution to the Siberian Expeditionary Force, the *Empress of Japan* and the *Monteagle* left Victoria for what was left of imperial Russia.

They arrived off Vladivostok in the early winter of 1919, only to find the port entrance frozen over. Jack McClure, the radio operator on the *Empress*, never forgot the sight of the Russian pilot coming out to the Canadian Pacific ship on a horse — followed by an icebreaker — then leading the convoy in, still on horseback. It would be April before the two ships, later joined by the *Empress of Russia*, began taking the troops home. It was a slow journey for the demoralized soldiers — made even longer when smallpox was discovered onboard and the troops were quarantined in Vancouver. For the Canadian Pacific and the merchant navy, the war effectively ended on October 21, 1918, when Admiral Reinhard Scheer, the victor of the Battle of Jutland and now commanding admiral of the German High Seas Fleet, called off the unrestricted submarine warfare campaign with the following message:

> To all U-boats: Commence return from patrol at once. Because of ongoing negotiations any hostile actions against merchant vessels prohibited. Returning U-boats are allowed to attack warships only in daylight. End of message. Admiral.

A precursor to the next war, the Imperial Navy's 274 U-boats had sunk 6,596 merchant ships, doing, for their size, more damage to the Allies than the whole German Grand Fleet.

Of the 52 ships that the Canadian Pacific Railway had entered the war with, 12 had been lost by enemy action. Of the 11,000 CPR employees who had been recruited, 1,115 had given their lives in the Armed Forces or had been lost at sea in the company's ships. The company could take pride in its war record: 2 Victoria Crosses, 6 Orders of the British Empire, 17 Distinguished Service Orders, and 327 other decorations. One of the Victoria Cross recipients had been Captain R.N.

Stuart who, serving in the Royal Naval Reserve on a decoy "Q" ship, had lured a U-boat to its destruction. Stuart was destined to become a commodore of the Canadian Pacific fleet in 1934, perhaps the youngest ever to achieve that position. To commemorate the heroism and sacrifice of all employees, the bronze statue "Winged Victory" by Canadian sculptor Coeur de Lion MacCarthy was unveiled by on April 28, 1922, by Governor General Lord Byng of Vimy in the concourse of Windsor Station, where it can still be viewed.

The worst CPOS sinking during the war had nothing to do with enemy action at all. Mirroring the *Empress of Ireland* disaster on the St. Lawrence, a Princess ship was involved in a sad maritime tragedy on Canada's west coast. Early on October 24, 1918, while travelling from Skagway to Vancouver in the midst of an early snowstorm, the *Princess Sophia* ran aground on Vanderbilt Reef in the Lynn Canal. At high tide, the ship was visible, perched on the rocks, its hull out of the water. With all power — heat and lighting — still functioning, the 268 passengers and 75 crew members were calm and awaited rescue. Captain Leonard Locke thought the ship was stable on the reef and did not order the passengers, described as important and wealthy citizens of the Yukon, and crew to abandon ship.

He decided instead to wait for the tides rather than subject his passengers to the inconvenience of being transferred to the waiting boats. In any case, with the weather worsening, the ships that came to transfer the passengers could only circle around the *Sophia*. At 4:00 p.m. the lighthouse tender, *Cedar*, received a radio message from the *Sophia* that it was taking on water. Passenger John Maskell, cited in a 2006 feature in the *Ottawa Citizen*, wrote to his fiancé in England about what was taking place around him:

> I am writing this dear girl while the boat is in grave danger. We struck a rock last night which threw many from their berths … the lifeboats were soon swung out in readiness but owing to the storm it would be madness to launch until there was no hope for the ship.

Soon, there were gale-force winds, and with the winter darkness the ship could no longer be seen. Then the waiting ships heard wireless operator Dave Robinson's plea for help: "Hurry, we are sinking. The water is coming in my room ... for God's sake, come quick!" The next morning at sunrise, when the *Cedar* got to it, only the masts of the *Sophia* were visible above water. It was assumed that, battered by the wind and waves, the *Princess* had slid off the reef, taking with it all its passengers and crew. The ship's only survivor was a dog which appeared at Tees Harbour two days later. The company, and especially Captain Locke, was severely criticized for the tragedy, but this was soon forgotten — the day that the recovery ship brought the bodies ashore in Vancouver (Maskell's letter was found on his), there was rejoicing in the streets. It was November 11, 1918, and the war had ended.

CHAPTER 6

The Inter-War Years

The decades between the wars were ones of unprecedented growth for the Canadian Pacific. The company had counted on ferrying thousands more immigrants escaping from war-torn Europe and would invest heavily in more ships. Unfortunately, in 1922, Ottawa put severe restrictions on immigration (except for agricultural workers), causing the flood of Europeans and Chinese labourers to decrease. But the prosperity of the decade had given birth to a moneyed middle class, who saw ships as the wealthy always had — not only for transportation but as part of the leisure industry.

Canadian Pacific dropped the former immigrant port of Antwerp and, although sailings continued via Greenock and Belfast, Liverpool remained its primary port. However, reflecting the focus on leisure cruises, the port of Southampton became the secondary terminal, with temporary stops at Hamburg and Cherbourg. This not only brought the more affluent London traffic closer to the ships via a short train journey, but the port itself was far superior to Liverpool's. As the ancient seafarers had known, the Isle of Wight, which sheltered the port entrance, was responsible for a double tide. To cater to the new class of leisure passengers, professions such as stewards, stewardesses, nurses, and nannies were also recruited locally.

It was a time for a renewal of the company's fleet. The original Canadian Pacific fleet, either bought from the Allan and Elder Dempster lines or built as the first Empresses in 1906, was also at the end of its useful life. Re-engineering the coal burners for oil fuel or converting to a single class were temporary solutions before selling them off. It took eight months to convert a ship to burn oil instead of coal and it was expensive for it owners (and disastrous for the collieries of that country), but the process changed ocean transport forever. No longer would there be the reeking smoke and burning cinders that passengers and crew detested. Below decks the profession of stokers — the "black gang" — would disappear, to be replaced by comparatively clean firemen.

When Canadian Pacific needed a large number of stokers for their first Empresses in 1903, the Liverpool Irish had cornered the profession and served in the deplorable black stoke holds until the conversion to oil in the 1920s. An exception was the coal-burning *Empress of Russia*, which suffered during the war when finding and keeping experienced stokers became a problem. While in the peacetime mercantile trade, the *Asia* was manned in part by a Chinese crew that signed on under Hong Kong articles (of agreement) and had filled positions in the engine, deck, and catering departments. As most ports would not allow the Chinese crew ashore, they remained with the company until paid off. When the ship was requisitioned, the Chinese crew (with the exception of four individuals) was discharged. These four became members of the delivery crew that sailed the ship to Liverpool for its conversion to a troop carrier. After the conversion they remained with the ship on the voyage to Suez and to Singapore.

By the early 1920s, the Canadian Pacific line had replaced its losses with new ships either built in Scotland (*Montcalm III, Montrose II, Montclare)* or given by the Reparations Commission from surrendered German fleets (*Montlaurier, Montreal II)*. The last of the Allan Line's ships, such as the *Sicilian* and *Corsican*, had been sold off and the first Empresses were scrapped. When the *Empress of Japan* was retired on July 18, 1922, it had served 31 years and crossed the Pacific 315 times — a record never to be equalled by any other CPR ship. It was to lie in Vancouver Harbour for four years and during the longshore strike of 1923 was used as accommodation for the stevedores. In 1926 it was sold to Victor Lamken and there were rumours that it was to be dismantled and its hulk used as a barge. Before that could take place, the *Empress* was slowly scrapped in North Vancouver by R.J. Christian. Two remnants of the ship still exist: the bell was bought by F.H. Clendenning and later presented to the Merchants Exchange. The distinctive nine-foot dragon figurehead was rescued by a group led by the publisher of Vancouver newspaper *The Daily Province* and in 1927 was installed in Stanley Park. But open to the elements, it was removed in 1960 and replaced by a fibre-glass copy. In 1960, the *Empress of Japan*'s original figurehead was given to the Vancouver Maritime Museum, where it can be viewed today.

On January 11, 1926, coming out of Shanghai, as the *Empress of Asia* was rounding Black Point on the Whangpoo River, the master saw three steamships coming upriver. The third, the *Tung Shing*, when three-quarters of a mile off the starboard bow of the *Empress of Asia*, blew one blast of her whistle and altered her course to starboard. The *Empress* replied with one blast and put her helm to port but, being sluggish on account of shoal water, this was barely noticeable. At half a mile the *Tung Shing*, still on the starboard bow of the *Empress*, again blew one blast and altered her course to starboard. The *Empress* replied with a blast and put her helm hard a-port and her engines to half speed. With a collision imminent, to reduce the impact, both ships then went full speed astern — but it was too late. The *Empress of Asia* struck the *Tung Shing* abaft the boat deck and abreast of her Number 3 hold. The smaller ship sank within two minutes in about 30 feet of water. There had been no lives lost and a court of inquiry found that the master of the *Tung Shing* was in error in not altering his course to starboard early enough.

To compensate for the wartime losses, in 1921 the company also bought former German ships from the Cunard Line. The *Konig Friedrich August* (9,720 gt) was renamed the *Montreal*, converted to cabin class, and kept in service until 1927, making voyages from Naples and Trieste to Montreal. The larger *Prinz Friederich Wilhelm* (17,500 gt) had been built at Geestemende in 1907 and was a twin-screw ship able to make a speed of 17 knots. It was her radio operator who in 1912 had sent out the ice report which should have saved the *Titanic*, but was ignored. In Norwegian waters when war began, in attempting to slip back home, the liner had run aground. After being refloated and evading the Royal Navy, the *Prinz Friederich Wilhelm* spent the time during hostilities in Kiel. As part of war reparations in February 1920, after bringing American troops back, it was sent to Liverpool to be reconditioned. The former German ship was then put under Canadian Pacific management and made several voyages — one as far as Bombay — before being bought outright by the company. In the course of her career, the *Prinz Friederich Wilhelm* would be given several names — *Empress of China II*, *Empress of India II*, *Mont Laurier*, and finally *Montnairn* — before being sold in 1928. Perhaps her best-known voyage was in 1922 when it rushed British troops to Turkey over the Chanak incident. By the 1930s, both would be sold to Italian companies to be scrapped.

But the real prizes were two future Empresses — the *Tirpitz* (21,498 gt) and the *Kaiserin Auguste Victoria* (25,000 gt). The latter began life in 1906 as the *Europa* until the owners, Hamburg-Amerika, asked the Kaiserin (the wife of Kaiser Wilhelm) to allow her name to be used and to launch the ship. Holding the title as the largest, most luxurious ship in the world at that time, fortunately the *Kaiserin Auguste Victoria*, like the *Tirpitz*, spent the war safely in port with all of its heavy, ornate mahogany fittings in place. Taken over by the United States as a troopship in 1919, and renamed the USS *Kaiserin Auguste Victoria*, it was then passed to Cunard as war reparations.

When Canadian Pacific bought both ships from Cunard, the *Kaiserin* became the *Empress of Scotland* and Canadian Pacific discovered why Cunard wanted to get rid of it: not only was the German liner coal-fired and its furnishings too dated, but it was top heavy — it had a high and bulky upper superstructure and needed 1,500 tons of permanent ballast to compensate. There was a story that the ship's tall bridge had been specially designed to carry the Kaiser and his entourage on a triumphal cruise after he had won the war to review the British fleet. As the Kaiser suffered from vertigo, perhaps it is just a story. By the late 1920s, when more economy-class berths were needed on the Pacific run, the *Empress of Scotland* was considered too expensive to make over. It was sold for scrap to Hughes-Blockow Co. Blyth on December 2, 1930, and the German fittings auctioned off. A week later, the ship caught fire and was demolished.

Like many of the German prizes, the *Tirpitz* had been sabotaged by its German crew. For years during its Canadian Pacific service, mirrors that had been almost unscrewed fell off walls in rough seas and nameplates that had been switched around allowed salt water to be inadvertently pumped into the boilers and bilge water to flood into the baths. This was not as dangerous as on Cunard's German ship *Berengaria*, which continually suffered from fires caused by sabotaged electrical short circuits.

Nonetheless, the *Tirpitz*, like the old admiral it was named after, was belligerent, contrary, and proved impossible to retire. On July 25, 1921, it was renamed the *Empress of China*, sent to John Brown & Co. to be converted to oil, and was refitted for the Pacific run between Vancouver and the Orient. With China in turmoil by the time the work was completed on June 2, 1922, CPS thought better of the name and the ship was renamed *Empress of Australia*. It initially joined the three other Empresses — *Asia, Russia,* and *Canada* — on the Pacific run and would go on serving the Canadian Pacific until 1952. But her fame was to lie in her early years. On September 1, 1923, as the *Empress of Australia* was about to cast off from Yokohama, Japan, the city was devastated by an earthquake. Although the wharf collapsed and the city burnt around her, the *Empress* remained in harbour to provide relief to the millions of homeless. Each morning for nine days its passengers and crew left the ship to search the city for women and children and bring them onboard. Master S. Robinson reported that soon the lower decks and alleyways all over the ship were covered with hundreds of badly wounded civilians. Two of the first ships to arrive in the devastated harbour were the *Empress of Canada* and the *Empress of Russia*, bringing with them supplies from the Canadian Red Cross and the Vancouver Japanese Association. The Canadian Pacific brought in food, nurses, and medicine without charge and donated $25,000 to buy supplies. Grateful British refugees later presented Master Robinson with a bronze plaque detailing the experience of the *Empress* in the disaster.

Along with other older coal-burning ships, the *Empress of Australia* was converted to fuel oil and in May 1926 was sent to the Clyde, where it was refitted with new boilers and single-reduction Parson turbines designed by the company's own engineer, the brilliant John Johnson. The ship was then put on the Atlantic run and in 1927 took His Royal Highness, the Prince of Wales, and British prime minister, Stanley Baldwin, to Canada to celebrate that country's 60th year in Confederation.

Less well known is the company's other contribution to Canada's anniversary. The centrepiece of the commemoration was to be the opening of the new Parliament Buildings in Ottawa and especially the Peace Tower Carillon. One of Canadian Pacific's "B" ships, *Balfour* (the cargo liners were given names like *Bolingbroke, Bantry, Bosworth,* and *Bothwell*), carried the 53 bells, including the "Great Bourdon," weighing ten tons, for the carillon that was to be put in the tower. The *Berwyn* had brought the 20 tons of structural steel to house the bells a week earlier.

The first post-war Empress, the *Empress of Canada*, was ready for service in May 1922. The largest, most opulent ship ever built by Fairfields up til then, her 444 first-class passengers enjoyed oak-panelled smoking rooms, a 30-foot indoor swimming pool, and hot and cold running water in each cabin. Mahogany from the Honduras panelled the "long gallery" that stretched from the main staircase to the public rooms and passengers could avail themselves of a laundry, barber, and manicurist — and for businessmen, a stenographer. There was even an exclusive kitchen for the Asian passengers in steerage. *Canada* was fast, as well, and in June 1923, broke the record for a Pacific crossing, doing Yokohama to Vancouver in eight days.

To replace the aging Princesses, *Irene* and *Margaret*, the British Columbia service connecting Vancouver–Victoria–Seattle received two modern ferries in 1925. Both were built, as with so many of the Canadian

Pacific ships, by William Pearce of Fairfields, also a director of the CPR. Lady Mount Stephen, wife of the first president of the CPR, launched the *Princess Kathleen* on the Clyde on September 27, 1924, sending her off via the Panama Canal to Vancouver. On November 29, 1924, the Honorable Marguerite Shaughnessy, daughter of the second president, inaugurated her namesake, the *Princess Marguerite*. Three hundred and fifty feet long and 5,875 gross tonnage, fitted for 600 passengers accommodated in overnight berths, each could carry up to 900 deck passengers. Their John Brown single-reduction geared steam turbines made them fast and efficient and initially they were fitted to carry upto 30 automobiles, as well. For 16 years both Princesses shuttled back and forth on the triangle run, with the occasional coastal cruise. But they were destined to make wartime journeys of Odyssian proportions, taking them to battles far from the British Columbia coast.

Canadian Pacific ships wielded a significant effect on the economy and society of British Columbia. Besides contributing to the emergence of Victoria and Vancouver as important cargo and tourist centres, the CPR also provided the chief means for the Chinese to immigrate to Canada. In Victoria, a vital pilotage station had grown because of the Empresses, which docked at the outer harbour before entering Vancouver, the CPR's Pacific terminus. Just before the First World War, the CPR built the Pier D complex next to the station to allow more ships to berth at the same time. In the 1920s, other piers were erected to deal with greater numbers and sizes of CPR ships now operating out of the port.

The Empresses also acquired much of their food and other provisions locally. When the second *Empress of Japan*, for example, victualed in Vancouver in the 1930s, it spent $75,000 on such goods every trip, the local CPR purchasing department keeping local butchers, farmers, and vintners well employed. When the Canadian Pacific ships, both Empresses and Princesses, required repairs, they went into dry dock at Esquimalt. Naturally, many Vancouver and Victoria families were employed by the Canadian Pacific, some as officers as well as crew.

The last years of the decade saw an escalation in ship size and luxury as each line attempted to outdo the other for passengers. In 1926, *Île de France* had been launched for CGT, to be matched the following year by Hapag's

Bremen. As both CGT and Cunard began investing heavily in larger and more luxurious ships to match their foreign competitors, the White Star Line returned to British ownership when it was bought by the Royal Mail Group. The Canadian Pacific was not to be left behind. Beatty pronounced that in 1927 Canada had "hit her stride" and it looked as if he was right. Between 1919 and 1928, his ships carried almost 1.3 million passengers, the highest the company ever would in its history. In 1927 alone, no fewer than 11 ships were launched, an achievement for a private company.

It was a boom year for the country. There were bumper harvests on the prairies, a leap in manufacturing, and a widespread expansion of railroads and steamship routes. Immigration numbers, wooed by the company if not the federal government, were once more climbing and the ships were filled to capacity. "My mother Dorris Pirra was a stewardess/interpreter for the immigrants — English, Italian, French, and German, mainly on the 'Monts,'" recalled Edmond Owen Humphreys, himself to be chief engineer one day. "They were wet boats due to a long working alley way on the main deck which was awash in the Atlantic winters, most of the time. The ships were cold with no heating and it was a long walk to the toilets."

One of the new ships built was the *Empress of Japan*, ready on December 16, 1929. Fast, with an average speed of 23 knots, it was also beautifully furnished, with a dome ceiling, Palm Court, ballroom, and cinema. Until the war, it served the company on the Yokohama–Vancouver run with Master S. Robinson, who had become well-known after the Yokohama earthquake as her first master.

It was no longer just the poor and dispossessed that travelled by sea. More Canadians had money to vacation than ever before, to enjoy not only the Canadian Pacific trains, hotels, and lodges, but also the Empress liners. The steerage conditions that so many thousands of emigrants had endured gave way to the improved facilities and better accommodations of "tourist class." The poorest (called "settlers" by the company personnel) paid £10 for the crossing.

The greatest threat to the Canadian Pacific in the inter-war years came not from its rivals like Cunard but from its friends — and its own government. The United States having been presented with a fleet of

German ships interned since 1914 — including the Blue Riband holder *Vaterland* (since renamed *Leviathan)* — now became a commercial maritime power. In the Far East, former rivals Russia and Germany had been replaced by the aggressive Japanese, whose ships carried passengers and freight anywhere for a fraction of the cost.

Because of the close ties that Sir John A. Macdonald's Conservatives had with the CPR, the company controlled much of the national transportation network. But when the Liberals came to power in 1921, they were intent on creating a state-owned rival on land and sea: the Canadian National Railway (CNR). Thus the groundwork was laid for a model in Canada (that would be followed in Australia), of two companies — one private, one public — in rail and shipping, and later in aviation and telecommunications. In a sparsely populated country that could barely support a single rail or coastal shipping network, the effects of having two meant decades of wasteful rivalry.

The company took measures to protect itself. In 1921(the year that George Stephen, its first president, died at his home in Hatfield, England) the company name was changed from "Canadian Pacific Ocean Services" to "Canadian Pacific Steamships Ltd." (CPS) and its fleet was (like that of the American-owned White Star Line) registered in Britain. The Waterloo Place offices in London were in the heart of the British Empire and gave greater access to investment and markets for passengers and freight than if they had been in Montreal. If many of the CPS crew were Canadian, the majority of the shareholders were British and would remain so until the 1960s, something that caused Ottawa much concern. But overall control would still be exercised from Windsor Station, Montreal, and the company's president would continue to reside (as Stephen, Van Horne, and Shaughnessy had done) in the nearby wealthy suburb of Westmount.

Canadian Pacific had advertised cruises around the world as early as 1891 when it used the delivery of its first Empresses from Britain to Vancouver via Suez to sell passages onboard. The idea was revived in 1920, when the *Empress of Canada* was being built at Fairfields, in a plan to sell cruise tickets on her maiden voyage to Vancouver, but it never came about — that is until 1924, when the ship was used on the company's first round-the-world cruise from New York. Joining the other lines, the Canadian Pacific met the prosperity of the 1920s by entering the cruise industry, operating around-the-world cruises and shorter ones from Britain to the Mediterranean or from Montreal to New York.

Empresses *France, Scotland,* and *Britain* were sent off in 1922, the *Empress of Canada* in 1924, and the *Empress of Britain II* in 1931. The old *Melita* and the "Monts" — *Montcalm, Montclare,* and *Montrose* — were put on cruises in 1932. With the latest in radio equipment, in 1924 the *Montclare* was the first company ship that allowed for music to be piped into any part of the ship. A sign that the Canadian Pacific was casting off its dowdy image was evident when the grey and black hulls were painted a tropical white. It was an opportunity to make money during the off-season and take passengers to the West Indies, Mediterranean, Canary Islands, and Scandinavia. Most notable were the number of around-the-world cruises by the Empresses: *France* (2), *Scotland* (2), *Canada* (1), *Australia* (4), and *Britain II* (8). "Go Empress" and "A Dozen Reasons You Should Go Empress" were two of the company's advertising slogans and a trip to Europe cost $260.00. Company ads told their readers to take sentimental journeys to Europe to see the old family home or tour the battlefields of Vimy Ridge. Appealing to women, one ad even proclaimed, "It Is Every Woman's <u>Right</u> to Visit Paris."

The railway understood that profit wasn't only in carrying passengers, and in 1928 it had five cargo ships built. All were 520 feet in length with a 62-foot beam; their hulls ice-strengthened, they were designed for a weekly London–Canada service. Their tonnage varied from 9,874 to 10,042 and they were easily recognized because of the five sets of twin king posts (masts that looked like goal posts) and for the fact that masts one and four had top masts. All had black hulls, white deck housing, and buff funnels.

Coal-fired, they were the first ships on the North Atlantic to have automatic stokers. Twin-screw, the five sisters were fast for their day, with Parsons turbines putting out a 14-knot speed. Their insulated cargo holds were the most modern available — 80,000 cubic feet for perishables like meat and apples. The ships could be converted to carry grain and cattle in specially built portable stalls between decks. To get cargo on and off efficiently, each ship had 27 derricks.

Called "Beavers" in memory of the Elder Dempster Line, they were built in three yards: the *Beaverburn* at W. Denny Brothers, Dumbarton; the *Beaverford* and *Beaverhill* at Barclay, Curle & Co. Whiteinch, Glasgow; and the *Beaverdale* and *Beaverbrae* at Armstrong Whitworth, Newcastle. The *Beaverburn* was completed first and launched by the wife of a Canadian Pacific director on September 27, 1927. The day after, the *Beaverdale* was launched at Newcastle by Lady Alice Northcote, the adopted daughter of Lord Mount Stephen. On October 27, 1927, a daughter-in-law of another company director launched the *Beaverford*. Miss Mavis Gillies, daughter of the general manager of the Canadian Pacific Steamship Services, launched the *Beaverhill* on November 8, 1927. The last Beaver ship *Beaverbrae* was launched on November 14, 1927, by Lady McLaren Brown, the wife of the Canadian Pacific general manager in London. All were completed by January 1928, and by that spring had been launched on their maiden voyages to earn their keep.

Through the 1930s, while the Empress and Duchess liners called at Southampton and attracted the glamourous and newsworthy passengers, the Beavers quietly plied their trade between Europe and Canada from the Surrey Docks at Rotherhithe, sometimes stopping to pick up cargo at Antwerp, Hamburg, or Le Havre. The historic peninsula of Rotherhithe on the Thames had been a port since Saxon times — the name Rotherhithe (sometimes called Redriffe) came from the Saxon words *redhra* ("seaman") and *hyth* ("haven").

Although the Surrey docks had been so named because it was from here that the garden produce from Surrey was once been shipped to London, by the 1920s its nine docks had spread over three miles. The quays bore the names of the countries from where the cargoes were unloaded — like Russia Dock and Greenland Dock (for the Arctic whalers). At Canada Dock, where the grain, meat, and timber arrived by Beaver ship, the Rotherhithe dockers (who spoke their own dialect) were distinguishable by the hats they wore for carrying planks of Canadian wood.

Annually, each Beaver made an average of six sailings to Montreal and four to Saint John (in the winter). They carried Canadian produce to Europe and returned with manufactured goods like motor cars. The *Beaverburn* made a record crossing in September 1928, from Le Havre to

Father Point, Rimouski, in seven days, eight hours, and 20 minutes, but it was usually an uneventful existence — "going about their lawful occasions," as it was called — and rarely did their cargo warrant any publicity. On October 7, 1931, the *Beaverbrae* left Hamburg with a dismantled Junkers 52 aircraft that had been bought for Canadian Airways. Dubbed "The Flying Boxcar," it would be the largest aircraft in Canada for the next decade. The aircraft was unloaded at Montreal and then barged across the river to be reassembled at the Fairchild plant at Longeuil. Another unusual cargo was the "Royal Scot," a fast British steam locomotive. In May 1933, rail track was laid on the deck of the *Beaverdale* to carry it and eight cars. The train and her passengers then toured Canada and the United States for eight months before returning home the same way.

Trade on the Pacific was not neglected either, and from 1931 to 1953 the company co-operated with the Union Steam Ship Co. of New Zealand to buy shares in the Canadian Australian Royal Mail Line. It operated the *Aorangi* and the *Niagara*, with the ships sailing every 28 days from Vancouver to both Australia and New Zealand via Honolulu and Suva, carrying passengers, butter, frozen meat, and fruit.

The company had always integrated its ship and train schedules to move mail, passengers, and freight as efficiently as possible and attempts to use aircraft to do the same was entirely predictable. It was estimated that three days could be saved if a mailbag was to be transferred to or from an awaiting seaplane with sufficient range. The first such experiment took place on February 21, 1927, when the *Empress of Asia* was 300 miles west of Victoria and a Curtiss HS-2L seaplane alighted alongside so that the purser could put in a can of newsreel film. The Curtiss then made for Seattle, where a land plane took the film on to Vancouver. The film depicted the fighting between the Chinese and Japanese armies in Shanghai and was being shown in cinemas a day before the *Asia* arrived.

The idea of speeding up transatlantic mail delivery with an aircraft meeting an Empress at Father Point, incoming or outgoing, also began that year. The *Empress of France* was the first Canadian Pacific ship to take part in such a scheme and was met on September 10 at Father Point by pilots H.S. Quigley and S. Graham (Canada's earliest bushpilot) in a Canadian Airways HS-2L. Unfortunately, the flying boat could not take off and the mail was taken ashore to be sent on by train. The opposite way was more successful: On September 21, 1927, an HS-2L left Montreal at 14:15, arriving at Father Point at 16:25. There the mail-bags were transferred to the *Empress of Australia*, which docked at Southampton on the 28th.

Ten experimental flights were carried out in this way but the HS-2L flying boats were too fragile for rough water and the seaplane meet was replaced with a land plane taking off from nearby Rimouski. Because of this, the little town was given Canada's second government-built airport (after St. Hubert, Montreal) and on October 27, 1927, H.M. Pasmore would carry the mail from Rimouski Airport to Ottawa in a Fairchild FC-2 land plane. The next summer, a regular air service connecting with incoming or outgoing ocean liners was begun.

Quick to capitalize on the air/sea connection, in May 1928, the Canadian Pacific Express Company advertised that first-class mail and express packages could be transported by air from its liners, not only to Montreal but on to Ottawa and Toronto, as well. The combined steam-ship/aircraft/train service worked so well that summer that when a Chatham, Ontario, store ordered a consignment of silk from a British tailor, it was onboard the *Empress of Scotland* on June 16, flown from Rimouski on the 22nd, put on a train at Windsor Station, Montreal, that same day, and delivered to the Chatham store on the 23rd — a total of seven days. By 1930, floatplanes were meeting the *Empress of Australia* in the Strait of Belle Isle, cutting 24 hours off the Rimouski meet.

But with the onset of the Depression, the government could not jus-tify such expense and killed off future such services. By the mid-1930s, only Germany's *Bremen*, which carried a catapult mail plane onboard and launched it 250 miles off New York, ever came close to the Canadian Pacific ship/air/train service. The last of the air/sea transfers took place in 1932 when Canada hosted the Imperial Conference in Ottawa. Official dispatches, carried by Canadian Pacific liners from Britain, were picked up by seaplane at Red Bay in the Strait of Belle Isle, flown to Havre-Saint-Pierre, Quebec, where another flying boat took them on to Rimouski for the regular land plane flight to Ottawa. Mail that had left London on July 13 was in Ottawa by the 18th.

The decades between the wars also caused a special type of passenger liner to appear: smaller than an Empress to access more ports yet equally luxurious. To serve Montreal and thus capture the Chicago and the American Midwest market, Canadian Pacific had four such "mini Empresses" built. They could sail up the St. Lawrence, past Quebec City, and all the way to Montreal, where train connections to Chicago made the trip faster than going through New York. The "Duchesses" — sometimes called the "Drunken Duchesses," because they rolled so much — were 20,000–gross tonnage liners. The *Duchess of Atholl, Duchess of York, Duchess of Bedford*, and *Duchess of Richmond* were equipped with hot and cold running water in all cabins and had accommodation for approximately 580 cabin, 480 tourist,and 510 third-class passengers.

Beatty must have been thrilled the first time a member of the royal family, HRH the Duchess of York — consort of the future king and better known to future generations as the Queen Mother — was persuaded to launch the ship named after her on September 28, 1928. Too late to change the name, the Canadian Pacific discovered that there was already a pleasure boat registered on the Severn River called *Duchess of York*. Fortunately, the owner was persuaded to sell it to the Canadian Pacific for £250 before the royal launch.

Crew Numbers

Departments	Duchess of Bedford, 1936	Empress of Scotland 1930
Deck Department	77	100
Engine Department	61	85
Catering Department	130	233
Cooks Department	35	115
Total	**303**	**533**
Stewardesses	13	21
Passenger capacity	1,800	1,473

Source: *George Musk, Canadian Pacific: The Story of a Famous Shipping Line.*
London: David & Charles, 1981.

The "Duchess" ships carried approximately 600 cabin-class, 500 tourist-class, and 500 settler-class passengers and the "Mont" ships could accommodate close to 500 in cabin class and 1,250 in third class. However, the passenger load on the Empresses varied according to cruise and season — on an average voyage the *Empress of Scotland*, for example, carried 459 first-class, 478 second-class, and 536 third-class passengers.

One such passenger was Walter "Babe" Woollett, an expatriate Englishman who between the wars pioneered bush flying in Canada. At a bon voyage party, Woollett's hand got stuck in a brass spittoon and he would embark with this encumbrance — but that is another story. After lonely months in the bush, he looked to luxuriating in the amenities that the Canadian Pacific ships were known for. He wrote,

> In the summer of 1934, I decided to take some time off, head for "Jolly Olde," and bought a round-trip ticket on the Canadian Pacific Steamship's *Duchess of Atholl*. Unlike some duchesses I have known, C.P.'s Duchesses had especially flat bottoms, so designed to enable them to navigate the shallow passage between Quebec City and Montreal, a privilege denied the Empress class. But with their flatter hulls [they] rolled all over the place and were known as the "Drunken Duchesses."

The *Duchess*'s master was "dear old 'Dobbie' Dobson," who upgraded him to a stateroom. "I didn't have much in the way of etchings, but what I did have was a portable gramophone and collection of Cole Porter records which proved to be irresistible 'bird bait,'" he would write in his autobiography, *Have A Banana!* At the end of the voyage, when Woollett was disembarking, "one of the old 'curry-shifters' from India, complete with burst mattress mustachio, stomped over and said, 'Sir, I just want you to know I think you're a cad and a bounder of the worst type! You have ruined my trip across the Atlantic with your bloody gramophone and raucous parties next door to me when you should have been in bed.'" Woollett didn't have the heart to tell him that for most of the voyage, he had been.

The decades between the wars saw the Canadian Pacific emerge from its 19th-century colonial personae and adapt to the changing conditions. Quebec was chosen over Montreal for the construction of the Harbour Terminal at Wolfe's Cove for summer passenger service on the transatlantic route (the winter terminal being at Saint John, New Brunswick). Although Canadian Pacific developed some freight traffic at the Cove, the building of a rail tunnel was primarily in conjunction with the introduction of the new Atlantic "Empress" ship, the *Empress of Britain*, which entered service in 1931. While the first train ran through the tunnel on May 26, the official opening took place on June 1, 1931, coincident with the first docking of the *Empress of Britain*. As well as being used by the Empresses, the terminal also served ships operated by Cunard and other companies. The reason that Quebec rather than Montreal was chosen as the location of the summer terminal for the Empresses was the height of the ships' masts — they were too tall to clear the new Jacques Cartier Bridge, located immediately downstream of the passenger terminals in the Port of Montreal.

But the company was steadily losing money as the Depression caused immigration, business, and tourist traffic to dwindle. Between 1919 and 1939, 1.26 million passengers travelled west on a Canadian Pacific ship, with 783,000 eastbound. As vast as these figures seem, it was a decline. Between 1924 and 1928, 580,000 passengers crossed; from 1929 to 1933 it was 437,000, and from 1934 to 1938, only 256,000. In 1929, 133,141 immigrants had been allowed by the federal government to enter Canada. In 1932, the figure had dwindled to 6,882 and immigration officers now saw more emigrants than immigrants during these years as many who had come to Canada returned home. The resplendent *Empress of France/Alsatian*, having carried royalty and happy vacationers on round-the-world and Mediterranean cruises, was laid up on the Clyde from September 1931 to October 1934, after which the company decided to scrap her.

It was a sad and unhappy time for shipping, the country, and the world as a whole. All over the world great liners such as the *Mauretania* and *Olympic*, the last of the three Cunard sisters, were cut up for scrap — a cost-cutting measure that governments would regret when the next war began and whole armies had to be moved across the ocean. Others were humiliated when their elegant surroundings were opened to the participants of what were called "whoopee cruises" — the United States was then "dry" and trips to Cuba and the West Indies, where drinking, gambling, and a no-holds-barred nightlife were commonplace, offered an escape for many North Americans.

Governments, whether democratic or fascist, could no longer afford to subsidize several national shipping lines and they were forced to merge. In Germany, the National Socialists made the Hamburg-Amerika and North German Lloyd combine as Hapag-Lloyd, and in Italy, Benito Mussolini directed that all Italian shipping lines amalgamate to form Italia. In 1934, the two fabled giants of the industry, Cunard and White Star, both almost bankrupted by competition, were married by the British government to become White Star/Cunard, the new company quickly sending to the breakers as many of the antiquated liners as it could.

CHAPTER 7

Fit for a King

Forty-two years old when he took over as Canadian Pacific's chairman in 1917, with film star looks, Edward Wentworth Beatty was a strange, controversial person who dominated the company in Depression and war until his death in 1943. He was educated at the University of Toronto and Osgoode Hall, joining the CPR's legal department in 1901. As son of the man who had provided the company with access to the Toronto money market and owned a Great Lakes steamship company before selling it to the CPR, Beatty was born to the job. And although he was the CPR's first Canadian-born president, he was an unabashed Anglophile, knighted in 1935 and idolizing two things: British royalty and his Empress ships. He was intensely disliked by the prime minister, Mackenzie King, who, while using the Empress liners to travel to London (filling his diary with copious accounts of the voyages) throughout his political career, worked with a characteristic vindictiveness to break what he saw as the CPR's stranglehold on the Canadian economy.

Beatty's pride and joy was the next Empress. Appropriately named *Empress of Britain II* (the first *Britain*, sister ship of the ill-fated *Ireland*, had been scrapped in 1924), it was the fastest, largest, most luxurious ship ever built for the Canadian Pacific, and represented the acme of British engineering, nautical architecture, and style. Her keel was laid at the John Brown Shipyard on November 28, 1928, just before the Depression began. On June 11, 1930, the radio broadcasts of the event were sent for the very first time throughout the Empire, and half a million people lined the Clyde banks to cheer the great white ship's launch as it was taken out by five tugs.

In a gesture typical of the prince who enjoyed many happy cruises on Canadian Pacific ships, on May 27, 1931, HRH the Prince of Wales personally flew to the Southampton docks to wish the crew bon voyage. The Empresses were host to royalty many times, but especially to HRH the Prince of Wales, the future King Edward VIII. Neither formal nor pretentious, and nicknamed "The Sunshine Prince," he seemed to be everything that the rest of the British royal family wasn't. The prince availed himself of the lifestyle onboard the Empresses on several occasions and once, on the *Empress of France*, even played the drums with the ship's orchestra, attempting to remain incognito as "Lord Renfrew." His Royal Highness did more to publicize the good life onboard the Canadian Pacific liners than any movie star — at least in Canada. "Where luxurious loafing charms" was a cruise ship advertisement, but the prince personified it. Cameras, both movie and still, recorded his unabashed enjoyment, and the sight of the heir to the British throne playing shuffleboard, lounging in a deck chair, and sitting at the master's table gave the Empresses a cachet that the company took pride in. Just before His Royal Highness arrived to see the *Britain II* off, a Rolls Royce entered the dock and majestically stopped at the foot of the ship's gangway. Onlookers sprang smartly to attention and the appointed dignitary stepped forward to open the car door. To everyone's horror, out poured four very drunk members of the crew.

The contemporaries of the Empresses were the French Line's *Normandie* and Cunard's *Queen Mary*. All three symbolized their countries: *Normandie* had the racy, chic look of a boulevardier, the *Queen Mary* was conservative and no-nonsense like the lady it was named after, the consort of King Edward VIII. The *Empress of Britain* was impressive, solid and a little stodgy — like the Canada it represented. Yet on the Luxury Index — a scale that took into account such standards as roominess, aesthetic appeal, food quality, crew courtesy, and the riding qualities of the ship — the *Empress* was classed second only to the *Normandie*.

Ship	Luxury Index
Normandie	2,945
Empress of Britain	2,211
Queen Mary	1,918
Europa	1,240
Majestic	1,226
Bremen	1,172
Île de France	1,083

Source: Ardman, Harvey, *Normandie: Her Life and Times.*
(New York: Franklin Watts, 1985), 181.

One of the reasons for the ranking, undoubtedly, was that the French ship had the most numerous crew ever carried — the ratio was one crew member for every 1.47 passengers. The *Queen Mary*'s was one per 1.94 passengers. But the *Empress*'s was a creditable one crew member for 1.61 passengers. "Such space per passenger is a unique feature," a company brochure explained. "In all three classes of accommodation, her staterooms are so unusually large that, together with the 16 public rooms, there are actually 36 tons of ship for each passenger when a capacity list is carried, a guarantee of comfort which is especially appreciated by world cruise passengers whose staterooms are their homes for several months."

The *Empress* was so huge that it became the largest ship to date to sail through both the Suez and Panama canals — squeaking through the latter with seven inches to spare on either side. Her masts had to be reduced by two feet to allow her to sail under the brand new Golden Gate Bridge in San Francisco. Her ten decks included a sundeck, sports deck, promenade deck, and much open deck space for tourist and third-class passengers.

"In the decoration of the *Empress of Britain*, particularly in the Public Rooms, the underlying thought is the provision of variety and interest consistent with good taste," the brochure stated. The more important rooms were distinctively named: the main dining saloon, which was able to accommodate 425 dinner guests, was named the Salle Jacques Cartier, in honour of the discoverer of the St. Lawrence. Designed by Sir John Lavery, the Empress Room was an entirely pillarless ballroom crowned by a large dome, which portrayed in deep blue and gold a representation of the heavens as they actually appeared on the night of the *Empress*'s launch. The stage at the after end of the room was covered with rose and turquoise-blue draperies, with coral, pearl, and diamond effects. At the forward end of the ballroom was the projection room for the cinema.

Aft from the Empress Room was The Mall — two long galleries that merged into the ship's main entrance. The walls were panelled in limed oak, with ornamental friezes, and heading the main stairway was a large painting by Maurice Greiffenhagen, R.A., depicting Samuel de Champlain, the founder of Quebec, welcoming his wife to the city. The Writing Room, aft of The Mall on the starboard side, was Georgian in style, with walnut-panelled walls, fluted oak pilasters, and a fireplace of Roman stone. On the port side opening from The Mall was the American or Knickerbocker Bar, where comic artist Heath Robinson had decorated the walls above the sycamore panelling with a panorama titled *The Legend of the Cocktail Bird*.

The Mayfair Lounge, the ship's central salon, had been inspired by the Temple of Minerva, with richly grained walnut panelling and green Scagliola marble columns. A dome in panelled amber glass rose from the centre of the room, each panel with a golden sun-ray centre, with the signs of the Zodiac in bas-relief on the intersecting panels. On a huge panel at the forward end of the room was a reproduction of a Gobelin tapestry that illustrated the hunting exploits of Emperor Maximilian I. Edmund Dulac had designed The Cathay Lounge, or smoking room, in a Chinese motif, and under its panelled ceiling of gold leaf were fretted walls panelled in grey ash and ornamented in black and red lacquer. In the centre of the room, beneath a four-sided clock suspended from the ceiling, was a carved rock formation, said to be "reminiscent" of Chinese jade. Even the furniture was specially designed in red and black lacquer, ornamented in pale gold and covered with coral-coloured material of Chinese design. The card room was "themed" in Spanish style with wrought ironwork, a series of mural arches in rough stone, leaded-glass windows, and a black and gold tiled fireplace.

The aft end of F-deck was filled with the Olympian Pool, the largest swimming pool on any ship. Lit from below, it was designed by P.A. Staynes in fluted turquoise-blue glass and mosaic columns, terrazo, teak, vitreous-glass, and parterre of different colours. To cap it all, a jet of sea-water poured into the pool from a large turtle made of Portland stone. Adjoining the pool were two modern gymnasiums, one for adults and the other for juveniles, each with a camel-riding machine, a horse-riding machine, and two cycle-racing machines. The Turkish Baths consisted of a laconicum, calidarium, tepidarium, vapour room, frigidarium, and a massage room. A rare shipboard provision was a regulation-sized squash/rackets court, up to "match-standard," while on the sports deck was a full-sized tennis court, complete with spectators' galleries and a café. Here, star players such as William T. Tilden II and Helen Jacobs practised.

On her maiden voyage, the *Empress of Britain* captured the Canadian Blue Riband by racing from Cherbourg to Father Point in four days, 18 hours, 26 minutes — ten hours faster than the previous fastest time set by *Empress of Japan* in 1929. Her eastbound passage to Southampton was only 17 minutes slower. Her master, Captain R.G. "Jock" Latta, was made commodore of the CPR fleet and after the maiden voyage named Tetoniatarakakowa, or "Swiftest Rider of the Mighty Waters," by the First Nations Iroquois at Quebec. In 1934, the *Empress* reduced the eastbound crossing to four days, six hours, and 58 minutes, and the westbound in four days, eight hours.

John Johnson, the company's own engineering consultant, had designed a unique engineering distinction for the *Empress of Britain*. The liner was propelled by four screws, each driven by an independent set of single-reduction geared turbines of Parsons type, developing 62,500 shaft horsepower (shp) to attain a sea speed of 24 knots. An overload power of 66,500 (shp) could be achieved to increase her speed to maintain schedules. Steam superheated to 725 degrees Fahrenheit was supplied to the turbines by eight Yarrow type and one Johnson boiler, the whole plant contained in two separate engine rooms. Two-thirds of the power was developed by the main turbines in the forward room, driving the inboard propellers. On cruises, when less speed was required than on Atlantic service, the two outboard propellers were removed, and the ship was driven solely by the main turbines and the inboard screws. The four diesel and two turbine generators were more than adequate to power, among other things, 12 elevators and 200 electric clocks.

The *Empress* was the first ship with a radio telephone service that connected passengers' rooms with anywhere in the world, and on May 31, 1931, the governor general of Canada, Lord Bessborough, personally phoned Beatty, who was onboard — the first such call in Canada. When the ship docked for the first time at the specially built wharf at Wolfe's Cove, Quebec, on June 2, the *Empress of Britain* was proof that the Canadian Pacific had matched Cunard and the French Line.

Stories of its eight round-the-world cruises were celebrated: it was said that the entire library was replaced at ports, and that when it docked, its cricket team played the locals — which in Los Angeles meant movie stars like Clark Gable, Laurel and Hardy, Joan Blondell, and C. Aubrey Smith. Both the *Empress of Britain* and *Australia* also feature in Mackenzie King's diary as he travelled aboard them to Britain to attend conferences and coronations. While onboard, King made ship-to-shore radio broadcasts from the radio cabin, ate at the captain's table, watched movies — he enjoyed *The Tale of Two Cities* and *Scarlet Pimpernel* — and read. On one voyage he was presented with a signed copy of the latest John Buchan novel — the author being the governor general, Lord Tweedsmuir.

On another occasion, King even visited third class to sign autographs for a charitable cause. As he noted in his diary on July 8, 1937, he was quite pleased in April of that year to have been given Suite 140 on the *Empress of Australia* — not only was it the finest onboard but it had been used by the former King Edward VIII the last time he had crossed the Atlantic as Prince of Wales:

Was up before 8 this morning. Shortly after twelve, the *Caledonia*, one of the flying boats which has made the transatlantic mail service came in sight of the *Empress*, following her up the river at great speed and after over-taking, circled around her once or twice, diving in salute and coming once so near the ship, it was possible to read the words: "Imperial Airways, London" as well as "Caledonia." As she approached the stern she looked like a great seagull; heaving in flight ... it was a historic moment to have had this transatlantic flight of the new air service which some day, will become regular first-class mail service between Europe and America.

Following the First World War, women — historically absent from seafaring, or only mentioned as prostitutes or stowaways — made their presence increasingly felt. When the transatlantic liners began to leave from Southampton, more and more women were taken on to cater to the passengers. Joining the stewardesses were bathing attendants, nannies, nursery nurses, laundry attendants (usually female), masseuses, and later hairdressers, swimming instructors, and stenographers. Even so, the ratio aboard the liners of male to female staff was 17:1. As married women were not supposed to work at sea, and as the stewardesses varied in age, marital status, education, and social background, all were addressed by passengers and staff as either "Missus" or "Miss."

For a woman to earn a living at sea — to even associate with seamen — invited controversy, for traditionally those who worked on the docks (or ships) risked being associated with prostitutes. Onboard, they weren't always welcome either, even when taking up what were traditionally "women's roles." Often working to support their children at home, if they dreamed of glamour aboard the ocean liners, they were mistaken. Up to 80 percent of vacancies available to them were as stewardesses which in effect meant nurse, waitress, cleaner, and chambermaid. There was little chance of glamour as female employees in all lines were forbidden on the public promenades or in the restaurants or from mixing with the male crew — outside of duty hours, they were expected to keep to their cabins.

As the Duchesses sailed from Liverpool, the majority of stewardesses on them came from that port, as well as Belfast, Dublin, and Bootle. For the Empresses out of Southampton, the stewardesses were from London, Bristol, Leicester, and Chertsey.

The working attire was more practical than stylish and former Canadian Pacific stewardesses can date their photographs from the uniforms. Before the 1930s, the morning uniform was a white and blue striped dress-overall. It had deep white cuffs and a white collar made of celluloid, or a similar material. In the afternoon this was exchanged for a navy blue dress-overall always worn with a high-necked, bibbed apron. It was essentially a nurse's uniform and bought from nursing out-fitters Hussey's at 116–118 Bold Street, Liverpool. After the 1930s, the firm decided that these uniforms were uncomfortable and "we got more comfy ones with short sleeves and brass buttons," remembered Ellen Laing. Post-war there was a further change to saxe blue with pleats.

A stewardess's role was to look after the female passengers and chil-dren — the newcomers were always sent either to the nurseries or to steerage. To actually work in the "rooms" (cabins) was a step up as it was it was more prestigious to be on A-deck. The wages were no better (and neither were the tips) but it was considered a promotion. Other stewardesses said that they went wherever they were sent — it could be first class one way and tourist class on the way back. But you only catered to the female passengers. A former stewardess recalled, "You only made the beds of female passengers — never those of men, not even those of women in a married couple." The bunks were three feet wide, and if a married couple — unlike other companies, the line did not allow the unmarried to share a cabin — the woman slept on the lower bunk. Stewards worked harder, as they always made the upper bunks and were responsible for cleaning the portholes and floor, the stewardess doing the basins and baths.

Each stewardess was allocated a section of the ship — the newest started off in steerage or looking after the babies in the nursery. A section consisted of at least 15 cabins, which they shared with a steward. But it was an unwritten law that staff were always on call. "Work and bed, work and bed, that's all there was," remembered one. The hours were long, the pace fast, and the chances of pleasure at sea were not great. "It was terribly hard work and not very pleasant; emptying chamber pots and cuspidors after the passengers had been sick."

On Canadian Pacific ships, the non-fraternization policy with passengers and male members of the crew was strictly enforced. Stewardesses and stewards (like all of the catering staff) were never permanent members of the crew, their employment dependant on how many passengers were expected: "You had to sign fresh articles of agreement for each voyage." But most went back on the same ship that they had worked on before. Interestingly, although they knew that passenger figures were declining through the 1930s, none of the women ever remembered any uncertainty about employment on the Canadian Pacific.

After the chief stewardess — who assigned duties, sections, and sleeping quarters — for the women the most important person was the catering superintendent onshore, as he decided promotions to the better paying position of chief stewardess. With hindsight, the women claimed that promotion to this was never based on seniority but instead on attitudes, skills, and "class" that the company wanted to foster. A good accent, coming from a well-off family, or being well-connected always helped. Former stewardesses said that they encountered male passengers who in return for certain favours promised to put in a good word for them with the company. Stewards on the other hand believed that being Freemasons would help them climb the promotion ladder. Then there was the ship's master. He inspected the cabins daily and on sailing day, remembered one woman, "all stewardesses went up on the square on 'A' Deck and the Master would inspect you to make sure that you looked alright [*sic*]."

Yet for its day, it was a comparatively advanced profession. Long before sex equality was legislated, stewardesses made the same pay as their male colleagues — something that their counterparts in Canadian Pacific Airlines did not achieve until the 1970s. In 1936, when women ashore in the catering and laundry professions were making (weekly) one pound, eight shillings, and eight pence and one pound, five shillings, respectively, the stewardesses on the *Duchess of Bedford* were quite well off, making seven pounds, 11 shillings, and sixpence, the chief stewardess £11, eight shillings, and the stenographer £11, eight shillings.

Besides this, they could also earn tips from grateful passengers. These varied from time of year, length of trip, and type of passenger. (It was accepted that royalty did not carry money on their person and thus did not tip.) Leaving Europe the tips would be in pounds, on return in dollars. The tips would not exclusively be financial — regular passengers formed friendships with the staff and exchanged letters, sometimes receiving marriage proposals. A good tip for looking after children for an excessive time or mopping up after seasickness would be from one to five dollars. The more discreet would leave the money in an envelope in the cabin, but most would hand out the tips upon leaving ship, when the staff was lined up. Where one worked onboard did not help: the tips in first class were not necessarily higher than what one got from steerage. What was different was the prestige and likelihood of serving the famous, especially the new royalty of the era — movie stars.

Besides emptying bedpans and cuspidors, the memories of two particular duties that stewardesses performed remained with them long after they had left the profession. All liners had a night-duty stewardess for the whole voyage and the Canadian Pacific insisted that a stewardess had to do one voyage of night duties annually. Work began at 10:00 p.m. when the day stewardesses went off duty and lasted until 7:00 a.m. the next morning. The night stewardess would sit in the bell room and answer the red bell (actually a light — red for stewards and green for stewardesses). The passengers' requests were usually for tea or a snack, both of which were made in the pantry near the bell room. The difficulties of sleeping at the wrong time of day, particularly in the cramped accommodation shared by five other stewardesses deep in steerage, made it a trying experience. "You were always aft and used to go mad listening to the noise of the propeller," one recalled.

On the other side of the scale was being a bath stewardess. This, too, could be any of the stewardesses; the choice, remarked one, depending on "whether the Chief Stewardess liked you or not." They had to prepare the female passengers' baths. As all baths were in saltwater, at the appointed time, the stewardess would bring a big tin bath of fresh water to the communal bathroom and leave it there. She would then knock on the cabin door and say, "Your bath is ready, madam." The passenger would finish her saltwater bath, using the special soap which was supposed to lather in salt water (but didn't) and then rinse off in fresh.

The stewardesses liked being in "baths" because "there wasn't much running around as long as the toilets were kept clean." There were three or four lavatories in the ladies toilet and the stewardess would have to mop the floors and clean the bowls. Of course all these duties were performed against the heaving seas and engine vibration. The constant motion of the ship meant that everything was twice as difficult to do as it would be on land because it required balance and the stewardesses coping with their own seasickness. Nor did work stop when the passengers disembarked. "In port," remembers one, "you had to clean the whole section for the new people boarding. It took a whole week, but you had every evening and Sunday off."

It took the Second World War, as the male members of the crew enlisted, for more positions to be opened to women. Again and again through that conflict, female employees demonstrated their courage in adverse conditions. When the *Empress of Britain* was sunk, stewardesses in its lifeboats, although in danger of being killed themselves if the vessel blew up, insisted on helping haul aboard other crew members swimming about and giving first aid to those suffering exhaustion after their ordeal in the freezing water. "They were real heroines," commented one survivor.

With another world war looming on the horizon, Beatty was preparing for what would be his crowning glory — the royal tour in early summer of 1939. Designed to cement Canadian ties for the coming war, King George VI and Queen Elizabeth used the *Empress of Australia* to begin a tour of North America. The battleship HMS *Repulse* had been chosen to convey the royal party across the Atlantic but as a former naval officer His Majesty refused to hear of it, saying that given the tense situation in Europe, Britain needed all her capital ships around her. The Canadian Pacific president gladly came to the rescue, making available at short notice the Empress which had already carried the former Prince of Wales and Prince George to Canada in 1927. His Majesty's parents had taken the *Empress of India* between Vancouver and Victoria 38 years before but this was the first time that a reigning monarch would use one of their liners for an extended period as a (however temporarily) royal yacht. Neither the P&O nor Cunard had ever been accorded such an honour and the company took great pride in being so designated.

When the press made the German origins of the *Empress of Australia* known to the British public, questions were asked in the House of Commons as to Their Majesties' safety, but British prime minister Neville Chamberlain, who had sailed to Canada for the Imperial Conference in 1932 on the *Empress of Britain*, was able to mollify the Opposition by replying that at least the engines had been made by Fairfield's on the Clyde — and that it would be accompanied by two destroyers. The liner had a normal capacity for 1,200 passengers and 400 crew members so the royal couple with their 18 staff was quite lost onboard, with extra ballast added to help assuage its "roll." It took a week of frenzied work to make it ready, but fortunately, as the *Tirpitz* the ship had had very large staterooms installed to accommodate the kaiser and his court. To fill them, furniture — namely the king's bed — was borrowed from the old Royal Yacht *Victoria and Albert*. The smell of the thousands of gallons of hastily applied paint was concealed with buckets of water filled with sliced onions.

But at 3:00 p.m. on May 6, when the *Empress of Australia* steamed out of Portsmouth for Quebec City, at its bow flew the Canadian Pacific House Flag, at the stern the White Ensign, and from its foremast the Royal Standard. In an admiral's uniform with the queen by his side, His Majesty stood on the *Empress's* promenade deck and waved at the crowds that had come to see them off. The pomp and circumstance served to mask the base realities of an impending war: few knew that the *Empress* was armed with depth charges or that one of the escort vessels, HMS *Southampton*, carried in its hold 3,550 gold bars from the Bank of England for safekeeping in Canada.

The *Empress's* catering supervisor, Mr. Abe Toole, ensured that the favourite delicacies of the royal couple were onboard — haggis, Black Sea caviar, 33 cases of wine from His Majesty's own cellar, and the king's hand-rolled Havana cigars. Once out in the Atlantic, the sea was stormy.

The *Empress*, travelling at a speed of 14 knots, bounced about, making the royal entourage seasick. Captain Archibald Meikle knew the best route to Canada in the spring was to be as far south as possible, away from the icebergs. But he was overruled by the Sea Lords in London who feared that German submarines prowling the Atlantic might kidnap Their Majesties. They wanted the *Empress* to be as far north as possible, and this meant, as Meikle knew, heading into fog and iceberg fields. On the fifth day out, as the captain predicted, the *Empress* and its two escorts ran into both thick fog and looming icebergs. As the entourage nervously watched the cathedral-sized icebergs off the bow — the destroyers having vanished into the mist — and the *Empress*'s foghorn blew constantly, everyone was well aware that the *Titanic* had sunk in these very waters, and at this very time of the year.

But Their Majesties seemed oblivious to the danger (to Meikle's relief) and both rested, walked about the empty ship, chatted with the crew, watched Walt Disney cartoons, and with the use of books and movies, studied up on Canada. Her Majesty Queen Elizabeth came into her own. She talked with everyone, asking questions and showing interested in everything. What, she asked the crew, were those large canisters on the deck of the *Australia*? Depth charges, they told her, and to demonstrate what they did, proceeded to fire one off — after alerting the accompanying destroyers, of course. The explosion directly below the *Empress*'s hull sent a torrent of freezing seawater up into its drains. The poor royal steward, Frank Knight, had been sitting happily on the toilet at that moment, and he felt a sudden flood and was uncomfortably soaked. He thought they had hit an iceberg and bolted out of the bathroom.

On May 13, just before a fog bank enveloped them, a gigantic iceberg came into view and Captain Meikle reversed engines around it and reduced his speed to five knots. He also radioed the waiting Canadian government that they were going to be two days late, arriving not on May 15 but possibly on May 17. Three long, nerve-wracking days later, ever-cautious (although the passengers could now see the lights of bonfires and automobile headlights along the shore), rather than risk making for Quebec City at night, Meikle dropped anchor 12 miles before Wolfe's Cove near St. Jean on the Île d'Orleans.

It was the last night onboard the *Empress*, and as if to relieve the tension of the voyage — and allow the packing to be done — the ship's dining room was decorated with balloons and streamers and a dance was held. Customary at the end of any royal voyage, the crew was given gifts, His Majesty making Captain Meikle (who had not slept for three days) a Commander of the Royal Victorian Order. The next morning, when the first bright, clear day dawned, wanting to get the voyage over with, the Canadian Pacific captain had the anchor hoisted at 8:15 a.m. and surprised the naval vessels by steaming toward Quebec City. The royal party might have arrived late to the reception at Wolfe's Cove (throwing out the careful timetables that the Canadian and U.S. governments had arranged), but thanks to the Canadian Pacific, it had arrived safely.

Beatty could not have been more pleased as in many ways it was a Canadian Pacific royal tour. Besides the *Empress of Australia*, the king and queen rode across Canada in his private railcar, "The Wentworth" (his middle name), and between Vancouver and Victoria the royal couple boarded the Canadian Pacific ferry, the *Princess Marguerite*. Its captain, Clifford Fenton, according to naval custom, proffering command to His Majesty who accepted, becoming the official master of the Canadian Pacific ferry for the voyage. The whole tour was a triumph and on June 15, 1939, Their Majesties embarked at Quebec City on the *Empress of Britain* for the journey home to Southampton. They so enjoyed the voyage that by express command of the king, the *Empress* was allowed to fly the Red Ensign (or "Duster") of the merchant navy instead of the White (Ensign).

But as the *Britain* made its way back to Southampton, there were those onboard who wondered what their immediate future held. One of them was the ship's second officer, Cecil Ernest Duggan. Duggan had graduated in February 1919 as a cadet from the HMS *Conway*, a British training ship located in the Menai Straits off the Welsh coast that prepared boys 14–16 years old for a career at sea. He had wanted to join the Royal Navy but his father had been advised that, because of the end of the war, the Admiralty was no longer accepting cadets and his son should consider entering the merchant marine with a view of later enlisting in the Royal Naval Reserve (RNR). The 16-year-old Duggan then wrote to Master T.V. Forster, the chief of CPOS in Liverpool, who was in the RNR himself, and asked for a job. Because of his training, he was accepted immediately and reported to the *Melita*, beginning a long and illustrious service both in the Canadian Pacific and the RNR. In 1926, he took a leave of absence to join the Royal Naval Reserve as a sub-lieutenant and had qualified in minesweeping. Within three months of the royal tour, with many in the company, Duggan was "called up" and found himself serving on HMS *Vernon*, sweeping the English Channel of magnetic and acoustic mines.

CHAPTER 8

War Service Once More

All was ruled by that harsh and despotic factor, shipping ... the stranglehold and the sole foundation of our war strategy.
— Prime Minister Winston Churchill

It is safe to say that the outcome of both world wars — the great victories of the Battle of Britain, of Alamein, and D-Day — would not have been possible without the merchant navy. It took between seven and 15 tons of supplies to support a single soldier overseas for a year, and before strategic air lift, the war would have been lost had there not been enough freighters and former liners to carry the soldiers, ammunition, and fuel needed. It was estimated that Britain would require 47 million tons a year of imports to survive. Food, fuel, and equipment vital to its survival came to the island in hundreds of ships ranging from tramp steamers to oil tankers and refrigeration ships. In 1940–41, thanks largely to the U-boats, it barely received a total of 31.5 million. For this reason, and because a U-boat was loathe to take on a fully armed naval vessel, the Kriegsmarine intentionally focused on the merchant ships that were initially escorted up to the "CHOP Line." Sinking an aircraft carrier or battleship made for good propaganda but starving Britain of essential food and supplies was strategically of more value.

In the decades between the wars, the theory of ships moving in convoys for protection had been so refined that the system was well in place when hostilities were declared and the first convoy was able to sail from Liverpool for Halifax as early as September 8, 1939. To the Royal Navy, a convoy was "one or more merchant ships sailing under the protection of one or more warships." The system of convoys was a broad front formation with several columns of ships with up to five ships in each column. The columns were 1,000 yards apart and the ships in each column 400 yards apart. This formation allowed the numbers of ships to be increased without having to add more escort vessels, as it did not extend the convoy perimeter. Convoy sizes therefore increased from an initial average of 35 ships to one of more than 60.

Merchant ships that could make more than 15 knots could sail independently. In November 1940, this was reduced to 13 knots, and loss rates of lone ships increased by 300 percent against those for convoys. But until the summer of 1941, the convoy system was only a theory. Those leaving Britain or Canada only lasted a few hundred miles off shore as it was believed that this was the limit of the U-boats' operational range. Control of North Atlantic convoys was exercised either side of a mid-ocean "Change of Operational Control Line" (or CHOP line) by Headquarters Western Approaches in Liverpool and Canadian and U.S. authorities. At this point, the escorts would leave to meet the incoming ships while their charges dispersed, put on all speed and made for the protection on the other side as best they could.

The *Empress of Britain* was on the high seas when the liner *Athenia* was sunk on September 3, and on arrival in Quebec City the ship was ordered to remain there. As part of the British merchant marine, Canadian Pacific was at war from that very day, a full week before the Dominion of Canada declared war September 10, all of its ships wearing the Red Ensign. Even before Hitler had invaded Poland, ship masters had been issued sealed instructions for the conduct of their ships in time of war. Marked A, B, and C, the envelopes were only to be opened when instructed by the port's naval officer and contained such instructions as blackening the porthole windows.

As with the previous conflict, Canadian Pacific threw itself whole-heartedly into the war effort. It had long encouraged its staff to train in the Royal Naval Reserve and Royal Canadian Naval Reserve, and in 1939, 40 of its officers held commissions. Sir Edward Beatty was appointed the representative in Canada of the British Ministry of Shipping and to the chagrin of Mackenzie King even found time to start the Canadian Pacific Air Service to ferry American-built bombers to Britain and have the CPR participate in the Commonwealth Air Training Plan. The British Ministry of Shipping requisitioned his vessels, from the luxury liners and the cargo ships to the British Columbia coastal ferries, and sent them to all corners of the globe with troops, fuel, and supplies one way and prisoners of war and refugees the other. In their respective classes — the company gave over to the Admiralty six Empresses, four Duchesses, two Princesses, and five Beavers. As with other shipping companies in the Commonwealth, Canadian Pacific was compensated with agreed-upon payments per gross ton per month, the Admiralty paying also for fuel, water, pilotage, and port charges. The company continued to pay the crew's wages and was responsible for provisions and maintenance.

On September 25, the Admiralty officially requisitioned the *Empress of Britain* as a troop transport. As the German blitzkrieg seemed unstoppable, General A.G.L. McNaughton's First Canadian Division was rushed en masse from Canada to Britain in the first troop convoy of which the *Empress of Britain, Empress of Australia*, and the *Duchess of Bedford* were part. The Empresses and Duchesses were ideal mass transit ships, able to carry whole divisions from the Dominions to either defend the Mother country or to distant battle fronts of the Empire. In October 1940, three Empresses — *Britain, Japan*, and *Canada* — were part of the historic "Multi-Million-Dollar convoy," sailing from Australia to South Africa with three other former luxury liners — Cunard's *Queen Mary, Aquitania*, and *Mauretania*.

They all suffered the indignity of having been painted grey with all luxurious furnishings removed (the *Empress of Britain*'s squash courts were converted to dormitories) and their catering schedules adapted to the new customers. On a "trooper" like the *Empress of Scotland*, 14,000 meals were served daily, the dining room was rebuilt to accommodate 1,060 men a sitting, the butter spread on the slices of bread with brushes. The company chefs attempted valiantly to keep to a semblance of pre-war luxury with chicken and ice cream followed by — instead of orchestras and jazz bands — movies, variety concerts, and "horse racing."

Because of their speed, as in the First World War, the great ships were in no danger of U-boat attacks and if they sailed in convoys, it was because of surface raiders, especially the pocket battleships. But their size and poor anti-aircraft armament made them prime targets for enemy bombers from which the company would suffer dearly. Of the 18 Canadian Pacific ocean-going ships and two vessels from its British Columbia coastal service that were requisitioned by the Admiralty, only five would survive to VE Day.

The tradition of sending British children to Canada for philanthropic reasons was well-established, and in September 1939 the first child evacuees began to arrive through private arrangements. This time they were fleeing not poverty but the imminently expected German air raids. If Ottawa was slow in extending an official invitation, private Canadians weren't. Sir Edward Beatty offered places in his fleet to move as many as wanted to come. Rotarians, schools, Anglican churches, and even Lady Eaton made available their institutions and homes. Naturally, many asked to look after the princesses, Elizabeth and Margaret Rose. In June 1940, in answer to government pleas that the princesses be taken to Canada, Queen Elizabeth famously replied, "The children could not possibly go without me. I would not leave without the King and the King will not leave under any circumstances."

On May 31, 1940, after the lobbying of charitable organizations like the Canadian Welfare Council led by a young Charlotte Whitton (a future mayor of Ottawa) and Lester B. Pearson at the Canadian High Commission in London, the federal government was forced into officially offering to accept the British children — Canada becoming the first

Commonwealth country to do so. Tax concessions were to be granted to any family who took them in, and 50,000 Canadians offered to do so. After this, events moved quickly. On June 19, the British Leader of the Opposition, Clement Atlee (who had once been a mayor of an inner-city London borough), presented the plan in the House of Commons for the immediate establishment of the Children's Overseas Reception Board (CORB). It was approved within a day — just France surrendered to Germany — and over 211,000 applications from frantic parents flooded into the CORB offices.

The first child evacuees destined for Halifax were taken to Greenock that July and put on the *Duchess of York*. On August 10, with 500 children onboard, the Canadian Pacific ship set sail in convoy, a total of 1,131 "guest children" spread out among other ships. After the austerity of wartime Britain, the children enjoyed life on the *Duchess* — there was good, plentiful food, movies, games, and hot baths in salt water. Their happiness was tempered only by the daily lifeboat drills and the stench of diesel fuel that contributed to seasickness. The convoy was escorted to the CHOP Line and then left to its own resources, upon which it was attacked by U-boats and one ship was sunk.

Ten days after leaving Greenock, the lights of Halifax appeared, looking to the children of the blackout like "a fairyland." They disembarked at Pier 21 and, after being processed, were overwhelmed by the generosity of Haligonians, the smell and taste of hot chocolate and giant cookies never forgotten. The CORB program was well underway when two tragic incidents occurred: the torpedoing of ships filled with Canada-bound children — the *Voledam* on August 28, 1941, and the *City of Benares* on September 17. With that the child evacuation program was curtailed, though children still came to Canada through private arrangements until the very end of the war. Of the 2,664 "Corbies" that were sent to the Dominions, 1,532 came to Canada.

On its next voyage, the *Duchess of York* transported 3,000 German POWs to Canada, the most troublesome of all the passengers that the Canadian Pacific had ever had. As only 250 members of the Home Guard (or "Dad's Army" as they were called) could be spared for the voyage over, the POWs were given complete freedom on the ship. Realizing the danger they were in, the Canadian Pacific crew protested and asked to be armed. But citing the Geneva Convention, the authorities refused. Halfway across the ocean a fight broke out and the Home Guard wounded the ringleaders, and in response to the crew's pleas the Admiralty ordered that the ship sail with all the lights blazing.

This time it was the Germans who protested that the display begged for a U-boat to sink them. But the *Duchess* arrived in Montreal without incident — where the local officials were completely unprepared for the POWs. A reporter from the *Globe and Mail* who met the ship recorded the scene in detail with some incredulity: "guarded by a few over age Tommies, the swaggering supermen boldly taunted their guards that Germany was sure to win the war."

On its next trip over, the *Duchess of York* brought 1,100 happy child evacuees. This time, with typical bureaucratic logic, all officers were issued with loaded revolvers.

Initially, the war had little effect on the Beavers' schedules, except that the pattern of cargoes changed drastically — heavy eastward and very little going west. It was only four of the sisters initially, as *Beaverhill* was out of service after hitting an iceberg. It had arrived in London on August 16, the repairs still incomplete. It would not be until May 1940 that the ship was declared ready — and this is what saved it from meeting its sisters' fate in those first terrible months.

It was during the *Beaverburn*'s fourth wartime crossing that it met its fate. The ship had left the Surrey Docks on February 1, 1940, and joined Convoy OB84 for Canada. The convoy's single escort was the destroyer HMS *Antelope*. The *Beaverburn*'s master was Thomas Jones, oddly enough known as "Farmer Jones." On February 5 at 13:12 a torpedo from *U-31* struck the ship. Farmer Jones takes up the story:

> We were zigzagging at nine knots (the speed of the slowest ship of the convoy, when there was a terrific explosion. It threw me up in the air. I ordered all hands to boat stations, rang the engine room telegraph to "Stop" and then "Finished with engines." (This was a warning to engine room staff that they should make their way to the boats).

The torpedo had struck right under the bridge ... the ship was breaking up; I ordered the boats to be lowered. She was still on an even keel as I walked aft to the engine room skylight where I could see water halfway up the engine room. I walked to the after rail, called to a boat to come closer, and leapt into the sea. She went down by the head and lifted her propellers out of the water and sank, about nine minutes after the torpedo had struck.

Chief Officer David Ewing later gave evidence:

I was on my way to the bridge and had my hand on the rail of the ladder when I felt the ship give a tremor, and lurch, and that was all I felt ... after cutting the lashings of two of the lifeboats I went up to the bridge where I found the Captain standing in the wheelhouse. I thought it better to get out of the wheelhouse and suggested that the Captain do the same. We did and a second later the wheelhouse collapsed as the ship was breaking in two amidships.

The 76 survivors were picked up by the American tanker *Narragansett*. Only the captain and third engineer, Henry Teare, had to swim for the boats — Teare had gone below to close off the valves and prevent an explosion. The *Narragansett* took them to Falmouth and along the way HMS *Antelope* radioed that it had sunk the U-boat that had torpedoed them. Months later, a postcard arrived at the Canadian Pacific's head office: "I picked up on this coast a name board that said *Beaverburn*. I have been told that there is a reward of £10 for its recovery. Will you please let me know if this is correct?" The general manager's red-pencilled minute reads, "If a stamped envelope has not been received with this query no reply is to be sent." This was the first of the Beavers to go and the first loss of a Canadian Pacific ship.

When the *Beaverdale* returned to London on May 28, 1940, the British Expeditionary Force was trapped on the beaches at Dunkirk. The ship's chief officer, Dave Ewing, took two of the lifeboats downriver and then across the channel to Dunkirk. For the next five days Ewing and the members of the *Beaverdale* crew helped with the evacuation, bringing the exhausted men off the beaches to the ships, all the while braving Luftwaffe attacks. He returned with both lifeboats intact in time for the ship's next sailing.

Unlike their colleagues in 1914–18, the merchant ships' crews that were central to the Battle of the Atlantic were now fighting not only the elements, the U-boats, and surface raiders, but long-range bombers, as well. After submarines, action by enemy aircraft was the second-highest cause of Allied shipping losses. Ships — especially the Empresses — were too large to miss and because of their design, could not adequately defend themselves. Typical was the case of the 42,000-ton *Empress of Britain*, which was equipped with one three-inch gun and four Lewis guns. The *Empress of Asia* was slightly better armed with a six-inch gun, six Oerlikons, eight Hotchkiss rockets, and depth charges, all of which proved to be of little consequence in an air attack.

And it wasn't only the great ships of the Canadian Pacific that were vulnerable to aircraft. On June 17, 1940, just after the Dunkirk evacuation, several thousand British troops and refugees still left in France scrambled onboard the 17,000-ton Cunard liner *Lancastria*. Bombed by Luftwaffe Dorniers, the ship caught fire and sank. German fighter planes then strafed the oil-slick sea, setting it ablaze. Estimates of soldiers, women, and children who died have ranged from 4,000 to as high as 6,000 — the disaster eclipsing that of both the *Lusitania* and the *Titanic*. Prime Minister Churchill had news of the sinking suppressed through the war.

The Focke Wulf Condor was the Luftwaffe's ultimate long-range maritime patrol aircraft. An adaption of Germany's pre-war commercial airliner, it was a low-wing, four-engine monoplane with fully retractable undercarriage, all metal except for fabric-covered control surfaces. In its maritime role, it carried bombs under the wings and was well armed. A lengthened ventral gondola held the gun positions, with a 20-mm cannon firing forward and a machine gun firing aft. Some aircraft were fitted with the earliest version of guided missiles and surface search radar. Only 276 Condors were built but their effect on Allied shipping far exceeded their numbers. With a range of 2,200 nautical miles (3,520 kilometres) they flew in loops over the eastern Atlantic, ranging from France to Norway. Condors searched for convoys from April 8, 1940, and not until mid-1944, when the Allies overran their bases in France, would they be withdrawn from the Atlantic. Their "happy time" was in 1940–41, when they sank over 363,000 in gross tonnage from August 1940 through January 1941.

Part of that tonnage was Beatty's pride and joy, the *Empress of Britain*. In March 1940, the *Empress* was sent to Australia and New Zealand to bring ANZAC troops to the Middle East to protect the Suez Canal. It was part of a "monster" convoy (so called because of the ships in it) that left Fremantle on May 12 in company with the Cunarders *Queen Mary*, *Aquitania*, and *Mauretania*. When Italy entered the war in June 1940, the Mediterranean was too close to Axis bases, and the *Empress of Britain* took the ANZAC troops via the Cape of Good Hope instead. On its return voyage, the ship stopped at Cape Town to pick up 643 passengers before making for Liverpool. A fighter escort had been promised off the northwest coast of Ireland but by October 26, none had appeared. They were almost home, but just 150 kilometres northwest of Ireland, at 9:20 a.m., the *Empress* was attacked by a Condor. Its pilot, Lieutenant Bernard Jope, dropped incendiary bombs onto the ship, setting it on fire.

In the *Empress*'s crow's nest, Able Seaman James Carroll had a "grand-stand" view of the bombing. He looked astern and saw the German plane diving out of the clouds toward the ship. The crow's nest was about 160 feet above deck and the plane came in so low that it was at his eye level. Carroll did not realize for a few minutes that any damage had been done, and did not hear an explosion. It was some time before he saw huge clouds of black smoke issuing from the deck. He ran down the ladder to his air raid precautions station but by that time the deck was blazing furiously.

Captain Sapsworth, who a year before had brought back the king and queen on the *Empress of Britain*, stood on the bridge encouraging his anti-aircraft gunners until they were all killed or wounded and the guns were out of action. The raider continued to machine-gun the bridge and the helpless passengers on deck and after the first bombing the Condor returned and dropped four more incendiaries. With the liner on fire, Captain Sapsworth gave the order to abandon ship, leaving only a skeleton crew aboard. The passengers took to the boats, some of which could not be lowered as they were ablaze. The youngest passenger, Neville Hart, aged 11 months, was tied up in a blanket and carried on the back of a seaman who slid down 60 feet of rope to a lifeboat.

An unknown steward would later write:

> It was like an inferno, and although I had been on the ship for a long time and knew every exit from the kitchen, I could not find my way out. All the staircases were ablaze, my only means of escape was through a porthole which I scrambled through and flung myself into the sea. The water was icy cold and I kept swimming to prevent myself from becoming frozen. There was a heavy sea and it was impossible to reach the boats against the swell, while those in the boats were unable to pull to members of the crew any distance away in the water. I and a colleague who followed me through the porthole, were in the water nearly an hour before we were picked up.

A survivor described the courage of another steward and the ship's doctor:

> The steward deserves the Victoria Cross with the kitchen crew trapped in their quarters and faced with throwing themselves through one of the doors into the heavy sea with no lifeboat nearby. The steward, aided by the electrician, climbed up a rope at the side of the ship to a lifeboat, impossible to reach from the decks. Although the side of the vessel was red hot from the flames inside, he made his way to the boat and lowered it. He was probably instrumental in saving the lives of 40 crew members.

The ship's surgeon, Dr. Edmund Delorme from Hamilton, Ontario, at great personal risk, climbed from lifeboat to lifeboat aiding the injured. "He performed an amputation on one of the survivors picked up by a warship and continued to treat the injured even after they reached port." Six hours after the order to abandon ship had been given, HMS *Echo* arrived and took the survivors onboard. Of the 643 that had been aboard the *Empress*, 598 were rescued by the escorting naval vessels, and 45 were missing — mainly Canadian Pacific personnel.

The Polish destroyer *Burza* and the two tugs, *Marauder* and *Thames*, took the burning vessel in tow and made for shore. But the Condor had given away the *Empress*'s position and soon the German submarine *U-32* was making all speed for the location. Its commander was one of the Kriegsmarine's aces, Kapitänleutnant Hans Jenisch, who had already sunk 17 ships. On October 28, Jenisch sighted the burning ship and fired three torpedoes into its hulk. One detonated prematurely but the other two found their target and the *Empress of Britain* sank, its name and reputation a propaganda coup for the Germans. The first to report the sinking was the German radio, the British declining to confirm it until two days later. Dr. Delorme's mother anxiously awaited news in Hamilton that he had been saved. She told the media, "If he is able to send me word I know he will do so immediately and every time the phone rings I think it's a message from him." The next day she heard that he had been rescued and was on his way to Britain.

The *Empress of Britain* would be the largest ship sunk in the Second World War and its loss shocked the world, with several newspapers publishing the obituary. "Goodbye *Empress of Britain*," G.Ward Price would write in London's *Daily Mail*. "Will anyone ever again be in the position to pay $1,500 for five days passage on such a ship? For me, you will always represent those far off times when, despite the Wall Street slump, which unfortunately preceded your appearance, the world seemed once again settled and secure." The *New York Times* editorial of October 29 agreed: "No ship ever fitted her name more truly than the *Empress of Britain*. She was indeed an empress with pride and grace and dignity in every inch of her. Her white paint was a coat of ermine that set her apart from the throng. It was always an event in our own harbor when the great white *Empress* came in."

On October 26, 1940, services were held in St. Patrick's Cathedral in Quebec, and on October 31 Sir Edward Beatty received a telegram from the governor general: "I have been asked by the King and Queen to convey to you and the Directors of Canadian Pacific Railway their sincere sympathy for the loss of that fine ship the *Empress of Britain* in which their majesties had such a pleasant voyage from Canada last year."

Beatty would never recover from its loss. On hearing that his *Empress* was gone, the president of the Canadian Pacific went into a slow mental and physical decline, his face contorted by a massive stroke on March 17, 1941.

On the same route were two other Empresses — *Canada* and *Japan* — both without escort, making for British air cover. The former escaped the attentions of the Luftwaffe but the *Empress of Japan* did not. At 09:00 hours on November 9, 1940, a Condor caught the liner off the north coast of Ireland and on his first run the pilot strafed the ship, his bomb just missing it. The second run proved more successful as the bomb exploded under the stern, damaging the *Japan*'s rudder, main bearings, and a condenser. Fortunately, the Condor then flew off, leaving the *Empress* crippled but afloat.

Working in darkness, Chief Engineer R.H. Shaw and his men managed to keep the ship underway and the next day Captain J.W. Thomas was able to bring it limping into the Clyde, where it passed its more fortunate sister, the *Empress of Canada*.

The day the *Empress of Britain* was torpedoed, the *Beaverford* was making its way to a convoy being assembled at Bedford Basin, Halifax. Of all the Canadian Pacific ships — Empress, Princess, Duchess, and Beaver — the *Beaverford* was destined to be the most celebrated, fighting a battle that has become the naval equivalent to the Spartans' sacrifice at Thermopylae. At 60 years old, Captain Hugh Pettigrew from Coatbridge near Glasgow had joined Canadian Pacific in 1910. He was a veteran of naval action at Gallipoli and had already been torpedoed as first officer on the RMS *Medora* in 1918. The other 37 ships gathering in the basin for Fast Convoy HX84 were former passenger liners, freighters, and oil tankers, crew and masters aware that the RCN's escort would end at the 350-mile mark and the RNs would begin at the Western Approaches.

In the vast tracts of ocean between, the fear was not so much U-boats but armed raiders, which it was hoped that the convoy's sole protection, HMS *Jervis Bay*, could cope with.

The 38 ships formed in nine columns and steamed out of Halifax on November 5. British Naval Intelligence were already aware that on October 27, the German pocket battleship *Admiral Scheer* had slipped out of the German naval base at Kiel making for Stavenger, Norway, and then ostensibly the Atlantic. Named after the victor of Jutland and commanded by Kapitän Theodore Krancke, the *Scheer* was heavily armoured, heavily gunned, and was equipped with highly secret radar. If let loose on the Atlantic, its 11-inch guns, which had a 12-mile range, promised to make short work of any convoy of slow and unarmed ships. On the night of October 30/31, Krancke received signals that HX84 was in the Atlantic and plotted a course to intercept it. Ensuring that there was complete radio silence, on November 4 he sent one of his two Arado float planes up to look for the convoy.

Although the day was clear, concentrating as they were on submarines and surface raiders, none of the ships' lookouts on HX84 noticed the little Arado. But the float plane's pilot saw them from 196 miles away and returned to Krancke with the convoy's location. It was mid-afternoon on November 5, with *Scheer* making full speed to intercept the convoy, when it came upon the tiny banana boat, the SS *Mopan*. Using a signal lamp, Krancke had the ship stopped, the crew removed, and the freighter sunk. The "kill" had cost valuable time and the daylight was fading. The convoy could escape into the darkness. Krancke knew that the next day the RN escort would appear and harry the battleship like so many terriers. He ordered full speed into the twilight, his radar picking out the prey.

It was 17:11 when the *Scheer* came in sight of HX84. Thinking that the battleship was part of the expected RN escort, Captain Fegen flashed out the signal "What ship?" When there was no reply, he had it repeated. At ten miles distant, the stranger turned broadside in the encroaching darkness. Then, at 17:15, six flashes lit up the horizon, followed by the sound of an oncoming express train. As the shells landed around the *Jervis Bay*, Captain Fegen sent out the rockets, signalling

"Scatter!" ordering the convoy to disperse. To buy enough time to allow the convoy to escape and the navy to arrive, he then made directly for the *Scheer*, the crew dropping off the canisters of smoke floats to complement the growing darkness. Six armour-piercing shells, each weighing over 600 pounds, hit the foredeck of the *Jervis Bay*, taking out its forward guns and the bridge. With an arm torn off, Fegen remained at his post, ensuring that his ship kept course toward the *Scheer*. The next volley killed him, but the former emigrant ship — now more a mass of burning metal than a ship — came on, altering course whenever the Germans tried to pass, paying for time for the disappearing convoy. It took the fifth salvo to stop it dead, its guns still not in range. It then began to sink bow first, taking 187 of its crew with it. The battle had lasted only 22 minutes.

Of the convoy's ships that were still within range of the *Scheer's* guns, the closest was the *Beaverford*. As the other ships made to put as much distance as they could between themselves and the battleship, the Canadian Pacific ship now turned about and took up the *Jervis Bay's* role, Captain Pettigrew and crew fully aware as to what their fate was to be. The *Beaverford's* wireless operator had been sending out detailed reports of the attack on the convoy and his last message was, "It's our turn now. So long. The captain and the crew of the *Beaverford*."

Throwing out a smokescreen to hide the remainder of the convoy, the Canadian Pacific freighter made directly toward the battleship and certain death. In clear view because of the tracer shells bursting above, the *Beaverford* was seen to absorb three massive hits from the *Scheer's* heavy guns and 16 from the medium. Yet somehow it remained afloat, Krancke guessing that the timber or wooden packing cases lashed to its decks under tarpaulins were keeping it above water. A captain of one of the fleeing ships later gave an eyewitness account of what happened next and this was published by journalist Norman Mackintosh in the magazine *Canada's Weekly*:

> For more than five hours she was afloat, followed by the raider, firing and fighting to the last. Using her big reserve of engine power for speed, and superb

seamanship for steering and maneuvering to baffle and evade the enemy's aim, hit by shells but hitting back, drawing the raider's fire and delaying him hour by hour while the rest of the convoy scattered fan-wise, made their escape into the rapidly gathering gloom.

So dark did it grow during the brave battle that the raider had to use star-shells; to illuminate his mark, and to maintain the range of his guns — a dread display of fireworks for the Fifth of November! ... when at 22:45 there arose a great burst of red flame from where (the *Beaverford*) had been and the fine Canadian freighter's splendid fight was over. It is thought that her end was due to the firing of a torpedo from the raider. But there is none left of her officers and crew to tell how that fierce, final explosion sent her to the bottom. She went down with all hands, in a glare of red flame with a shower of enemy starshells above her as she sank. She had fought the good fight: she had finished her course.

The *Scheer* was already racing to its next target even as the torpedo hit the fore part of the *Beaverford*, lifting it out of the water:

> Water rushed now rushed into her gaping side and the deck cargo slipped as she keeled over. There was a great sound of bursting and cracking now as the wooden cases broke up ... the ship's stern rose higher out of the water and then the whole vessel slid under the surface....

Krancke managed to catch up to the convoy, sink four more ships, and then lose himself in the vastness of the South Atlantic and later the Indian Ocean. The German captain correctly guessed that the British were rushing capital ships to the area and making all speed to the convoy where the battleships HMS *Nelson*, HMS *Repulse*, and HMS *Hood* — the last soon to meet its demise with the *Bismarck*, the *Scheer*'s sister ship — searched for survivors of the *Beaverford* but found none.

Captain Fogarty Fegen was awarded a posthumous Victoria Cross and in remembrance of the *Jervis Bay*, its commander, officers, and crew, a service was held in Liverpool Cathedral on November 18, 1940. As it should be, the *Jervis Bay* is commemorated in Canada at Ross Memorial Park in Saint John and in Owen Sound, Ontario. In the Royal Australian Navy several ships have been named after it, including the latest, the fast sealift catamaran.

As for the *Beaverford*, many naval historians are of the opinion that the whole crew deserved a posthumous George Cross. But the heroic ship's memorialization was to be more personal. On May 20, 1944, the students and teachers of Downhills Central School, near the London docks in Tottenham, gathered in the school hall for a special service for "their" ship. The school had adopted the *Beaverford* through the British Ships Adoption Society, keeping up a correspondence with the crew through the 1930s and, when the *Beaverford* was in port, taking tours of the ship and receiving visits from the ship's officers.

During the service, Alderman Morell, JP, chairman of the Tottenham Education Committee, presided and spoke of the valuable work done by the Merchant Navy, and a former member of the staff gave an account of the school's interaction with the ship and read extracts from letters received from members of the crew. The ceremony ended with a stirring account of the *Beaverford*'s last fight with the German pocket battleship. Finally, as a lasting memorial, a watercolour painting of the *Beaverford* coming round the Nore into the Thames Estuary and a bronze plaque were unveiled.

Hugh Pettigrew's name appears on a memorial to the Merchant Navy near the Tower of London, on the Tower Hill. And in Point Pleasant Park, Halifax, visible to all ships approaching, stands a granite Cross of Sacrifice more than 39 feet high dedicated to the 3,257 Canadians who during the two world wars have no known grave but the sea. Two of the *Beaverford*'s firemen, William Lorne Thibideau and Clifford Carter, are listed there.

In faraway New Zealand, the Canadian Pacific liner *Aorangi* had been requisitioned as a troopship and would survive the war. Not so the liner's sister ship, *Niagara*. In June 1940, it was setting out from Auckland to Britain with war supplies. The British Army had lost most of its small arms ammunition at Dunkirk and with an invasion impending that summer the New Zealanders had, with typical generosity, loaded all of their ammunition onto the Canadian Pacific ship and sent it off to the mother country. Also aboard were 295 boxes, each containing two ingots of gold, the total valued at £2 million, which had been contributed by New Zealand to help pay for British war supplies. On June 18 at 3:30 a.m., as it set off from Auckland, the *Niagara* struck a mine in Hauraki Gulf between Hen and Chicken Islands. The minefield of 162 mines had been laid seven days before by the German surface raider *Orion*. The ship remained upright and a calm sea allowed all 136 passengers and 200 crew to take to the boats. The gold bullion would be salvaged in 1941 — less it is said, five ingots. The *Niagara* now lies 260 feet below the surface on its port side, a favourite of divers who still hope to find those missing ingots.

The *Empress of Japan* was in Shanghai on September 3, 1939, and the captain, fearing internment by the Japanese, omitted calling at Yokohama on the way home, prudently returning to Victoria. Like its sisters, the *Japan* was then painted grey and armed, prepared for service as a troopship. In that role, on November 9, 1940, off western Ireland, it was pounced on by a German bomber, close to where the *Empress of Britain* had been fatally hit just two weeks earlier.

During the air raid, Captain J.W. Thomas and Ho Kan, the Chinese quartermaster, manned the wheelhouse, steering the ship into evasive action. Because of this, the two bombs that hit the *Japan* were deflected off the stern rail into the sea, causing little damage. After the attack on Pearl Harbor, on October 16, 1942, at the express order of Prime Minister Churchill, the *Empress of Japan* was re-christened the *Empress of Scotland II* — much to the disappointment of its crew, who were proud of their ship and its name. The company explained that, "its object was to rid so fine a ship of so unfortunate a name." With its new identity, the *Empress* began nine years of carrying troops, ironically surviving the Luftwaffe's attentions to be sold in 1958 to the Hamburg-Atlantic Line and renamed the *Hanseatic*.

Courtesy Library and Archives Canada/C-35115.

Right Honourable William Lyon Mackenzie King and Ernest Lapointe greeting King George VI and Queen Elizabeth at gangway of CPS *Empress of Australia,* Wolfe's Cove, Quebec City, May 1939. For the Royal Tour of 1939, Canadian Pacific President Sir Edward Beatty gladly provided the *Empress* to transport the royal couple. Neither the P&O nor Cunard had ever been accorded such an honour.

Courtesy Library and Archives Canada PA-205855.

The *Duchess of Bedford* was part of the first troop convoy that rushed the First Canadian Division from Canada to Britain in September 1939. The Empresses and Duchesses were ideal mass transit ships, able to carry whole divisions from the Dominions to distant battle fronts. The *Duchess* is the only Canadian Pacific ship believed to have sunk a U-boat, on August 9, 1942. After the war, the ship's bell was presented to Divisional Movements, Canadian Army Headquarters, in Ottawa. Photo *circa* 1928.

Courtesy Clifford M. Johnston/Library and Archives Canada/PA-056816.

The CPS *Beaverford*, Montreal, Quebec, 1933. Destined to be the most celebrated of the CP ships, the *Beaverford* fought a battle that has become the naval equivalent to the Spartans' sacrifice at Thermopylae.

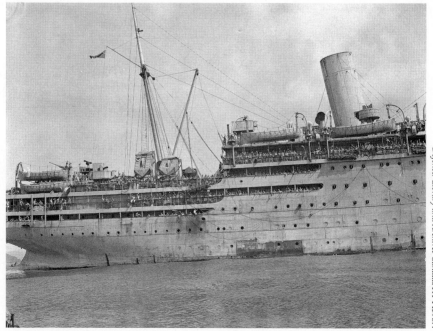

Courtesy Jack Hawes/Canada Department of national Defence/Library and Archives Canada/PA-145987.

Liberated Canadian prisoners of war and internees line the rails of the *Empress of Australia* to wave goodbye as the ship heads for Manila in the Philippines. Hong Kong, China, September 1945.

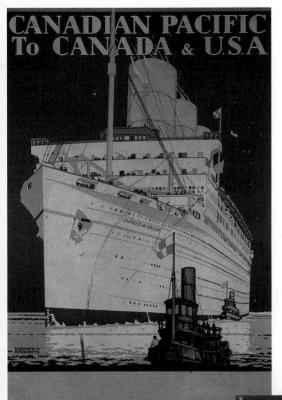

The *Empress of Britain*. Kenneth Shoesmith created important publicity work for Canadian Pacific's largest-ever liner, famous for her enormous funnels. The *Britain* was torpedoed off the coast of Ireland in October 1940. The largest ship sunk in the Second World War, its loss shocked the world. *Canadian Pacific.*

The *Empress of Britain*. Because they were in competition for passengers with the New York–bound ships, the company spared no expense with the *Britain* and its sister ship, the *Empress of Ireland*. Each cost £375,000 to build and were equipped with complete libraries, a café, leather upholstery in the dining room, ornate ceilings, and a two-level atrium. Artist: Colin Ashford.

"Canadian Pacific Spans the World."
Advertisement for the Canadian Pacific
Line. *Canadian Pacific.*

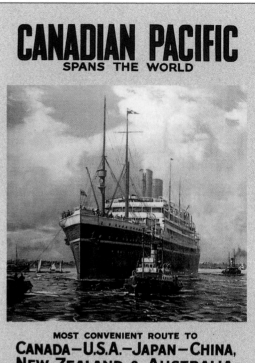

"Insist on Travelling by C.P.R." Advertisement for the Canadian Pacific Line.
Canadian Pacific.

Canadian Pacific steamship RMS *Empress of Canada* was built in 1928 by John Brown & Company Ltd., Clydebank. The last Canadian Pacific ship left Montreal on November 23, 1971, marking the end of almost seven decades of CP passenger shipping. From a painting by J.K. Byass.

Canadian Pacific steamship RMS *Empress of Britain*, built in 1931. The *New York Times* once wrote, "No ship ever fitted her name more truly than the *Empress of Britain*. She was … an empress with pride and grace and dignity in every inch of her. Her white paint was a coat of ermine that set her apart from the throng." The ship was torpedoed by the German submarine *U-32* in 1940. From a painting by J.K. Byass.

"Only Four Days Open Sea." In its advertising, Canadian Pacific liked to exploit the fact that by the sheltered St. Lawrence its ships plied a shorter route across the Atlantic. *Canadian Pacific*.

The first container ship, *Ideal X*, a converted oil tanker with 58 containers, sailed on April 26, 1956, from Port Newark, New Jersey, for Houston, ushering in the container revolution. Soon ports worldwide saw the potential of containerized trade and built specialized handling facilities for the new container ships, beginning in 1960 in New York.

Nothing demonstrates the purpose-built ship designs to accommodate the maximum number of containers more than this aerial shot of a CP ship in 2002. For a multi-modal company like CP, the introduction of containers in 1964 meant that the same container could be transferred from its ship to a flatcar and even sent by a truck trailer directly to the customer.

Canadian Pacific Ships Archives.

The familiar red-and-white-checkered House Flag of the Canadian Pacific ships. The pattern evolved from the way that land on either side of the railway track had been allocated between the government and railway in alternate blocks — on a map this was coloured red and white. Van Horne chose the pattern as the shipping line's flag, reasoning that it might be easily recognized when hanging loose.

Canadian Pacific Ships Archives.

In September 2002, CP Ships Limited took delivery of the 4,100-TEU *Contship Aurora* built by Daewoo in South Korea. Built under the company's $800-million ship-replacement program, the *Aurora* was the first of three ships specially designed to carry a high proportion of refrigerated containers. The TEU (twenty-foot equivalent unit) represents the cargo capacity of a standard container 20 feet long and eight feet wide.

At the parish church of Forfar, Angus, Scotland, is a brass plaque that states:

IN PROUD MEMORY, CAPTAIN N.A.C. HARDY RN, 41 OFFI-
CERS AND 143 MEN OF HMS FORFAR, 2 DECEMBER 1940.
HONOR TO ALL BRAVE CAPTAINS AND TO ALL INTREPID
SEAMANS AND MATES AND TO ALL THAT WENT DOWN
DOING THEIR DUTY.

Few parishioners may know that the *Forfar* was the Canadian Pacific passenger ship *Montrose II*. Built in 1922 and named after the ship that Crippen had almost escaped on, the *Montrose II* had been requisitioned by the Admiralty as an armed merchantman and renamed HMS *Forfar*. On December 2, 1940, when meeting an incoming Halifax convoy, it was torpedoed at 3:50 a.m. by *U-99*. With 47 victories, Kapitänleutnant Otto Kretschmer was a star within the U-boat fraternity and had earned the nickname "Silent Otto" for his approach to merchant vessels. Kretschmer's motto was "One torpedo — one ship," but the former Canadian Pacific ship's death proved to be a slow one and it took four more precious torpedoes to sink it. After this attack, the Admiralty saw the vulnerability of armed merchant cruisers and took its two sister ships off this role.

Because of that decision, they survived the war. The *Montcalm II* had been requisitioned as an armed merchant cruiser in 1939 and, purchased by the Royal Navy in 1942, was converted into a submarine depot HMS *Wolfe*. It spent most of the war on Holy Loch and was paid off in 1949 and broken up in 1952. The *Montclare* had a similar history but remained a Destroyer Depot Ship, serving with the 3rd S/M Flotilla at Rothesay. It was eventually broken up at Inverkeithing in 1958.

Since the outbreak of war, the *Beaverbrae* had been commanded by Captain B.L. Leslie, and March 25, 1941, found it on its 12th wartime voyage between Canada and England. At 8:05 a.m. a Condor dived out of the sun and dropped a stick of bombs on the Beaver ship's deck. The explosion tore through the upper and shelter decks and blew out the side of the ship, fracturing the steam and water pipes and flattening the engine bulkhead. The Condor then returned for a second run, strafing and bombing. A third attack followed, after which the aircraft flew off.

The *Beaverbrae*'s crew fought the fires onboard for 35 minutes before the chief officer decided that they were spreading too quickly. At 8:45 a.m. the order was given to abandon ship. The ship's company took to the lifeboats with the exception of the captain who remained on the bridge until 10:00. Royal Air Force aircraft dropped provisions to the lifeboats and at 17:15 two destroyers arrived to take the entire ship's company onboard. Captain Leslie was reluctant to leave the *Beaverbrae* and deliberated with the destroyer captain the possibility of towing the burning ship into port. After circling the *Beaverbrae*, it was decided that this was not possible and the ship was abandoned to sink the next day. The survivors were taken to Scapa Flow and were able to catch a train at Truro. It was somehow ironic that the *Beaverbrae*, the ship that had carried the giant Junkers aircraft to Canada, was sunk by another German aircraft.

The *Beaverdale*'s last voyage began March 26, 1941, with Convoy SC26 out of Saint John for London. Captain Draper had survived the previous war and had even been sunk in 1916 off Cherbourg. Early on April 1, his ship was hit by a torpedo from the *U-48*. It settled and remained afloat, allowing all of the 79 crew to safely disembark in the three lifeboats. Rowing away, they watched as two U-boats surfaced around them and began shelling the *Beaverdale*. There was a huge explosion and the ship sank. In the darkness, Number 2 lifeboat separated from the other two and disappeared. The next morning the two remaining boats made for Iceland, which the master thought was about 300 miles away. The two boats lost contact with each other and on the sixth day, Captain Draper's boat sighted Iceland and landed on a beach, from where the survivors were taken to a farmhouse. Number 3 lifeboat sighted the Icelandic fishing fleet a day after losing contact with Draper and its crew was rescued by an Icelandic trawler that took them to Reykjavik. The remaining lifeboat with 21 onboard vanished. It was assumed that it had been hit by shells from the submarines when the Germans were trying to sink the *Beaverdale*.

The last Beaver remaining, the *Beaverhill* was deemed unsinkable. Between May 1940 and November 1943, it carried a total of 268,652 tons and 3,680 passengers in 26 voyages. Since its sea trials in May 1940, the ship had led a charmed life, going unmolested back and forth across the Atlantic as though it were peacetime. No U-boat or Condor attacked and it never fired its guns in anger. Its reputation as a lucky ship was so well-known that just the news that the *Beaverhill* was to be part of the convoy was enough to convey a general feeling of relief. However, the crew couldn't be insensitive to events around them and en route to Liverpool on May 26, 1941, a lookout in the crowsnest reported "a small flat object. Bearing fifteen, sir." It was an inflated raft with two figures onboard, waving frantically. The *Beaverhill* was made windward to the raft and a scramble net was fastened to the port side. Two volunteers from its crew went over the side to grab the raft and eventually all four men were dragged onboard. The rescued were a pilot and observer from the Fleet Air Arm who had taken off from the aircraft carrier HMS *Victorious* looking for the *Bismarck*. They had run out of fuel and ditched and a 57-hour ordeal had followed. Just as they had given up hope, the *Beaverhill* appeared.

Despite its bulk, the *Empress of Canada* found itself involved in a commando raid. On August 6, 1941, it took the Canadian Army's K Section, 1 Divisional Signals on "Operation Gauntlet," the British and Canadian raid on the Norwegian island of Spitsbergen to prevent the Soviet-owned coal mines from falling into German hands. The military disembarked from the *Empress* and, led by the Norwegian underground, destroyed German radio stations as well as strategic supplies, including 540,000 tons of coal and 275,000 gallons of petrol, oil, and lubricants. The 2,000 Russian workers on the island were evacuated by the liner to the port of Archangel, in the intervening eight days. When the *Empress of Canada* returned from Archangel the military force then withdrew, taking with them the Norwegian civilians from the island.

CHAPTER 9

The Pacific Arena

The fast BCCSS Princess ferries had been requisitioned as troop carriers by the Admiralty in late November 1941, and sent off to the Middle East, across the Pacific via Honolulu. The entry of Japan into the war while they were at Honolulu meant that both ships had to dodge enemy warships in the Dutch East Indies. By January 1942, the Princesses *Marguerite* and *Kathleen* found themselves "working" the eastern Mediterranean, either taking aviation fuel to the besieged island of Malta or shuttling along the North African coast with the Eighth Army as it fought Rommel.

The start of the war found the old *Empress of Asia*, which had once searched for the *Emden* in another world war, continuing to cross the Pacific to Hong Kong, now under threat by the ever-encroaching Japanese. On September 14, 1940, a year before Japan entered the war, the Japanese Air Force bombed it in error while it was in the Gulf of

Tokyo. Arriving in Vancouver on January 11, 1941, having completed its 307th (and last) crossing of the Pacific, it was requisitioned by the Admiralty as a troop transport and painted grey. The Chinese crew of engineers, firemen, greasers, and trimmers and part of the catering department all had been recruited in Asia and signed on under Hong Kong articles (of agreement). With the exception of four individuals, all were discharged and an entire crew was brought to Vancouver from the Canadian Pacific's Great Lakes fleet to replace them.

On February 13, 1941, the *Asia* sailed for Britain through the Panama Canal, by way of Jamaica and Bermuda, where it bunkered, reaching the Clyde in late March 1941. Then it sailed for Liverpool, where the modifications for its troop-carrying duties were made. Basic accommodation and cooking facilities were built in, the bridge was reinforced with protective concrete, and armaments in the form of a six-inch gun, six Oerlikons, eight Hotchkiss, a three-inch anti-aircraft gun, several Bofors, four PAC rockets, and depth charges were added. On November 12, under Captain J.B. Smith, the *Empress* sailed from Liverpool with troops for Bombay, via Freetown and Durban. There, it discharged them and embarked 2,235 soldiers for Singapore. Fearing hostilities with Japan, the British were rushing reinforcements to the island fortress and evacuating civilians.

The Japanese entered the war while the *Empress* was loading in Bombay. From there the convoy left on January 23, 1942, the *Empress of Asia* now joined by four other Canadian Pacific ships — the *Aorangi*, *Empress of Australia*, *Empress of Japan*, and *Duchess of Bedford* — the whole convoy protected by two destroyers and the heavy cruiser HMS *Exeter* (one of the victors at the Battle of the River Plate). The other Canadian Pacific liners successfully landed their troops and got away from the ever-advancing Japanese — the *Empress of Japan* was the last major ship to quit Singapore on January 31. The *Duchess of Bedford* would narrowly escape the Japanese air force to evacuate 875 women and children to Batavia.

But, coal-fuelled and slower, the *Empress of Asia* was not as fortunate. At 11:00 hours on February 4, as it was passing through the Banka Straits, a *V* formation of 18 Japanese twin-engined bombers appeared at about 5,000 feet. Incendiaries aimed at the *Asia* were dropped, but none hit the ship. The next day, February 5, was bright with good visibility and smooth sea. In a single line, led by the cruiser HMS *Danae*, the last of the convoy approached Sultan Shoal at a reduced speed, ready to embark pilots. Then, at 10:45, another *V* formation of Japanese Mitsubishi Navy 1 twin-engined monoplanes (code-named "Betty") flew over at a high altitude and disappeared into the clouds. Returning 15 minutes later, they bombed the convoy from all directions.

Every ship was hit, but the *Empress of Asia*, as the largest target and well known to the Japanese, took the worst. Concussions shook it as there were direct hits, and at 11:05 thick, black smoke poured out of its starboard side, near the forward funnel. Fire parties fought the blaze as best they could, but as the old ship had not been fitted with a sprinkler system, the crew had to rely on fire extinguishers, fire buckets, and axes. The troops had been sent below but now Captain Smith ordered that they assemble at their muster stations on A-deck. At 11:30 the engineers reported that the engine room and stokehold were filling with smoke and that they could no longer remain at their stations. The *Empress* was now approaching the Ajax Shoal buoy between the minefields that protected Singapore from the sea. Fearing that, out of control, it would venture into them, the captain ordered the ship be swung around and anchored near the Sultan Shoal Lighthouse.

By noon, 11 miles west of Singapore, with the entire midship from bridge to after funnel ablaze, its ends packed densely with troops and crew, the captain ordered that those lifeboats that were not on fire be lowered. Two of the escorts, HMAS *Yarra* and RINS *Sutlej*, now came up beside of the *Empress*, the commander of the Australian sloop bringing his ship alongside the liner's port quarter, making fast with lines as soldiers and crewmen swarmed over onto his decks. At the same time the Australian anti-aircraft gunners kept up a strong fire that brought down three bombers.

With thousands now crammed on his deck, the *Yarra's* captain yelled a warning that no one was to move for fear of capsizing. W.H. McArthur, engineer on the *Empress*, later said, "If the *Yarra's* commander had not taken enormous risks in a close proximity to a minefield, most of the crew and hundreds of British soldiers would have lost their lives. I take my hat off to the *Yarra's* commander." By 13:00, all personnel were off the *Empress* and Smith then boarded HMS *Danae*, from where he ordered a sweep around his ship to make sure that no one had been overlooked by rescue craft. "Packed on the *Yarra* like sardines," McArthur related, "we crawled into Singapore. Our ship was still blazing in the distance."

The *Empress* remained afloat and on fire for four days, drifting ashore west of Keppel Harbour before the fires burnt out. Fifteen soldiers had been killed but the only crew casualty was D. Ellsworthy, a Canadian pantryman, who died in hospital from injuries and was buried at Singapore. Incredibly, a total of 2,772 personnel onboard had been rescued.

By the time the Japanese made their first landing on the island on the 8th, many of the *Asia's* catering personnel had joined with the ship's doctor to volunteer to work in the hospitals, and when the city fell, along with the troops they brought, many ended up in Changi Prison.

One of those to be rescued by the *Yarra* was John Drummond. Born in Edinburgh in 1882, Drummond had already worked aboard ships before immigrating to Canada with his family in 1922 on the CPS *Victorian*. They settled in Vancouver, where in 1926 Drummond signed articles of agreement to join the *Empress of Asia* just months after the ship's collision out of Shanghai. As senior sanitary engineer, he was responsible for maintaining the labyrinth of pipes and equipment that moved cold, hot, and waste water about the ship. After his rescue, Drummond was landed in Singapore — which was fortunate, as later both the *Yarra* and the *Exeter* would be sunk in separate actions, the Australian sloop paying the ultimate price for taking on three Japanese destroyers by itself. Drummond met other *Empress of Asia* survivors and escaped the doomed city with them in the *Hong Kwong*, a small Straits Steamship Company freighter.

The Canadian Pacific crew raised steam, started the engine, and in spite of bombing attacks, arrived at Batavia on February 15. Here they joined another ship and sailed to Ceylon, took the ferry to the Indian mainland, and travelled by train to Bombay, where they had started out a month earlier. On March 14, 1942, the remnants of the *Asia*'s crew sailed for South Africa, where at Cape Town they boarded the *Queen Mary* for New York. Here they took a second train, this time across the North American continent, arriving home in Vancouver on May 18, 1942. Also successfully repatriated were two of the *Empress of Asia*'s remaining four Chinese crew members, with two, Chan Kam and Chan Lam, arriving in Vancouver that day.

In 1943, the Japanese attempted to make use of the beached *Empress* as a storage depot, and had it towed off the shoals. But during the operation a tropical storm suddenly came up, the tow lines broke, and the *Empress of Asia* sank into 80 feet of water. Salvage operations were begun on March 4, 1960, to retrieve scrap metal from the hulk. It was unsuccessful and another attempt was made in 1996, at which time it was discovered that the old ship had almost disappeared into the seabed. The dredgers did bring to the surface several artifacts, including the *Empress*'s anchor and pieces of Canadian Pacific china — some of which are on display in a Singapore museum.

Allied fortunes were as hard-pressed in the Mediterranean, where both the BCCSS ferries, Princesses *Kathleen* and *Marguerite*, were hard at work, rushing aviation fuel to the embattled island fortress of Malta and moving troops back and forth as the Eighth Army's fortunes waxed and waned. On August 17, 1942, the *Marguerite* was en route from Port Said to Famagusta with 1,000 troops onboard as the British were attempting to reinforce Cyprus. The convoy was well escorted but did not reckon on Kapitänleutnant Hans-Werner Kraus getting the *U-83* through the protective ranks of destroyers, and at 15:00 hours he torpedoed the former British Columbia ferry. The torpedo hit the *Princess*'s fuel tanks and it was soon ablaze, the engine room filling with smoke.

The two engineering officers, E.E. Stewart and W.B. Harris, both from Victoria, British Columbia, were on watch when the vessel "took a tin fish," as they later reported. The explosion drove them to their hands and knees as the engine room filled with steam and smoke. The lights went out and all communication with the bridge was disrupted. Through the hissing, screaming inferno both groped their way toward the emergency throttle. "I put my hand on the throttle," Steward said, "and found that Bill Harris was already there." In stopping the engines before coming on deck, the two men had kept the ship from running down the survivors and spreading fire among the lifeboats. In March 1944, Harris, Stewart, and Captain R.A. Leicester of the *Princess Marguerite* were awarded MBEs (Member of the Order of the British Empire) for "conspicuous courage, coolness and resource."

When the fire reached the *Marguerite*'s munitions store, the ammunition began to explode and the ship was given up. The captain of the escorting destroyer, HMS *Hero*, came as close as he could alongside the ferry to take off survivors, and because of this, of the 1,000 onboard, the death toll was limited to 49. Some of those rescued were taken to Suez and there put on a ship going to Durban. Here they boarded the *Duchess of Atholl* and had the misfortune to be torpedoed once more on October 10, 1942. For whatever reason, the sinking of the *Princess Marguerite* was withheld from the public until January 22, 1945.

The *Marguerite*'s sister ferry *Princess Kathleen* continued working away — helping evacuate civilians from Alexandria in the face of Rommel's advance in 1942 and then bringing the first troops into besieged Tobruk in 1943. Later the ferry would serve as the home for the Emir Mansour, son of Ibn Saud, when he and his entourage were in Suez. The emir wanted to thank the captain of the *Kathleen* personally for his hospitality by sending him a herd of 50 live sheep but was convinced to substitute bags of rice instead. On October 10, 1943, the ferry's Canadian crew was finally returned to Canada to be replaced with a British one. The *Kathleen* remained in the Mediterranean until VE Day, when it became the first Allied ship to reach Greece and take aboard the surrendering German general staff. After a short refit in Malta, it made its way back to Vancouver where, in Canadian Pacific service once more, it returned to coastal duties. In commemoration of its wartime service, a plaque was hung in the forward lounge showing the *Kathleen*'s around-the-world adventures and all the ports it had called at.

As of June 30, 1943, the number of Canadian Pacific Steamships employees who had enlisted in the Armed Forces was:

The Admiralty Service	4,488
On the "Mont" ships used as armed cruisers	1,010
Shore Staff	87
Total	**5,585**
Grand Total of all company enlistments including Railway, Express, and Airlines	17,387

Source: Company minutes, summer 1943.

In early 1943, the news went around the company that one of their
own had, as the newspapers put it "bagged a sub." On January 17, at a
classified location, Captain W.G. Busk-Wood, commanding the *Duchess
of Bedford*, sighted the conning tower of a U-boat some 400 yards away.
A heavy sea was running and the captain guessed that the big wash made
by his ship had lifted it out of the water. "We didn't open fire immediately," he later said,

> but I swung my helm hard to starboard and swung the
> ship around. We then opened fire at a range of only 100
> yards. The first shell hit the water but the second struck
> abaft of the conning tower with a terrific explosion. Two
> more shells hit the submarine, one entering the hull and
> the other striking the fore side of the conning tower.

Immediately after these explosions the U-boat's bow rose 30 feet out of
the water and the submarine sank. "It all happened so quickly. He showed
no fight at all," the captain concluded. "After these actions we stood on our
course again and reached our destination without further incident."

Its sister ship, the *Empress of Canada*, was not as charmed. The former hospital ship during the Yokohama earthquake in 1923, the *Canada*
had been requisitioned for trooping in November, 1939. Its last voyage
was to be far from the Pacific when, on March 1, 1943, it left Durban

for Britain with 1,892 passengers. These included 400 Italian POWs and 200 refugee Poles who had been released by the Soviet Union after Germany invaded. Escorted by the same HMS *Antelope*, the ship's ordeal began when Captain George Goold received radio messages telling him to proceed to the port of Takoradi, Ghana, specifying the exact route to be followed.

At 11:54 on the night of March 13, 400 miles south of Cape Palmas, near Liberia, the *Empress of Canada* was torpedoed on its starboard side, its engines destroyed as the engine room flooded. Goold later said that the first torpedo burst a fuel tank and the heavy oil saturated the water. Fortunately there was no fire. The order was given to lower the lifeboats and abandon ship. The torpedo had been fired by the Italian submarine *Leonardo da Vinci* and it now surfaced near the Number 6 lifeboat. Wing Commander E.R. Edmond, returning home from duty with an RCAF Catalina squadron in Ceylon, remembered,

> They shouted to us in a marked Italian accent to iden-
> tify our ship and say which boats contained the master
> and chief officer. We did not reply but an Italian military
> medical officer shouted all the information and began
> yelling "Viva Italia!" They also asked for one of the ship's
> officers but we couldn't find one of them. They seemed
> very disappointed at this and then fired another torpedo
> into our ship.

He said that the sub took the Italian doctor onboard and then, "booted off a bunch of Italian seamen who were also trying to gain the submarine's deck." After the war it was learned that the Italian doctor had been signalling from his porthole and that the messages to change course were sent by German radio.

At about 12:50 a.m. the second torpedo hit the ship, also on the starboard, and it then began sinking rapidly. The *Empress* sank 20 minutes later with Goold the last to leave. In the wing commander's boat were 14 Polish army women who "did a bit of singing to keep up spirits up and so did some Cockney sailors in another boat. There were 92 of us in the open water and we were all violently sick from oil fumes — for the water was covered in a thick, oily slime."

Adrift for 15 hours, they lived off biscuits and water while

> all around us were bodies of men and women who had been attacked and killed by sharks and barracuda. After a day in the equatorial sun, we were pretty worried about [the] future. Then the Catalina dipped over us and we knew that rescue was near. It stormed that night and we were afraid of being tossed over board or swamped in the waters that were boiling with sharks.

Of the 392 fatalities, 340 were passengers, including most of the Italian prisoners of war. Many of those who had jumped into the water died after being attacked by sharks and barracudas, which the crew had to fight off with guns. The survivors were picked up by a destroyer and taken to Freetown. The most successful of all the submarines in the Italian navy, the *Leonardo da Vinci* continued on to the Indian Ocean, scoring more victories, but on the way home it was sunk by HMS *Active* in the Bay of Biscay.

The loss of yet another *Empress* dealt Sir Edward Beatty the fatal blow. Paralyzed after the sinking of his *Empress of Britain*, no longer able to talk, humiliated by requiring help for his personal and corporate functions, Beatty died on March 23, 1943. Feared by his employees and hated by the prime minister, the childless president had given away millions of dollars, much of it from his own salary, to children's charities and to McGill University. He would have been gratified to know that thousands of Montrealers lined the streets for his funeral cortege. Ever the politician, Prime Minister Mackenzie King, who had rebuffed Beatty's help on many occasions, eulogized him:

> Few men of our country have given so much of their time and energies to serious and useful work for the benefit of the community. His patriotism was of the highest order, his example of quiet and efficient public service will long be remembered.

Beatty would be succeeded by D'Alton Corry Coleman, a former newspaper editor, and under him the company would add a third arm, that of Canadian Pacific Air Lines, to its transport empire. But there would never be another Canadian Pacific president who so loved ships as Sir Edward Beatty.

It wasn't only the grand Empresses or lowly Beavers that suffered during the Second World War. The *Duchess of Atholl* left Cape Town in Convoy WS17 on October 3, 1942, with a crew of 296 and 529 passengers, including 58 women and 34 children. It was spotted by the *U-178*, then on its first patrol, some 200 miles east of Ascension Island. At 6:29 a.m. on October 10, the *Duchess* was hit by three torpedoes. The ship turned on its side, and at 9:25 a.m. sank by her stern. Although four lifeboats were unusable, the ship was efficiently abandoned within 20 minutes with the loss of only five lives.

The *Duchess of York* had a narrow escape in 1942 when, during an air raid, chief officer Robert V. Burns and eight volunteers had wrestled overboard an unexploded bomb that had penetrated its four decks. The following year the *Duchess* was part of Convoy OS51 "Faith," sailing from Plymouth to Freetown, Sierra Leone, on July 9, 1943. Toward evening on July 11, the convoy and its escorts were steaming a zigzag course some 300 miles west of Vigo, Spain, in calm, cloudless weather. At 8:35 p.m. a Focke Wulf Condor was sighted shadowing the convoy and hovering just out of gun range. Half an hour later it was joined by two more Condors and shortly afterward the planes came in to attack. The aircraft concentrated on the troop transports *California* and *Duchess of York*, both of which were soon ablaze.

On such a clear night, the flames illuminated the survivors struggling to get away from the burning ships and their rescue looked simple. But the fear among the captains of the escorts was that this would also attract a U-boat wolf pack and the destroyer HMCS *Iroquois* swept the area before coming as close to the burning *Duchess* as it could, taking 854 men off. The action made the *Iroquois* a target herself and as the bombs fell astern, the destroyer's four-inch-high angle guns and multiple pom-poms kept up a heavy barrage that convinced the Condors to give up and leave. At 1:35 a.m. on July 12, orders were given to sink the burning hulks of the *Duchess* and *California* with torpedoes, with the *Iroquois* making for Casablanca where the survivors (some of them seriously wounded) were disembarked. The *Duchess of York* would be the 12th and final Canadian Pacific ship to be sunk.

When Canadian Pacific president D.C. Coleman announced the sinking at the annual company meeting in Montreal on May 2, 1944, 12 decorations and "mentions in despatches" were added to the CPSS honour role. There were two double decorations of Officer of the Order of the British Empire (OBE) and the Lloyd's War Medal and three awards of the British Empire Medal. Chief Officer S.W. Keay, who had once "won the stick" in an early harbour opening in Montreal, and Chief Engineer E.E. Vick were made OBEs, Keay for "fighting fire till forced from his post" and Vick for standing by his engines and boiler rooms "throughout the deadliest danger." For their courage on wresting the bomb on the *York* overboard, Burns was awarded the George Medal, First Officer Robert McKillop was made a member of the Order of the British Empire, and William Hughes (boatswain) and George J. Keggan (carpenter) were presented with the British Empire Medal.

Having survived four years of dodging U-boats and the Luftwaffe, the *Beaverhill* finally met its nemesis, which was nothing more sinister than a hawser. On November 24, 1943, while getting out of Saint John Harbour, a towing hawser split and wrapped itself around the *Beaverhill*'s propeller. This, combined with the wind and tide, trapped the ship on Hillyard's Reef. When the tide ebbed, it broke in half, the final Canadian Pacific ship to be lost during the war.

But the very last great ocean liner to be sunk was German and the total loss of life has never been equalled — or accurately known. As the war drew to a close in January 1945, the former luxury ship *Wilhelm Gustloff* was pressed into service to evacuate the remnants of the German military and refugees ahead of the advancing Russians. En route from Gdynia to Kiel it was torpedoed by a Russian submarine. To this day, no one knows how many refugees, soldiers, and crew were drowned, but a conservative estimate is put at 6,000. While packing so many onto a defenceless ship was a desperate measure on the part of a desperate nation, the liner's sinking was a salutary lesson of the vulnerability of the great ships in war.

With VE Day, the ships began the happy task of taking the British "guest" children home and returning with the Canadian troops — and their war brides. Between August 1944 and January 1947, the Department of National Defence took control over transportation of servicemen's dependents to Canada. Several of the great ships were involved as "war-bride ships," including the *Île de France*, the *Georgic*, both of the Queens, the *Empress of Scotland*, and the *Duchess of Richmond*. In a program that would defy modern logistics (let alone present-day bureaucratic efficiency), in the midst of a war the department shipped 61,334 dependents from the United Kingdom to their new homes in Canada — at an average cost of $140.29 each. This sum included transportation in the United Kingdom, ocean transport and meals, and train fares, berths, and meals to destinations in Canada.

The ports of Halifax and Quebec saw many homecomings that September. On September 9, the *Empress of Scotland* was steaming slowly past the heights of Dufferin Terrace and the Citadel on her 2,108th day of war service and 484,914th mile of war travel. Swing tunes blared from loudspeakers, cannon boomed from a battery on the Plains of Abraham, and RCAF aircraft "buzzed" overhead to greet the big "trooper" as it nosed into its berth. Where the CPR immigrant trains had once stood were eight troop trains to carry 4,066 passengers (including 40 women, one baby, one pram, and two dogs) that would disembark and make for distant parts of Canada. The *Empress* had been in every ocean and visited 24 countries, carrying altogether 210,068 personnel, including 30,000 Americans in seven trips between the United States and Casablanca. It had made three complete trips around the world — in 1941, 1944, and 1945 — and some of itscompany had been with the ship through the entire war, including the master, Newfoundland-born Captain J.W. Thomas, OBE, who had not been "off the articles" since 1939.

It would be a quick turnaround for the *Empress of Scotland*, as on September 11, it left Quebec, now with a vice-regal flag waving from its foremast. The governor general, the Earl of Athlone, had boarded to return home to Britain. As a young man in 1901, he had been part of the entourage of the Duke of Cornwall and York (later King George V) and sailed on the new *Empress of India* from Vancouver to Victoria. In a time-honoured custom, his flag was hoisted in a ball and then when he came aboard it was broken out by the ship's quartermaster.

Among the passengers on the *Empress* was 21-year-old Vera Kissell who was sailing to England to be wed. Packed away in the hold was her wedding dress, trousseau, and wedding presents. She was going to marry a 24-year-old RAF pilot, Flight Sergeant Roy Cartwright, who she had met when he was on the Montreal–Bahamas bomber ferry run. Hardly had the ship moved downriver when Miss Kissell found a telegram waiting for her on her bunk. Thinking it was from her fiancé, she tore it open. It was from his commanding officer in Wales who informed her that Cartwright had been killed in a flying accident the day before. So shocked was she that she probably did not realize that the gentleman who later came down to comfort her was the Earl of Athlone. In the small hours of a foggy morning, Vera Kissell disembarked from the *Empress* at Father Point.

Going in the same direction as the governor general were some of Canada's POWs, distinguishable by their field-grey greatcoats with a big red POW patch on the back. The last 2,000 of the approximately 35,000 POWs that had been brought to Canada embarked at Halifax on December 22, 1945, on the *Duchess of Bedford*, for some the same ship that had brought them to Canada five years before.

In the Pacific, even before VJ Day, on September 5, 1945, 11 days before the formal surrender of the Japanese forces in Hong Kong, the *Empress of Australia* once more entered the Fragrant Harbour. It carried 3,000 RAF personnel, including airfield construction units to get the colony's Kai Tak Airport open as soon as possible. The Canadian merchant cruiser HMCS *Prince Robert*, part of Rear Admiral Harcourt's liberation fleet, preceded it to tie up in Kowloon on August 30, exactly where it had done so in 1941, bringing the ill fated Canadian force to

CHAN, For Sui, No. 1 Saloon Boy — **British Empire Medal (BEM)** — Awarded as per *Canada Gazette* of 13 January 1945. *Canada Gazette*, Department of Transport file 18-2-7, Volume 2, (National Archives of Canada, RG.12, Volume 1,106) a memo from Mr. Arthur Randles (Director of Merchant Seamen) to Mr. Robert Dorman (Secretary, Sub-Committee on Awards to Merchant Seaman, Department of Transport, Ottawa) dated 4 April 1944.

I am attaching hereto the original letter I have received from Captain E. Aikman, Assistant to the Chairman, Canadian Pacific Steamships, bringing forward the case of Chinese seaman Chan For Sui, now serving on the SS *Princess Kathleen*. This seaman, in a period of over fifty years, has served about 33 years on Canadian Pacific vessels and his name might be brought forward for recognition in view of this long, meritorious service, as well as over two years continuous service in the Mediterranean area, during which time he experienced a torpedoing. Supporting documentation indicates that Chan For Sui was a No.1 Saloon Boy, born October 1871 in a village near Canton. He has served on the *Empress of China* (1892–1900), *Monteagle* (1903–10), *Empress of Russia* (1925–41), *Princess Marguerite* (eight months in 1942, ship torpedoed and sunk, 17 August 1942), and *Princess Kathleen* (1942–44). This had included two years continuous service in the Mediterranean. It was noted that earlier in the war, when the *Empress of Japan* (later renamed *Empress of Scotland*) had been bombed, the British government had made an award to the Chinese Quartermaster who had displayed courage and coolness. Elsewhere in files it is noted that the *Princess Marguerite* was on passage from Port Said to Famagusta with 1,124 passengers. Although described as "abandoned successfully," 55 lives were lost.

ATKINS, Maurice Dudley, Second Officer — **Member: Order of the British Empire (MBE)** — Canadian Pacific Steamship *Whitehall Park* — Awarded as per *Canada Gazette* of 6 January 1945 and *London Gazette* of 1 January 1945. Home: Brentwood Bay, B.C.

Joined RMS *Empress of Asia* April 15, 1941, as a cadet and served in that ship until she was attacked by Japanese bombing planes in Singapore and burned February 5th, 1942. Arrived back in Vancouver, B.C. May 12th, 1942, and joined S.S. *H.F. Alexander* June 2nd, 1942, served in that vessel until August 15th, 1942, and joined RMS *Empress of Canada* the following day. Was serving in that vessel when she was torpedoed March 14th, 1943. Returned to Vancouver, B.C. May 6th, 1943, and joined SS *Mohawk Park*, as Third Officer June 18th, 1943. Mr. Atkins was not quite 17 years old when he joined the R.M.S. *Empress of Asia* and is now just 20 years old.

defend the colony. The crews were witness to the liberation as Chinese flags and Union Jacks flew everywhere and garlands of firecrackers were tossed by the locals at the British soldiers in the streets. As there were still Japanese units unaccounted for — Kai Tak Airport remained partially under enemy control — the city was under curfew. Only the fittest POWs were to go to the *Prince Robert*, with stretcher cases carried into the hospital ship *Oxfordshire*, and the walking sick told to "toddle as best they can" (as the senior medical officer put it) to the *Empress of Australia*. The ship took them directly to a hospital in Manila, where the Canadians were reunited with their comrades who had been taken to Japan.

Their grey paint stripped off, the guns removed, and the pre-war decorative panels and overlays re-installed, the great ships returned to their roles. In the Far East, Canadian Pacific ships entered the devastated ports of Hong Kong and Yokohama, making their way through sunken wrecks to wharves crowded with starving refugees. In six years, the company's ships had been from Narvik to New Zealand, embarked troops in Spitsbergen and Singapore. They had endured bombs, torpedoes, and shells. Of the 17 liners that were requisitioned by the Admiralty, only five remained afloat in 1945. Their crews had witnessed landings in Oran, Madagascar, and D-Day. The ship's dining halls and smoking lounges where royalty and movie stars had luxuriated had endured refugees taken off at Brest, Odessa, and Batavia. The luxury state rooms and suites that in pre-war days had accommodated two or four passengers had tolerated up to 16, with some decks dismantled to fit the "standee" berths — canvas sheets tacked to steel frames.

What to do with the ships rails also puzzled the company. For carved on all of them without exception were myriad initials, names, and "I Love _____s" (not to mention some that were much less wholesome) executed with gusto by thousands of pocket knives. While there were those at Canadian Pacific who wanted this vandalism filled in or new rails put up, there was a suggestion: "Leave them there permanently," wrote one company executive, "as a perpetual reminder for another generation of travelers to marvel at."

The last Canadian Pacific coal-burning liner, the *Empress of Russia*, despite presenting itself as a target with its huge columns of smoke, survived the war intact. In 1943, in its greatest wartime role, the *Russia* took part in a successful exchange of POWs. Brightly lit and with a huge Union Jack painted on the side, on October 18, under escort of the German navy, it took German POWs from Britain to neutral Gothenburg, Sweden. The *Empress* returned to Leith, Scotland, on October 25 with Allied POWs, among them British and Canadian troops, many of whom had been captured at Dunkirk and Dieppe. Second wireless operator Robert Kendrick aboard the *Russia* remembered the exuberant POWs expressed just three sentences before breaking into a rendition of "God Save the King": *Who won the International* (Soccer Tournament)? *Was there any beer aboard?* and *God bless the Red Cross!*

The last Pacific Empress remaining was the *Empress of Scotland* and, anticipating its return to civilian life, the company sent it to the Vickers-Armstrong yard at Barrow-in-Furness in June 1945. At 32 year of age, like an elderly dowager it was in need of a complete makeover — especially in the passenger accommodation. At 2:00 a.m. on September 8, a fire spread quickly throughout the ship, which, as the *Normandie* had been, was defenceless. Fought by her crew, the Vickers-Armstrong fire brigade and hoses from SS *Manxmaid*, a ship that was brought alongside her, it would be 1:30 p.m. before the fire had been extinguished and two bodies found in the aft end. But because of the water pumped into her, the *Russia* was close to capsizing and her funnels and masts were swiftly removed. So much of the old ship had been burnt or destroyed by fire and water that the decision was made to scrap her.

As in the previous war, Canadian Pacific had served the Allied cause well, but at great cost. Not only had CP managed for the Canadian government its fleet of 22 Park ships — freighters named after Canadian parks — from 1942 onward, but its own ships had seen ports far from their usual call, like the Iraqi port of Basra, the fjords at Narvik, and the Soviet naval base at Odessa. All that was left of its grand fleet were two Empresses (*Australia* and *Scotland/Japan*), two Duchesses (*Bedford* and *Richmond*), and one Princess (*Kathleen*). One of those was the old coal-burning *Empress of Australia* — once the kaiser's *Tirpitz* — that had aided Yokohama in the earthquake. In total, as Empress, Duchess, and Beaver, they had steamed 3,729,843 miles and had carried 977,133 tons of cargo and 1,009,271 passengers. These last were not only troops but as diverse a load as airmen for the Commonwealth Air Training Plan, refugees, scientists such as professors Sir Henry Tizard and Sir John Cockroft (who brought to the United States the secrets on splitting atoms, radar, and antisubmarine devices), 3,700 Russians who had been POWS in France, frightened child evacuees, and ecstatic war brides.

Seventy-one Canadian Pacific employees had been decorated either by the British or Canadian governments and 236 had given their lives. By 1945, company officers had achieved the following ranks: commodore, 2; captain, 6; commander, 6; lieutenant commander, 17; and lieutenant, 8. Typical in the advancement was Cecil Duggan, the Conway cadet who, as the conflict unfolded, had risen to the rank of commander, having served in minesweeping flotillas in the Mediterranean Sea and in the Far East — the last under Vice-Admiral Lord Mountbatten — before returning to Canadian Pacific.

The Canadian Pacific building on Cockspur Street at Trafalgar Square survived the war, too. In October 1940, a bomb landed on the street between it and Canada House but burrowed deep into the ground, the explosion leaving a huge crater and only breaking a few windows. After the war, with little accommodation and transportation available in London, returning Canadian Pacific staff found it impossible to live in the city and commute to Trafalgar Square. As Waterloo Place had been bombed, as well, when hostilities ended the company kept on the Cockspur Street office, but in June 1948 it moved its headquarters from London to Liverpool, obtaining offices in the port's distinctive Liver Building. Liverpool also became the Canadian Pacific's only European passenger terminal, to be used until its very last passenger ship docked there in 1971.

CHAPTER 10

The Age of Air Travel

No one could have paid much attention in February 1909, when J.A.D. McCurdy in Baddeck, Nova Scotia, using a flimsy contraption called "The Silver Dart," became the first person in the British Empire to sustain a controlled flight. Much more spectacular was Charles Lindbergh's 1927 Atlantic crossing, accomplished in 33 hours and 39 minutes. But his "Spirit of St. Louis" Ryan monoplane contained no dining room done up in art deco style, nor a grand piano or indoor swimming pool. For his evening entertainment the lonely airman did not have the choice of dancing to a jazz band, listening to the ship's own orchestra, or enjoying whatever movie was being played that night — and the phenomena of "talkies" were just coming in then. At the time, no one in their right minds would prefer such an uncomfortable, unsafe method of travelling the ocean as flying over it.

Then, in 1937, the world witnessed the first successful crossing of the Atlantic by Imperial Airways. Who could have guessed that this was the beginning of the end of the great ships? The seaplane airliner had flown from Foynes, Ireland, to Botwood, Newfoundland, in 15 hours and three minutes and was going on to Montreal. There were already a dozen airlines in the United States that were actually making money. What must have galled the shipping companies was that these transportation upstarts attempted to steal the status associated with travelling by ship by dressing their flight crews in nautical uniforms, designating their pilots as captains, their attendants as stewards, and wooing customers with the exclusivity of airport lounges called "Admirals' Clubs."

Soon, Pan American Airways breached the New York–London route and both companies were running scheduled Atlantic services using flying boats. The flying boats were themselves to soon disappear but no ship could hope to match the speed at which land planes were now regularly flying across the Atlantic, carrying up to 30 passengers in comfort.

With the advances in aviation brought by the Second World War, the demise of the great ships was assured. In fact, the monopoly of the ship on the Canada–Britain service had been broken two years before the war ended. On July 21, 1943, a Canadian airliner took off from Montreal Airport and 12 hours and 26 minutes later landed at Prestwick, Scotland. Although not a true commercial flight (it was a "civilianized" Lancaster bomber) and operated by the Canadian Government Travel Air Service (in reality, Trans Canada Airlines) and its passenger list was confined to VIP government personnel, it was the first blow.

By 1946, with its new Canadair North Stars, Trans Canada Airlines (TCA) operated the transatlantic flights under its own name and advertised for paying customers. The aircraft were ear-shatteringly noisy and had to refuel in Gander, Newfoundland, and Shannon, Ireland. The trays of pre-cooked food that TCA offered its passengers were nothing compared with the sumptuous fare available on an Empress. To while away the journey, the TCA passengers contented themselves with smoking, reading, and trying to make conversation above the engine noise.

But the aircraft was still faster than any ship and the airline's advertisement said it all: "Europe in Only a Day: Fly TCA!" The fault lay not with the ships themselves — now upgraded with enlarged staterooms, hulls painted white (with a green riband), and flying the red-and-white-checkered flag — but with the public's raised expectations and impatience at travel. Sam Cunard would have been pleased to know that in 1946 the average Atlantic crossing westbound was four days, 11 hours, and east four days, eight hours. But it was still four days more than what the airline passenger was prepared to tolerate. The truly global scale that the war had been fought on had given the world an appetite for flying long distances, made possible by the navigation aids and landing fields in the most remote corners of the globe. All shipowners knew that it would not be long before the thousands of long-distance troop transport aircraft would become available for use by commercial airlines. The future for travel by ship looked unclear indeed.

It was worse in the Empresses' old haunts in the Far East, where the Chinese and Japanese economies — like the ports of Yokohama, Shanghai, and Hong Kong — had been destroyed by war. The possibility of North Americans ever visiting Japan as tourists was thought unlikely and no Japanese were allowed to leave the country as tourists or emigrants. The future of Shanghai and the British Crown Colony of Hong Kong looked even more tenuous, especially with the Chinese civil war raging at their doorsteps. Because of this and the company's lack of Empress ships, the decision was taken not to revive its Far East service. The closest that the Canadian Pacific beaver logo would ever be seen in Asia again was in 1949 when Ottawa permitted Canadian Pacific Airlines (CPA) to fly from Vancouver to Honolulu, Tokyo, Hong Kong, and Sydney. Ever mindful of its historic antecedents, CPA christened their Canadair North Stars "Empresses," and like the ships, Canadian Pacific's airline became famous for its cuisine and service, the best on any airline until the late 1970s.

The granting of the Pacific air routes to Canadian Pacific Airlines was by no means largesse on the part of Mackenzie King's government. They were given because Canada had promised the Australians that there would be an air connection between the two dominions, but Trans Canada Airlines had turned what was sure to be a money-losing route down. With the Korean War and the economic resurgence of the Far East all of that changed and it was a decision that Ottawa later regretted.

On the British Columbia coast, Captain O.J. Williams, manager of the B.C. Coast Steamship Service, estimated that it would take many months and over 2,000 gallons of paint to return the coastal ships to their white, black, and buff colours of peacetime — in some cases three full coats would be necessary to cover the grey. Before that they would have to be "demunitioned" — the removal of guns and gun turrets and the protective armour that had covered the wireless cabin and pilot house. Most difficult of all was the training of new crews — the service having lost so many experienced employees to the war.

After a refit at Malta and another long voyage, the *Princess Kathleen* resumed its duties on the Vancouver–Victoria–Seattle run. In 1949 it was replaced by the *Princess Marguerite II* and the *Princess Patricia II*. The old warrior was then transferred to the Alaska run. On September 7, 1952, running between Juneau and Skagway, the *Kathleen* hit a reef 18 miles north of Juneau and ran aground off Lena Point. The Coast Guard took all 387 passengers and crew off and put them on a local beach, where buses took them back to the city. As the tide fell, the ship slipped off the rocks and sank, stern first, rolling on its port side. The ship's captain stood on the shore, according to legend, and saluted the *Kathleen* as it went down. Scuba divers have since located the ship, which is still well-preserved in the cold waters.

But by 1951, demand for expanded services between Vancouver Island and the mainland led to the addition of the auto-passenger ferry *Princess of Nanaimo*. Side-loading like her predecessors, the *Nanaimo* was already obsolete. For the growing rail and truck traffic, the Vancouver–Nanaimo route received the stern-loading *Princess of Vancouver* four years later, which was equipped with a high-clearance car deck and railway tracks. The end came abruptly in 1958 when a strike by Canadian Pacific ferry workers and the threat of a simultaneous strike by the employees of rival ferry company Black Ball led the provincial government to create the British Columbia Government Ferry Authority. At taxpayer expense, it was soon equipped with the most modern fleet on the coast, something that no private company could compete with. On October 1, 1962, the Canadian Pacific left the British Columbia ferry and coastal steamship business forever.

In contrast to this, in the Atlantic, the old shipping lines were being resuscitated. Cunard had managed to emerge from the war with both its Queens intact and put them into service as soon as they were "civilianized" — the *Queen Elizabeth* in 1946 and the *Queen Mary* in 1947. As there was little food to spare in Britain, all the meat and vegetables served on the Queens had to be brought over from North America first. The French took over the North German Lloyd *Europa* as war reparations and renamed it the *Libertie*; the Dutch brought out the *Nieuw Amsterdam*. In 1950, having resisted for so long the competition to build the fastest ship to cross the Atlantic, the Americans entered the race with their liner, *United States*. Two years later, it broke all records by crossing the Atlantic in three days and ten hours, becoming the last commercial passenger ship to capture the Blue Riband. Unfortunately, these returns were the last hurrah for the great ships — with airliners soon able to fly nonstop across the Atlantic, almost no one believed that "getting there was half the fun" anymore.

Canadian Pacific speedily replaced its Beaver cargo vessels, either with war reparations such as the *Beaverbrae II* (9,034 gt), taken from German Hapag lines in 1945, or bought from other shipping lines — the *Beaverlodge* (9,904 gt) from Shaw, Savill & Albion and *Beaverford II* (9,881 gt) from the British Ministry of War Transport — or built more at Fairfields, such as the *Beavercove* (9,824 gt). Britain needed to export, and whatever the depressed situation regarding passenger liners, there was always a need for freighters.

The *Beaverbrae II* (formerly the *Huascaran*) was comparatively new, having been built in 1938 and used as a depot ship, living out the war in a Norwegian fjord. Given to Canada as part of war reparations, it was purchased by Canadian Pacific and outfitted in Sorel, Quebec, as a refugee ship. From 1948 until 1954, it made eight trips annually to war-ravaged Germany, bringing out an average of 500 to 700 displaced persons each time who had been forwarded to the Canadian Pacific office in Bremen from depots across Europe. Sponsored by friends and family in Canada, they would be put on CPR trains at Montreal, destined for Toronto and Winnipeg — and a better life in Canada. The former German ship completed a total of 52 voyages and carried 38,000 refugees before being sold by the company in 1954.

Even the tradition of the gold cane had suffered because of the war. Throughout the hostilities, the captain of the first ocean-going ship to enter the Port of Montreal continued to receive the cane annually. Montreal newspapers duly reported that the port manager, Alex Ferguson, had combed the city, looking for a few ounces of gold (as all supplies of precious metals were going to the war effort); however, the gold cane was replaced with a silver one. Interviewed later at his home in Ottawa, Ferguson admitted that the substitution had occurred to save money — the order had come from a bureaucrat in the National Harbours Board. "I was so incensed," Ferguson said, "that the following year I paid for the difference out of my own pocket."

Even in 1945, after VJ Day, the cane remained silver as Captain Walter Keay discovered when his ship the *Beavercove* won that year. On April 18, 1950, the *Beavercove* once more captained by Keay received the cane — now gold once again. The award for the first ship to enter the port lost some of its uniqueness in 1962 when the Coast Guard began keeping the channel clear to protect the communities along the river from the annual spring floods. Combined with ships that had reinforced hulls, the building of ice-control works, and better navigation aids, winter navigation of the St. Lawrence became possible and when the *Helga Dan*, a Danish vessel, sailed into port on January 4, 1964, a new era had begun.

In the face of the advances in air transport, it was obvious that the shipping companies could only operate with heavy government subsidies — an advantage that the Canadian Pacific did not have. In 1944, in an air-raid shelter under Waterloo Place, the engineering staff had optimistically drawn up designs for two 20,000-ton Empresses. But after the war, the company decided that rather than invest in the building of ships of whatever size, they should "make do" with what there was. Britain still had thousands of troops stationed across her Empire and the demobilization of Allied forces meant that there was still a demand for trooping to Africa, Asia, and the Far East, a task that the great ships were ideally suited to. Between 1947 and 1951, the company's ships carried 179,000 passengers, the "austerity" contracts as they were called, keeping the passenger side of the company afloat — but just barely.

One veteran of trooping, the *Duchess of Bedford*, which escaped the Japanese at the evacuation of Singapore, survived the war and after a refit on the Clyde in 1948 was elevated to an Empress. Initially, it was to have been called the *Empress of India II* but as that country had just become independent — and was soon to be a republic — it was renamed *Empress of France II*. It was put on the Montreal–Liverpool route in the summer, using Saint John in the winter. With Canada's NATO commitments in Europe, once more Canadian troops were carried on the former Duchess. After 186 transatlantic voyages, in December 1960, the 32-year-old *Empress/Duchess* was scrapped by the British Iron & Steel Corporation at Cashmore, Newport.

In the early 1950s, Montreal had become the main summer ocean terminal for Canadian Pacific. Liners continued to call at Quebec, but boat trains to that port were now infrequent. As of 1964, the St. Lawrence was kept open year-round above Quebec and in to Montreal. The years 1952–56, when traffic numbers reached 234,000 passengers, gave the directors at Canadian Pacific some hope. In 1952, with bookings pressing for the Coronation of Princess Elizabeth, when thousands of North American tourists were expected to travel to London to witness the event, and as the airlines could not hope to accommodate the numbers, all the shipping lines expected to do well — if they could find enough ships to handle the demand. Orders were placed at Vickers-Armstrong, Newcastle, by Canadian Pacific for their first post-war company liners, both first drawn up in an air-raid shelter, the *Empress of Britain III* and her almost identical twin the *Empress of England*, the latter a new name in the company's fleet.

The year 1957 was a good one for the company. There were now four Empresses on the Atlantic: *Britain*, *England*, *France*, and *Scotland* — ships that were majestic and streamlined, but too slow for the jet age. Few passengers wanted to spend six days "lounging, snoozing or reading," as the company brochures promised, in its glass-enclosed promenades. That summer Canadian Pacific began negotiating with Vickers-Armstrong to build what would be its last passenger liner. In Canada, the Conservatives, the party of Sir John A. Macdonald, always sympathetic to the Canadian Pacific, returned to power. The new prime minister, John Diefenbaker, had campaigned against what he perceived as the tyrannies of the state-run Canadian National Railway and Trans Canada Airlines, which in order to operate at a profit (and thus not burden the taxpayer) were always given preferential treatment by the government in choice routes.

Passengers Arriving in Canada from Europe

Year	By Sea	By Air
1955	55,000	47,000
1960	56,000	149,000
1965	26,000	351,000

Source: Statistics Canada

There was now definite warmth in Ottawa toward the Canadian Pacific. Proof of this was the granting of permission to Canadian Pacific Airlines to fly across Canada, breaking the transcontinental monopoly that Trans Canada Airlines held since 1937. It was thus no surprise that Mrs. J.G. "Olive" Diefenbaker, the wife of the Canadian prime minister, launched the *Empress of Canada III* (27,300 gt) on May 10, 1960, with a bottle of Canadian white wine.

On the other side of the Atlantic, however, labour troubles began to plague the CP. Seamen's strikes in Liverpool in August 1957 stranded all three Empresses — *England, Britain,* and *France* — in port, causing the company to lose hundreds of customers to the airlines, most of whom never returned. Again, in August 1960, seamen at Liverpool staged what was termed an "unofficial" strike over employment conditions. They wanted an abolition of the 1947 service scheme of hiring, the abolition of the 1894 Merchant Shipping Act on the maintaining of discipline onboard, and a promise that there would be no victimization of strikers.

The *Liverpool Echo* of September 1 reported that pickets were out in force on the Gladstone Dock to prevent the *Empress of France* from sailing, but it "got away to Montreal with cargo but no passengers." A Canadian Pacific spokesperson admitted that there had been a "scuffle" on the *Empress of France* between some of the crew and that it was being manned entirely by officers. The company's general manager in Liverpool, Captain R.V. Burns, gave out a press statement that they "were extremely satisfied of the loyalty of a large number of the company's regular employees that enabled her to sail." When asked why 30 of the crew of the *Empress of France* were being flown home, he said that it could be that they were needed to take another Empress — *Britain* or *England* — out of port. Cunard in Southampton was unaffected, and the *Queen Elizabeth* embarked with a full crew destined for New York.

The Seafarers International Union (SIU) in Montreal sent funds to the strikers — paying the fines, providing bail and legal aid. Hal Banks, the Canadian director of the SIU, addressed "dissident" British seamen in Montreal, allowing them use of the SIU hall, paying for their meals, lodging, and cigarettes. This was strange as the SIU had long held that Canadian Pacific should fly the Canadian not the British "flag of convenience" in Canadian waters and wanted to replace the British crews with Canadians. But Banks said that helping the British seamen was not to do them out of a job but to act as mediators between the strikers and the Canadian Pacific. He did not want to see hard-pressed British seamen, he said, turn to the Communists for help.

Around the same time, in the mid-1950s, a man named Malcolm Maclean came up with an invention that would revolutionize world trade, its impact to be felt from the "big box stores" to the Japanese car manufacturers, but nowhere more spectacularly than the shipping industry.

From the earliest days of maritime commerce, cargo, whether in crates, jars, or sacks, was shipped as "break bulk," which meant it was loaded onto a vessel piecemeal and then secured with the hope that there would be as little breakage, pilferage, and spillage as possible. The inconvenience of loading and unloading the cargo and shipping it to and from the hinterland, not to mention its transhipment to other vessels, was accepted as normal and a consignment arriving at its ultimate destination would have passed through several companies, requiring many personnel and invoices to track it. The whole system was inefficient but had been throughout history — ever since quinquiremes from distant Ophir had unloaded their cargoes of ivory, apes, and peacocks.

Maclean's company, Sea-Land Service, Inc., changed all of that. Packages, drums, and bags could now be packed into weatherproof, water-resistant metal boxes that were almost invulnerable and easier to track. Sealed at the point of departure, they were unsealed only at the final destination. The first container ship, *Ideal X*, a converted oil tanker with 58 containers sailed on April 26, 1956, from Port Newark, New Jersey, for Houston, heralding in the container revolution. Soon ports worldwide saw the potential of containerized trade and built specialized handling facilities for the new container ships, beginning in 1960 with the Port of New York Authority (Port Elizabeth Marine Terminal).

For a multi-modal company like CP, the introduction of containers meant that the same container could be transferred from its ship to a flatcar and even sent by a truck trailer directly to the customer. Even before the sale of the last Empress, the company was focusing on freight and on shipping by container as opposed to bulk and tanker. In 1964, its first container ships were able to carry approximately 12 containers each. CP even developed containers that were smaller and lighter than the standard so that its trucks could carry them. Within five years, the company began converting its freighters to container ships and renaming them: the *Beaverpine* became the *CP Explorer* and the *Beaveroak* the *CP Ambassador*.

CP Ships also entered the bulk shipping trade to transport lead concentrate and later newsprint from Vancouver to Japan. A new company based in Bermuda was formed to own and operate large-capacity bulk carriers. Two of the 28,000-dwt (deadweight tonnage) bulk carriers had historic connections with the founders of the company. In August 1966, the *Lord Mount Stephen* was launched in Nagasaki and two months later, so was the *Lord Strathcona*. When the latter first visited a British port on May 1, 1967, Lord Strathcona, a grandson of the founder, presented a silver rum keg and goblets to the ship. On December 16, 1967, the *R.B. Angus*, a second-hand bulk carrier that the company had purchased to move zinc, lead, and forest products from British Columbia to Japan, was lost in a storm on the Pacific with all 39 of its crew saved.

The year 1968 was an auspicious one for Canadian Pacific. The first of its three 28,000–gross tonnage dry cargo bulk carriers, the *H.R. MacMillan*, entered service on January 26 to be followed by *J.V. Clyne*

What Is a Container?

Containers come in two sizes: 20 and 40 feet long. They are eight feet wide and range from eight feet to nine feet, six inches in height. Most containers are constructed from steel — about 2.5 tons of steel is used in a 40-foot container. Each corner of a container is designed to withstand a load of 96 tons, the equivalent of five fully laden containers. The floors can withstand loads of about 350 pounds per square inch.

Containers mainly carry dry general cargo like boxes, crates, drums, pallets et cetera; however, bulk in the form of grain can also be loaded into a container. Containers specially designed to carry liquids are called "tanktainers." Some containers can also carry liquified gas. Containers designed to carry refrigerated or frozen cargo are called "reefer" containers. These containers can be cooled down to minus 20 degrees Celcius. Open containers with collapsible flaps at each end are called "flatracks." These are used to carry cargo that might be slightly overwidth or overweight or a large piece of machinery that cannot be transported in a fully enclosed or open-top container.

Containers are shipped on specially designed ships called cellular container vessels. Third generation cellular container vessels can be quite large and steam at speeds up to 20 knots. There are limited means of securing cargo within a container. Cargo can be packed/unpacked using forklifts. Containers can be loaded under deck or above deck. Above-deck containers can go as high as five or six. They rest on specially fabricated container fittings and are secured onto the ship's structure by means of twist locks and lashing rods.

and *N.R. Crump* the next year. The two 57,000-ton coal/ore carriers, the first to be built in Japan — at the Nippon Kokan Kaisha Ltd. Shipyards — were almost ready to be launched and were named after *T. Akasaka* (the president of the Nippon shipbuilding company) and *W.C. Van Horne*. In September, Canadian Pacific ordered three 14,000-gross tonnage container ships from Cammell, Laird & Co. of Birkenhead. Each ship would carry up to 700 containers between London, Rotterdam, and Quebec.

At the same time, under CEO W.J. Stenason, the sprawling Canadian Pacific empire was put through a corporate "makeover." In keeping with the Swinging Sixties, the Van Horne checkered logo was replaced by a dark green triangle enclosed within a white semicircle. The company's various divisions share the same design but the colour of the triangle differed: CP Rail was red, CP Air orange, CP Transport blue, CP Hotels grey, and CP Telecommunications yellow ochre. As CP Rail still ran some coastal shipping, its vessels were in red. On July 3, 1971, the parent company changed its name to Canadian Pacific Limited (CPL) to reflect its conglomerate status.

None of this could stem the decline, though, and less than a decade after the *Empress of Canada*'s launch, all three of the new Empresses has been sold off, ending their days as cruise ships. In 1963, after only 109 Atlantic crossings, the *Empress of Britain III* was put up for sale. The *Empress of England*, after 149 crossings, suffering the same fate in 1970. The causes were obvious: that year only 23,732 passengers took the Empresses across, compared with 98,000 ten years before. Citing the devaluation of the American dollar, the tapering off of immigration from Britain, and most of all affordable air travel and cheap charter flights (especially with the advent of the new jumbo jets) Canadian Pacific announced on November 9, 1971, after its 121st crossing, that the *Empress of Canada* was being withdrawn and the 1971–72 Caribbean cruise schedule cancelled. "We regret" said Stenason, "that the economic circumstances have made it impossible to achieve a viable passenger ship operation, despite a determined effort to promote the service and attract increased business." Besides speed, what ultimately sank the last Empresses was economics: that year the single transatlantic fare on an Empress ranged from $250 to $417 while that on a charter flight cost $200.

On January 1, 2003, at 12:04 precisely, the *Canmar Courage* entered the port of Montreal, the first vessel to reach the port after December 31. Captain Ashwanik Engineer at its helm would be awarded the coveted gold-headed cane a week later. This was the fourth time that a ship belonging to Canada Maritime, the company owned by CP Ships, had accomplished this honor. Onboard the vessel were 2,220 twenty-foot-equivalent (TEU) containers that had been loaded in Hamburg and Antwerp. (TEU are the industry standard of measurement for containerized trade.)

It was a far cry from the Canadian Pacific ships that had habitually won the cane. No longer made at Fairfields or Vickers Armstrong, they were now built by Daewoo Shipbuilding, in Okpo, South Korea. The Marconi wireless operators had been replaced by satellite telephone, fax, telex, email, and mobile phone. Their gross tonnage was 3,914, the length overall was 804 feet, and its average speed of 21.30 knots came not from Parson turbines but from an engine built by Korea Heavy Industries. The break with the past could not have been more complete than among the crew. Chief officer, engineer, fitter, bosun, oiler, and steward — they came no longer from Liverpool, Southampton, or even Canton, but from India and Vietnam and were employed to run the ship by the Anglo-Eastern Ship Management Ltd. A century before, it had taken 118 crew to run the *Empress of India*. In 1931, 630 men and women in deck, engineering, and catering, were necessary to run the *Empress of Britain II*, and 30 years later its successor, the *Britain III* had a crew of 460. Now there were 22 crew members onboard the *Canmar Pride*, sister ship to the *Courage* (including a training seamen). Not surprisingly, to cater to so few, the ship's chandler was a "mom and pop" store in east-end Montreal.

That most of the crew was from India was no surprise. British seamen had to be paid a British standard of wages and as a result in 2003, only 39 percent of seamen and fewer than 50 percent of officers serving on British registered ships were actually from the United Kingdom.

The loss of maritime skills and experience had become such a threat to Britain that only after intense lobbying by the British trade union NUMAST (National Trade Union of Marine, Aviation and Shipping Transport) did the government decide to link its tonnage tax-benefit scheme for companies to providing training and employment opportunities for locally recruited (British) cadets. In this, CP Ships had led the way. Beginning in 2001, it had several cadets in a British cadet training program managed by Lothian Shipping Services, all of whom would be joining CP vessels as third officers or fourth engineers to eventually progress to shipmaster and chief engineer positions. Anglo-Eastern Ship Management Ltd. would soon take over the role of training provider with NUMAST general secretary Brian Orrell welcoming the commitment of CP Ships to the continuing employment and training of its "tonnage tax cadets."

What was definite was that in their whole careers, none of the cadets were ever likely to encounter more than a dozen passengers on any one crossing. For despite the advances in air freight, in the first years of the 21st century, 95 percent of world trade by weight or volume went by sea — 5.88 billion tons in the year 2000 alone. And in the same year, 70 percent of general cargo was containerized, this figure expected to be 90 percent by 2010. The world container fleet was 2,755 ships having a total carrying capacity of 5,356,650 TEUs. To benefit from the economies of scale, as they had once done with the passenger fleet, ships kept getting larger. In the 1970s Canadian Pacific chose to build its main Atlantic service intermodal container terminal at Wolfe's Cove, transatlantic passenger service having disappeared by then. It was to be short-lived, closing when Canadian Pacific transferred all container operations to Montreal in 1978.

Unfortunately for the traditional ports of Canadian Pacific, Quebec City, and Halifax, the decision was taken to move its container operations completely to Montreal, which, thanks to the St. Lawrence Seaway, was deeper into the North American continent and closer to the American Midwest. Another reason was more historic: the CPR had never been very strong in the Maritimes but already owned vast facilities in Montreal. In 1978, it opened its Montreal Gateway Terminals at Racine in the city's east end to handle the container traffic. It was cheaper to carry containers as far as possible by sea, and Montreal, with its huge CPR rail connection to move them on to the hinterland of North America, was ideal. On 30 acres of land in the east end of Montreal Harbour, a common-user terminal was erected operated by a company subsidiary, Racine Terminals (Montreal). The last CP ship to leave the Quebec terminal was the *CP Discoverer* on November 9, 1978, ending the company's historic association with Quebec City.

CHAPTER 11

The Last Great Ships

In the late 1940s, the *Empress of Scotland II*, last of the three funnellers to ply the ocean (with the exception of Cunard's *Queen Mary*), was being refitted at Liverpool with the gross tonnage increased to 26,313. From 1950–57, as the flagship of the Canadian Pacific fleet, it was assigned to the prestigious transatlantic services. Crossing the Atlantic in five days, it plied between Liverpool and Montreal — its masts shortened to get under the Jacques Cartier Bridge to do so — making it the largest ship to ever go that far up the St. Lawrence.

On November, 12, 1951, on her regular Atlantic run, it was called to stop at Conception Bay, Newfoundland. Her master, Captain Cecil Ernest Duggan, manoeuvred her as close off Portugal Cove as he could, and at 1:10 p.m. noneother than Princess Elizabeth and the Duke of Edinburgh boarded for their journey home. The Royal Suite on the A-deck starboard side had been prepared at Quebec with some of the furniture taken from the *France*. It was on the sunny side, homeward-bound with three rooms in pastel shades: the princess's bedroom, the duke's bedroom, and a common sitting room.

Princess Elizabeth was impressed to know that during the war Duggan had served under Mountbatten. The Duke of Edinburgh, Mountbatten's nephew, was equally impressed. Along with Duggan, there were others on the *Scotland* with memories of the princess's parents on their Canadian tour. Chief stewardess Lillian O'Brien, who attended to Elizabeth, had 33 years of uninterrupted service at sea and had attended to the queen, the princess's mother, during the 1939 Canadian tour. But Duggan's chief engineer, James Thompson, had other memories. He had been temporarily blinded and scalded when the *Empress of Canada* was torpedoed off Liberia.

This would not be the last time that Captain Duggan would see the queen. After the voyage, he was appointed aide-de-camp to the princess, and attended her coronation at Westminister Abbey in 1953. Duggan left the sea to become the Canadian Pacific Marine Superintendent in Montreal from 1955–63 and when the St. Lawrence Seaway was opened, he supervised the extension of service to the Great Lakes.

John MacPhail worked on the Empresses in the 1950s as a tourist-class steward, starting his day at 6:00 or 6:30 a.m. with "a wake up call and a cup of tea from the 'Glory Hole Steward' whose job it was to look after so many steward cabins." The first job was to restock the ship's bars, each steward carrying a crate of spirits, wine, or beer from the stockroom in the bowels of the ship to the bars, which were usually situated on the top decks. "We were not allowed to use the lifts in case we woke the passengers," he recalled. Then came the "scrub out," when each steward on hands and knees with a bucket and brush had to be scrubbed out an assigned area of floor. Then the stewards showered, put on their CP uniforms, and prepared the tables for two sittings of eight passengers each. The stewards' own breakfast came next, followed by jobs in the dining saloon, mainly cleaning the woodwork, mirrors, brass, and silver.

Officer Ranks Onboard a Passenger Ship

Peter Roberts joined the *Empress of Scotland II* in July 1952, under the command of Commodore J.P. Dobson, and would serve on all the Empresses at various times and ranks, both on the North Atlantic Liner service, the Caribbean Cruises out of New York, and the Island Cruises out of Liverpool. He left his last passenger ship in April 1966, the new *Empress of Canada* (27,300 gt), with the doubtful honour of being the last staff commander of the Empress fleet before the company diversified into a trading fleet. Noting that although the ship's captain "was of course the ultimate boss, final arbitrator, judge, jury, and hangman," there were many "chiefs" onboard and "one quickly learnt that anyone with a 'Chief' prefix had to be treated with due reverence."

Below Roberts describes the different ranks of a passenger ship:

Deck Department: The Deck Department, charged with the safe navigation of the ship was led by the Chief Officer who was responsible for the general maintenance of the decks, cargo gear deck machinery, hatches, lifeboats, safety equipment etc. It was his job to organize Boat and Fire drills for the crew and passengers (without trying to frighten the life out of them). On our passenger ships there were 5 watchkeeping officers. The First Officer would keep the 4:00 a.m. to 8:00 p.m. and his main function was navigator. Though the ship's position was officially recorded at noon, the most reliable sights were taken at twilight when both the horizon and stars etc. could be observed together. The Second Officer would keep the "graveyard watch," the 12:00 p.m. to 4:00 a.m. shift. His daytime job was being responsible for Bullion and Mails. Third Officer would keep the 8:00 a.m. to 12:00 a.m. shift and his other responsibility was cargo, and be responsible to the Chief Officer for the maintenance of safety equipment. He also had to compile the Muster

Station List before sailing, an arduous task long before word processors were invented. That usually kept him up all night as new crew members would be signing on right up to sailing time. These would be the senior watch-keeping officers and would all have Master Mariner's Certificates. Then would come the 4th, 5th, and possibly 6th Officers who would double up the watches.

Ratings: The Chief Officer would have ratings in his charge, the most senior being a Chief Petty Officer, known in the trade as the Boatswain, or Bosun for short. He was the power behind the throne and had probably been aboard the ship since it was built. I think it would be safe to say that it was his ship. A good bosun had an enormous influence in the running of the ship. Amongst the ratings there were the Quartermasters who steered the ship (we didn't have auto-pilots in those days, it was very much "handomatic"), and Petty Officers who maintained the Promenade and Boats Decks. In the evenings they helped out with various fun and games that were devised to prevent boredom amongst the passengers. We also had carpenters, joiners, and a "lamp trimmer." The name was a left over from the days of sail when oil was the only form of lighting. The lamp trimmer was exactly that, but as we moved into the hi tech world, in addition the tending the lamps (for emergency use and DoT requirements), he was mainly the deck store keeper, who tenaciously guarded his hoard of ropes, wires, paints, shackles, and a million other bits and pieces that a ship carried and accumulated.

Master at Arms: Another crew member who was virtually a law unto him was the Master at Arms. These gentlemen were usually ex-policemen whose duties were to maintain order onboard. Though he had to make daily reports to the

Chief Officer, I suspect that he had a private line to the management and no one escaped his prying eyes and inquisitive ears. His logbook contained some interesting reading and investigating the entries was a task that one had not really been trained for, i.e. Judge, Jury, Hangman, Marriage Counsellor, Priest, Detective, and Undertaker etc.

Staff Commander: There was one other officer that was peculiar to the passenger ship and this was the Staff Commander. A very senior officer (his next job was command of a ship) his was a job undefined and not even mentioned in the official manning requirements laid down by the Board of Trade, in fact a ship could go to sea without one. It was a position ordained by the Company as the staff commander was there to represent the Captain on the passenger decks. On the North Atlantic as the weather demanded much attention of the Captain, the Staff Commander's main function apart from preventing awkward passengers from bugging the Captain, was to be a presence on the passenger decks, show the flag and generally be nice to the customers. When they saw someone wandering around covered in gold braid apparently unconcerned as all hell let loose in bad weather, the ship belting through the ice track at breakneck speed, they were reassured. He was necessarily a diplomatic "charm man" and every one wanted him at their cocktail parties (if they couldn't get the Captain), and as such had to acquire the ability to (apparently) tuck away a prodigious quantity of booze and canapés day and night without showing any effect from the stuff. We had some highly revered heroes amongst them. A fact not really appreciated is that should the Captain "snuff it" or otherwise become incapacitated, the Chief Officer could legally take command. Actually, should this happen the Company would, if they knew about it, most likely authorize the Staff Commander to take over, and due entry made into the Official Log book (a very important and legal document)

Chief Engineer Officer: The Chief Engineer Officer, who was the next most responsible person onboard, wore four bands of gold on his sleeve but with purple bands between. He and the captain were of comparable seniority, though of course the buck eventually ended up in the Captain's lap. "The Chief," as he was universally known, had some considerable explaining to do if the ship was delayed through mechanical failure. He had a large staff, including a Staff Chief Engineer. With two engines, HP Steam Turbines, and boilers etc., there would be several Engineer Officers on watch at any one time. Amongst them would be Electricians and Sanitary Engineers. There was a vast amount of pipe work and plumbing onboard a passenger ship. On our later ships we had evaporators to condense seawater into drinking water and sewage plants that purified waste to a stage were it was drinkable … not that any one other than manufacturers were prepared to demonstrate. The "Chief's" staff increased when we began to get air conditioning, cinemas, casinos, and massive refrigerated storerooms to maintain.

Chief Petty Officer: The Chief Petty Officer in charge of the Engine room work force was called the "Donkeyman" and this again stemmed from the days when the first piece of machinery on a sailing ship was the donkey engine, a primitive steam-driven pump for bailing the bilge water overboard. The Donkeyman looked after it and I suppose he was the first engineer on ships. He, like the Bosun, was the king of the Engine room.

Chief Purser: The next in line was the Chief Purser who ruled the Purser's Bureaux with his staff of Junior Pursers and Stenographers. He was virtually the ship's banker and invariably the poor Joe that would receive the first complaints from the clients. In those days he was also very much in the forefront of the entertainment business and would arrange various deck games, frolics in the Empress Room during the evening, and organize the Masquerade Ball towards the end of the voyage. I never ceased to be amazed at the ingenuity of some of the passengers who could create the most astounding costumes from anything that they could acquire onboard. It was the Staff Commanders job, apart from judging, to inspect this lot before they were allowed to parade before the public. Needless to say some of their "gear" was not only highly original but not quite in keeping with the decorum of the generally staid atmosphere onboard.

Chief Steward: The Chief Steward, in charge of the Catering Department, had the most staff onboard. He would liaise closely with the Chief Purser, in fact in later years the two departments combined when Hotel Managers, Restaurant Managers and Entertainment Managers etc. appeared on the scene. The most important member of his staff, if not the most important man onboard, was THE CHEF who had a staff of his own. The company very carefully preserved a good chef and God help anyone who upset him (as I did on one occasion which terrified me, but that's another story). He used to preside in his special little house raised above the kitchens where he could keep an eye on everything going on in his realm. I swear that the chef was a better meteorologist than any of the navigators, he seemed to be able to predict the weather long before us and would know exactly what and how much food was to be prepared.

After a short break, they were back to serve two sittings of lunch and then their own lunch: "We would order from the passenger's menu and one of the kitchen staff (who would be tipped at the end of the trip) would keep it in the hot plate to be eaten later or standing up in the galley." Stewards served afternoon teas on alternate days so that each man got a rest every other day. The day closed with two sittings of dinner with an occasional game of cards after. Then to bed. "It was a ten hour day plus overtime," MacPhail concluded.

Brian Scott joined the *Empress of Scotland II* in 1956 as a junior cargo officer and remembered how hectic the quick turnarounds made his life:

> There was tank cleaning after discharging the tallow, hold cleaning after the grain plus the requirement to work out the vessels' stability a.m. and p.m. due to ballasting/deballasting, refueling and taking on fresh water. Outward cargo was high value goods such as mails, crockery, textiles, woollen goods, motor cars and machinery. This was exchanged in Quebec for grain, sawn timber, apples, bulk tallow, mail, gold and silver bullion for Liverpool.

No longer able to compete with the newer, faster liners on the passenger runs, *Empress of Scotland II* was soon put on cruises to the West Indies. Peter Roberts, who obtained his Master's Foreign Going Steamship Certificate in September 1956 and was despatched as 3rd Officer to the "mighty and elegant" *Empress of Scotland*, was witness to the ship's transformation:

> We made one North Atlantic trip to Quebec and then into dock for overhaul and fitting out for Cruising. Though it took a month, little was apparently done — basically the hatch boards were removed from No. 5 cargo hold and a prefab swimming pool inserted in the space. What the passengers didn't realise was that there was an 80-foot drop under the pool to the bottom of the hold.

As a cruise ship, the *Scotland II* only carried about 500 passengers and had more lifeboats than were required (under *Titanic* rules). The surplus boats were put ashore and converted to launches that would carry the passengers to shore at the many ports in the Caribbean that had no docking facilities. To outfit the launches, Roberts was told to ensure that the bottom boards on the floor of the boat were raised at least 16 inches. "I never queried this, assuming it was for the added comfort of the passengers. The reason became clear when we went to our first tropic island and the surf flooded in through the bottom," he said.

Laundry facilities were also installed:

> Quite a comely staff was specially employed to run this torture chamber, affectionately know as "Steam Queens." There was a constant rise of steam and the deck was awash with soapy, dirty water slurping back and forth. It looked like Dante's *Inferno*, and flitting around this lot were these poor girls in their white coveralls, looking like a flock of swans.

The heat was so fierce that the crew would keep a shell door open when conditions allowed. This had a heavy steel grill that dropped down over the gap to prevent anyone falling overboard, and in port, to stop unauthorized entry. "The girls would sometimes lift the grill and stand in door space to cool off and enjoy the scenery or chat with the locals," Roberts remembered. Many of these young women had been attracted by the recruiting adverts extolling the pleasures of cruising in tropic seas and exotic islands with board and lodging thrown in.

On January 13, 1958, after 27 years of service with Canadian Pacific, the *Empress of Scotland II* (once the *Empress of Japan*) was sold to the Hamburg Atlantic Line, the same line that its predecessor, the *Empress of Scotland I* (as the *Kaiserin Auguste Victoria*), had been built for. (It had been laid up at Liverpool and later drydocked at Belfast since November 1957.) Renamed *Scotland* on January 19, 1958, it was sent under a German flag to Hamburg for a refit. Completed in July, the former *Empress* emerged from the Howaldt Shipyard under its new name,

Hanseatic. Put on the company's Cuxhaven–Le Havre–Southampton–Cobh–New York route, on September 7, 1966, the old liner caught fire in New York Harbor. It was towed back to Hamburg and scrapped.

The other Empress, *Australia*, was sent to Harland & Wolff, Belfast, to be refitted and returned to trooping on the Liverpool–Port Said–Egypt route. Born as the top-heavy *Tirpitz* in 1922, it had been renamed the *Empress of China*, a title kept for only a year. In 1950, almost a full half-century after it had been laid down at the Vulkan-Werke yard in Stettin, it gamely took on its last trooping run, carrying a British brigade and some 2,000 military personnel to Pusan, Korea, for yet another war. Finally, on April 29, 1952, the *Tirpitz/Empress of China/Empress of Australia* was sold for scrap and towed to Rosyth to be cut up. In the service of Canadian Pacific, it had seen the worst as the saviour of Yokohama after the earthquake and the best as the royal yacht for the 1939 tour of North America — and risen equally well on both occasions.

Some of the *Empress of Australia* lives on at the Glenfarclas Distillery in Scotland, five miles south of Aberlour on the A95 Grantown-on-Spey Road. The oak panels from the first-class smoking lounge were built into the British Legion Hall at Rosyth. When the hall was dismantled in 1972, the *Empress*'s oak panels were put up for auction on Radio Scotland. This was just as plans were in place to build a visitors' centre at the distillery, and the late George Grant purchased the panels for the centre, which opened in 1973. Then, in 2000, in what was called the Ship's Room, a reunion was held. The original blueprints for the *Empress of Australia* were discovered just five miles from the distillery at the Archiestown Hotel.

The end of the Second World War saw the *Duchess of Richmond* bringing British troops and civil servants back to Singapore The next year, as India was preparing for its independence, the ship went twice to Bombay, taking out British troops and civil servants. Returned to the Canadian Pacific the following year, the ship was sent to Liverpool to be rebuilt for the civil market. On July 16, 1947, the *Duchess* was reborn as the *Empress of Canada II.*

Besides the new name, it was also the first ship to sport the old house flag — Van Horne's red and white squares — on her buff funnels. Completely booked to bring Canadian tourists to the United Kingdom, the *Duchess of Richmond/Empress of Canada II* was sent to Fairfields, where it had been built in 1928, to be refurbished. After the major work was completed, it was moved to the Gladstone Dock, Liverpool, on January 24, ready for the busy season to begin.

With the threat of fire a major problem at sea, all liners now had extensive detection and suppression systems — from crew training to fire control centres. But as with the *Normandie* and the *Queen Elizabeth*, they were at their most vulnerable when in harbour with their trained crew no longer onboard and fire control centres inoperable. At 15:35, the day after the *Empress of Canada II*'s arrival, workers on shore saw smoke swirling up from below her decks. As it was known that there were welders working below decks, no alarm was given. When the fire was eventually discovered, someone was sent ashore to phone the local fire brigade. With the ship's water main not connected, the crew onboard could not fight the fire and were evacuated. The local fire brigade arrived at 16:30, only to discover that both B and C decks were filled with smoke. Additional fire brigades were called. The water being hosed into the *Empress of Canada II* caused her to list, so a decision was taken to stop fighting the fire — just as the fire brigades claimed that they had it under control. By 20:00, now abandoned, the ship was ablaze and the listing unabated. At 01:40 hours, early on January 26, 1953, it toppled over on its side, with only the starboard side above water.

Salvage work on the *Empress* began immediately with divers sealing off open ports and doors so that the ship could be pumped out and made watertight. Nine-inch-thick hawsers were welded to her side and winches on the opposite side of the dock wound the hawsers, and finally, on March 6, 1954, at 12:35 hours, the *Empress* was turned upright. It was vertical but stuck in the mud of the dock bottom. It took two months for the liner to be refloated and made watertight. After all that, Canadian Pacific concluded that it was fit only to be scrapped. On September 1, 1954, the *Empress of Canada II* was towed to the breakers in Genoa, Italy, arriving there on October 10. An inquiry into her loss was held in

December that year, with the committee finding that there had been no phone lines between Canadian Pacific and the local fire brigade, that the fire main had not been charged, and that the fire doors and watertight doors had not been closed.

With another Empress gone and the Coronation impending, Canadian Pacific looked to acquire some extra tonnage — and quickly. As a stop-gap measure (until their two ships could be built), Canadian Pacific bought the *De Grasse* from the French line in 1953, renaming her *Empress of Australia II*. The *De Grasse* had been named for François Joseph Paul, the Count de Grasse, who defeated the British at Chesapeake Bay in 1781, only to have surrendered his ship the following year and ended his days in disgrace in a prison in London. The *De Grasse*'s early career on the South American run was successful, but like its namesake, fortune deserted her soon after.

In mid-Atlantic on the day that the Second World War began, rather than face a U-boat and share the fate of the Montreal-bound *Athenia*, the *De Grasse* turned around and made, not for New York as its sisters the *Normandie* and *Île de France* had, but for Halifax. Returning to France in the period known as the phony war, the *De Grasse* was used as a barracks ship in the Gironde River, near Bordeaux, only to be sunk on August 30, 1944, by the retreating Germans. Pumped dry in 1946, the liner was towed to St. Nazaire, on the French coast, for repairs and (minus one funnel) put back into service. This new life proved to be short, and in 1949, with the *Île de France* now in service, the *De Grasse* was put up for sale. After three seasons on the Liverpool–Montreal circuit, in January 1956 it was sold to the Italian Grimaldi-Siosa Line. Renamed the *Venezuela*, the unlucky ship ran aground off Cannes in 1962 and was sent to the breakers at La Spezia.

The *Empress of Britain III* (25,516 gt) and the *Empress of England* (25,585 gt) cost £5,500,000 each, measured 640 by 85 by 48 feet, and were built to accommodate 150 first-class and 900 tourist-class passengers. Unlike their predecessors, they were aerodynamically sleek, single-funnelled, fitted with gyro-controlled stabilizers, and completely air-conditioned. The third ship to bear that name, the *Empress of Britain III*, gleamed white with a single buff-coloured funnel that sported Van

Horne's checker pattern. It was designed to cross the Atlantic in the summer season and cruise in the West Indies/South America during the winter. The *Empress of Britain III* was launched at Fairfields on June 22, 1955, by Her Majesty the Queen and was in service in April 1956, with her first cruise from New York to the West Indies taking place in January 1960.

One hundred and ninety two first-class passengers were accommodated on the *Britain III*'s decks, within which were four blocks of suite rooms and six verandah suites. Tourist class was no longer far below in steerage but in the upper, main, and restaurant decks. To serve the necessary 5,000 meals daily, 26,000 cubic feet of insulated storage space held 25,000 pounds of meat, 3,000 gallons of fresh milk, 6 tons of flour, 12 tons of potatoes, 9 tons of vegetables, and 5,000 oysters — a far cry from the cows and chickens that the first Empresses carried. By dividing the boiler- and engine-room casings on either side of the ships, a huge panorama from the forward end to the bulkhead was created. The appearance of space was maintained in the central alleyway on the upper deck, which was called "The Broadway." A painting of Queen Elizabeth II hung in the Empress Room and a mural of Windsor Castle on the cinema's bulkhead. There was a sun lounge on the boat deck and a swimming pool on D-deck.

On May 9, 1956, *Britain III*'s twin, the *Empress of England*, was launched by Lady Eden, the wife of Sir Anthony Eden, prime minister of Britain. It made its maiden voyage on November 18, 1957, and that summer crossed the Atlantic in record time: four days, 15 hours eastbound, and four days, 15 hours, and 30 minutes westbound. Her first cruise took place on January 15, 1958, from New York to the West Indies. Proving that the danger of collision with another ship was still possible, even in 1965, the *Empress of England* hit the Norwegian tanker *Norska* outside Quebec, not far from where the *Empress of Ireland* had been torn open by another Norwegian collier, the *Storstad*.

Said retired CP chief officer Pat Adair,

> Waiting to leave Quebec in a heavy snow storm, the *Empress of England* was told by Quebec Control to un-berth, move upstream and follow a "laker." We could

hear the laker as it came past the Citadel then when we saw her, the tugs pulled us off the berth and we cast off…. Just as another ship looked into view. The starboard engine was rung astern in an effort to swing the ship away but it was too close. Quebec Control had not said anything to the *Empress*, Pilot or Master — I know this for a fact, as I was on the bridge. The vessel came back alongside, discharged passengers and baggage, sending them to Montreal by train. The *Empress* then went to the Davies dry dock at Lauzon across the river for temporary repairs. We then went back to Montreal for the passengers.

With the danger apparently past, the *Empress of England* headed out into the Gulf of St. Lawrence. It was then discovered that the dummy bow had split wide open. The ship headed back to Quebec to offload the poor passengers and await more repairs. The offending dummy bow was cut out, the forepeak around the damage was covered with heavier plate, and the space around it was filled with concrete. Ship and crew then headed home to Liverpool, without passengers, where the ship was put into the Gladstone Graving Dock and a new bow section installed.

Then, in December 1960, after 186 Atlantic crossings (the highest of any Canadian Pacific ship) another Empress, the *Empress of France*, was scrapped. That winter the company had only two Empresses in operation.

The next year was better and in May 1961 the *Empress of Canada III* came into service. Now with three of the most modern ships on the Atlantic, never before had Canadian Pacific looked so prosperous. The *Empress of Canada III* (27,300 gt) was launched from the Walker-on-Tyne yard of Vickers Armstrong on May 10, 1960, and embarked on her maiden voyage from Liverpool to Quebec and Montreal on April 24, 1961.

When Terry Foskett joined the *Canada III* on August 4, 1961, at Gladstone Dock, he recalled that his first duties were helping with the "sign-ons" for the new voyage:

During those halcyon days before containers and ten-hour turnarounds, CP passenger ships spent five days in their home port on a turnaround. They arrived on Thursdays and sailed on the following Tuesday from Liverpool during the Atlantic season. During the winter the ships usually deployed to the Caribbean out of New York. CP kept one ship sailing on cruises out of Europe or on charter but during the first few years I was there all three ships sailed on the Atlantic during the season.

The Empresses would leave Gladstone Dock in the morning and, all being well, reach Prince's Landing Stage by midday, commence embarkation, and then sail at 5:00 p.m. if tides were favourable — if not, they would go to mid-river and wait for the tide to get the ship over the Mersey Bar. Foskett recalled that as a cadet he would sort the arriving passenger flowers into cabin order in the gymnasium with the help of an older man, a former public-room steward:

> He would turn up in his uniform with the blue facings and tell me what to do. I think he had had an accident as he had a steel support on his leg and hobbled around the gymnasium sorting the flowers. As he was no longer fit to go to sea, I suppose CP had given him the job to make a little money. They were very good at that in CP. In those days steamship companies had a legacy of care and concern for their employees in return for which they received loyalty.

The ship would then sail for Greenock, arriving early the next morning. The passengers were brought out by tender and within a few hours the ship was off across the wide Atlantic for the St. Lawrence River and Quebec and Montreal. As the ship carried many immigrants, processing would take place at Quebec not to far from Wolfe's Cove under the Heights of Abraham. The whole run to Montreal from Liverpool took seven days, with a three-day turnaround in Montreal — arrive on one day, a full day in port, and sail the following day.

Among Foskett's social duties were the evening bingo games and, once each crossing, the "Atlantic Derby":

> Naturally, the Pursers took their slice of the "commission," depending how far up the command structure you were. When I first started on the *Canada* as a cadet I was given a few dollars out of the float at the end of the Bingo which was my "commission." The games took place in the First Class Windsor Lounge, starting around 9:00 p.m. after dinner. Tourist Class was run separately which was where the big money was. The First Class Bingo was under the First Class Purser usually assisted by two cadets or one cadet and an Assistant Purser. The other two games were Tourist Class Bingo held every night at 9:00 p.m., and the "Atlantic Derby," which was run on a tote system. In a backhanded way, the commission also benefitted the company. In those days, unlike today, everyone paid for their own uniforms and kit. Thus the Pursers Department were the best turned out of all the officers and as they were very much "front of house," they presented a smart appearance and impressed our passengers.

Not only was the uniform not provided but for most of the company's history, laundry was only free when the ship was in Canada. In the 1930s, when an assistant cook made £7.35 a month and the kitchen boy £5.40, this was a hardship.

Foskett later worked as purser in the crew office: "There had been some kind of snarl up in the accounting for the Crew wages and so I was assisting the 2nd Purser Crew and Assistant Purser to sort it out. The night before arrival in Liverpool we worked all night. By the time I finished sometime the following afternoon I was exhausted and went to bed." The crew of 500 was paid every six weeks, receiving cash advances in between payoffs. Deductions included the "Penny in the Pound"(a kind of insurance scheme) and "Allotments" to be sent home, as dictated in the "Red Sets," the ship articles that all seamen signed to obey the master, and that had details about next of kin, wages, et cetera.

"It was a laborious task," Foskett recalled.

> One of my jobs in the early years was to be drafted to write these up. On a general "sign on" this took every day we were in port on a weekday — not over the weekend, thank God! We stayed until about 2:30 or 3 p.m. and then finished for the day. Some crew being what they were, would go off the ship on arrival at Gladstone Dock around 11 a.m. or 12 noon after disembarking our passengers at Princes Landing Stage, find the nearest pub, and not return until 2 or 3 p.m. and expect to be paid off. Any wages not collected would be taken by the Crew Purser early the next morning and deposited at the Board of Trade Shipping Office with the Shipping Master cashier. You would take a taxi and someone else with you.

Peter Roberts's first impressions of the *Empress of Canada* were of a ship that, though not quite in the luxury-liner class, had great character: "something of a wonderland," with glass-enclosed promenade decks, two huge funnels, rows of lifeboats, acres of dark wooden panelling, jalousie doors, nooks and crannies, pantries, hidden spiral staircases through the decks, ironing rooms, and wooden decks marked out for deck tennis and quoits. It was built for the carriage of passengers from point A to point B in an age when it was the only way to cross the oceans (except for the wealthy and the brave) and the only competition was from rival companies plying the same routes. By today's standards it had little to offer the passengers. Strictly two classes, first and second, two bars, two restaurants, two accommodation spaces, which were divided by deck levels, with the first class on the upper decks. There was, however, the Empress Room, where the passengers could dance to the orchestra, or play cards or bingo:

> As a junior deck officer, you don't (officially) have much social contact with the passengers [though] you do meet

them in your general course of duties … Lifeboat Drills, visits to the bridge etc. You also have to make rounds of the ship during the night watches (there are two Officers on watch, senior and junior). I used to find this fascinating, visiting the hallowed places that were normally completely out of bounds. Walk the now usually deserted promenade decks, the bars, public rooms, walk the many passageways where the passenger cabins are situated, check the gyrocompass, which was down in the bowels of the ship, close to the centre of gravity, and generally ensure that all was ship shape and free from hazard and that no unauthorized personnel were on the prowl. During these wanderings it was likely that you would meet the odd late night reveler, insomniac, lonely lady who for some reason wanted to visit the Gyro Room, new found lovers seeking solitude, stowaways and on one occasion a deranged passenger who was armed with a pistol taking pot shots that anyone that hadn't taken cover. The Chief Officer, Eric Connerton, a Canadian, received a medal for his bravery in disarming the man.

Captain John Arton remembered the Empresses as being nightmares for the crew because of their accommodation standards:

In those days when building passenger ships, the welfare of the crew was probably the last thing that shipowners/designers thought of. I remember that on the *Empress of Canada* some crew cabins held up to ten seafarers, all in metal bunks with metal fittings, and communal washrooms that served maybe 50/60 persons. In stark contrast with the passengers' accommodation where even the worst cabins held a maximum of four and were quite nicely furnished with wooden fittings … as a junior deck officer, 9 officers share two showers and two toilets — and we thought it quite luxurious!

What was unchanged since the turn of the century was the economic and social difference among passengers. Nurse Margaret Knox noted:

> The First Class on "A" Deck [was] mainly Americans with a few affluent British among them. The tourist accommodation was a mixture of emigrants from Britain hoping for a better life in North America. On one trip there were hundreds of Hungarian refugees with everything they possessed wrapped up in a handkerchief — I remember realizing that we had some of the richest people in the world onboard and some who had nothing: it was a great shock to me. But I never really got to know any of my patients. The crossing was a short one and most of the patients only needed one or perhaps two visits.

One exception stayed with Knox all her life. A "lovely wee girl" of three, who was travelling with her mother and big brother and sister, had become very unwell and was brought into the hospital with her mother where it was quiet. The father had immigrated to Canada ahead of them to get himself established before they joined him. She had serious intestinal problem but there was nothing that could be done to help her.

A day later a terrible storm came up off the south of Iceland and the ship was just turned into the wind to ride it out. Approaching Canada, it was decided that the girl would be taken ashore on the pilot cutter at Father Point and flown to Quebec. However, the captain had other ideas: he realized he could make Quebec in about the same time with far less trauma for the child. Nurse Knox debarked with the child in her arms:

> The minute the gangway was down I was ashore with her wrapped in a blanket into a waiting ambulance with her mother and other siblings. The surgeon was ready for her when we got to the hospital and I was rushed back to the ship to continue on to Montreal. For two days I pestered officials coming onboard at Montreal about that

child and eventually one was brave enough to tell me that it had been too late. She had died and had been buried in a pauper's grave. Needless to say both the doctor and myself were very upset and I have always since hoped that the family have had a successful life in Canada.

When the *Empress of Canada* left Montreal for Liverpool for the last time on November 23, 1971, it marked the end of almost seven decades of Canadian Pacific passenger shipping. Renamed the *Ocean Monarch* with Shaw Savill Line, the former *Empress of England* had a short career as a cruise ship but was scrapped in 1975. The *Empress of Britain* would become the *Queen Anna Maria* for the Greek Line in 1965 and in February 1972 the *Empress of Canada* was sold to Carnival Cruise Lines to become the *Mardi Gras*. Both ships would be reunited when *Britain* was sold to Carnival to be renamed the *Carnivale*. The trendy Canadian Pacific funnel logo was modified to become Carnival's logo, but the ships remained white and kept their "Empress Decks."

Both ships now worked as "budget" cruise ships, with the former *Empress of Britain* suffering through other renamings as the *Fiesta Marina* and the *Olympic*. Thompson Cruises took her over as the *Topaz* and in 2003 the old ship was chartered as the "Peace Boat." Under this name, the last remnant of Canadian Pacific passenger glory now travels the world on educational voyages. Her sister, the former *Empress of Canada*, was less fortunate. It was sold by Carnival in 1993 to Epirotiki Lines and renamed *Star of Texas* and later *Lucky Star*. By 1999 it was sailing once more from Liverpool, working for Direct Cruises as the *Apollon*. This proved to be her last identity change as, after being laid up in Greece in December 2003, it was sent to India and scrapped.

Even Cunard was not immune and in 1971 it was taken over by Trafalgar House PLC, which was bought by the Norwegian group Kvaerner, which in 1998 was itself taken over by Carnival Cruise Lines of Miami.

With shipping lines turning to cargo handling and passenger cruising, there was no longer a demand for greater speed on the ocean and the Hales Trophy was retired to the American Merchant Marine Museum in New York State and, except for Richard Branson's attempt to capture it in 1986, the Blue Riband was all but forgotten. For a while, the Soviet *Alexandr Puskin* and the Polish *Stefan Batory* took up the Rotterdam–Le Havre–Southampton– Quebec City–Montreal route. But by 1980 they, too, had gone the way of the Empresses, accepting their fate as floating casinos and cruise ships.

In the face of this decline, and fighting to keep their jobs, the crews on the last Empresses worked hard to keep the passengers they still had. Roberts would sum it up:

> As the competition with the jet plane increased and before it was necessary to employ entertainment managers, artists, hostesses, and other comics, not only did the captains have to take note, but also the staff commanders and pursers take a more active role in entertaining the passengers, in some cases far beyond the remit of their original job titles. Some were natural and others developed certain manners, which they adopted in pursuance of their job and was, in the main, to impress the passengers. This did create some quite memorable situations. But first and foremost, they were all good seamen and could be depended on when the chips were down.

EPILOGUE

More than 100 years after an Act of Parliament had brought it into being, CPL was a conglomerate behemoth — the seventh largest company in Canada in terms of assets, the fifth largest in terms of profits, and the largest in terms of revenue. Its diversification policy had been so successful that it was now more than 160 companies and had more than 127,000 employees. It was the last acquisition made in 1981 that forced it to change course. Buying Canada International Paper just as commodity prices went into a tailspin proved so disastrous that CPL began to mount huge losses and its shares began trading at a discount.

As CP Ships consolidated operations with the purchase of two major freight lines — Dart Containers and Manchester Lines, in 1984, it co-founded Canada Maritime. While its shipping divisions was still making acquisitions, the parent company was selling off subsidiaries and in 1987 Canadian Pacific Airlines went for $300 million, ending one branch of the company's cornerstone, multi-modal transport. In July 1996, no longer headquartered at CP Railway, the company was de-structured into five divisions — PanCanadian Energy, the holding company CPL, CP Hotels, CP Ships, and Fording Coal.

At a dramatic news conference at the Fairmont Royal York Hotel, Toronto, in August 2001, Canadian Pacific Ltd.'s executives unveiled the conglomerate's "starburst" breakup. The five divisions of the company, CP Rail, PanCanadian Energy, CP Ships, Fording Coal, and Fairmont Hotels (bought by CP Ltd. in 1999), were spun off as independent concerns — the feeling was that each was mature enough to generate more investment by itself than as a group. All divisions later suffered in the aftermath of the September 11 terrorist attacks in the United States, but by January 31, 2006, when the last of the "starburst" Fairmont Hotels was acquired by Kingdom Hotels, owned by a prince of the Saudi royal family, each had done very well for investors.

CP Ships had grown from a North Atlantic niche carrier to one of the world's top ten container carriers, with principal markets in transatlantic destinations, Australasia, Latin America, and Asia, and within these operated in 22 trade lanes, most of which were served by two or more of its seven brand names: ANZDL, Canada Maritime, Cast, Contship Containerlines, Italia Line, Lykes Lines, and TMM Lines. By 2003, it was one of the world's leading container-shipping companies with a fleet of 89 ships and employing 4,400 staff worldwide. Its stock prices, just over $11 in 2001, were now on a high of $30, it was about to move out of its Trafalgar Square corporate headquarters for Horley near Gatwick Airport and, for the first time since 1968, the company also revived the red-and-white-checkered flag. Van Horne would have liked that.

Who would have guessed that a year later the company would be (in the parlance of ship's emergency drill) ordering all onboard to lifeboat stations? What mortally wounded the old shipping company were not U-boats, Luftwaffe Condors, or even Boeing 747s, but missteps in corporate governance and strategic blunders in business. When the first-quarter profits were announced on May 11, 2004, there was a minor revelation that new accounting software had forced the removal of US$8 million from the previous year's profits. Then, in August, shareholders were shocked to hear that US$41 million would have to be taken off from previously reported profits over the past two years.

"For years, it had been an open secret in industry circles that CP Ships had not taken the difficult decisions to combine IT systems as it headed off on the acquisition trail," said an opinion piece that month in *Lloyd's List* , later cited in a *Canadian Business* Special Report. Criticisms that the directors of CP Ships should have spent less time acquiring other lines and more on integrating their accounting and IT systems into the fold were rife, to be followed by rumours that senior officers had beneficially traded stocks with certain knowledge of inside information. Both did much to shake shareholders' confidence and damage the credibility of a company that had always prided itself on very high standards of disclosure, transparency, and corporate governance. The Ontario Securities Commission (OSC) called for a hearing just as CEO Frank Halliwell resigned on December 1, 2004, followed by the announcement that company managers would repay the profits earned by inside stock trading.

When CP Ships Ltd. announced on April 28, 2005, that it was going to retire its seven operating brands by the end of the year and re-brand its container shipping services under the CP Ships name, industry analysts knew it was setting itself up for a sale and there were suggestions that the rebranding was a last-ditch defence mechanism. All owned and long-term chartered ships in the fleet would be renamed over the next several months and repainting of funnels and hulls would take place during regularly scheduled dry-dockings in 2006. Suitors were said to include Shanghai's giant China Shipping Group (with 400 ships) that were said to be interested in getting a container company to build in routes where it had less strength, such as Europe and Australia — where CP Ships was strong.

Company chairman Ray Miles explained: "A single CP Ships brand will help us to streamline our corporate structure, improve further our accounting and related business processes and information systems, save costs, strengthen our company culture, and more closely align how we communicate with all of our customers. We look forward to re-establishing the historic CP Ships brand." New standards were also to be introduced for ship names and livery. For the first time in more than 20 years, ship names would be prefixed with "CP," replacing existing brand names. The *Canmar Venture*, for example, would become the *CP Venture*. Ship funnels would carry the CP Ships red and white checkered flag against a field of dark blue and the new colour for hulls would be the same red as in the flag. "We are proud to be establishing a new CP Ships tradition that also connects us to our historic past," Miles concluded.

The company's co-operation convinced the OSC to decline to open a formal hearing just as in July 2005 CP Ships Ltd. confirmed that it was in discussions regarding a possible sale. On August 21, its board of directors unanimously recommended that shareholders accept an offer from Hamburg-based TUI AG to acquire CP Ships in an all-cash transaction for US$21.50 per share or about US$2 billion (1.7 billion euros) on a fully diluted basis. Including the assumption of net debt of $0.3 billion on June 30, 2005, the transaction had a total value of $2.3 billion. The buyer was Hapag-Lloyd AG, which had been created on September 1, 1970, by a merger of the historic shipping lines Hamburg-Amerikanische Packetfahrt-Actien-Gesellschaft (Hapag) and Norddeutscher Lloyd (NDL). Its owners, TUI AG, a European tourism group, said that they planned to combine Hapag-Lloyd and CP Ships to create the world's fifth-largest container shipping company, with a fleet of 139 ships (and a further 17 on order) and a capacity of approximately 400,000 TEU on 100 routes spanning the globe.

On December 14, 2005, the board of CP Ships recommended that their shareholders accept the offer. The final meeting was held at the Fairmont Royal York Hotel in Toronto — the hotel chain itself would be sold off within the year. When the holders of 99.8 percent of the shares approved the sale, the company called CP Ships, formerly Canadian Pacific Steamships and Canadian Pacific Ocean Services, effectively ceased to exist. Historians might argue that the knell of Canadian Pacific's shipping arm came when Adolf Adrion, an executive board member of Hapag-Lloyd took over from Ray Miles, the last British CEO, on January 1, 2006. The company was de-listed on the Toronto Stock Exchange and its shares were no longer available to Canadian investors. Whatever the date, a part of Anglo-Canadian history had ended. The other Canadian institution, the Hudson's Bay Company (HBC), which traced its origins to 1670, barely outlasted Canadian Pacific. On February 27, 2006, CanMaple Leaf Heritage Investments Acquisition Corporation, based in South Carolina, announced that it has been successful in its offer to acquire HBC.

With CP Ships's 82 vessels capable of carrying approximately 195,300 containers and Hapag-Lloyd's 57 units with 215,500 container capacity, the sale was described as a perfect "strategic fit," the fleets complementing each other satisfactorily. While CP Ships had mainly vessels with a capacity up to 4,000 containers, Hapag-Lloyd focused on mega-ships with up to 8,750-container capacity. The joint fleet comprised 139 ships with a total capacity of over 400,000 TEU. The marriage had created the world's fifth-largest container shipping company. And when the job cuts came, inevitable in integrations, most were at CP Ships's former headquarters at Gatwick. On April 19, 2006, TUI AG slashed 2,000 jobs at CP Ships. While reductions affected around 200 sites worldwide, the most — 500 — were at the British office.

Soon, all that will remain of the multi-modal Canadian Pacific conglomerate will be CP Rail — the very beginning of the company — and now the very last.

BIBLIOGRAPHY

Appleton, Thomas E. *Ravenscrag: The Allan Royal Mail Line.* Toronto: McClelland & Stewart, 1978.

Ardman, Harvey. *Normandie: Her Life and Times.* New York: Franklin Watts, 1985.

Boswell, Randy. "Divers Plunge 'Titanic of the West Coast.'" *Ottawa Citizen,* April 27, 2006.

Bowen, Frank C. *History of the Canadian Pacific Line.* London: Sampson Low, Marston & Co. Ltd. 1955.

Canadian Pacific Railway. Department of Colonization and Development (brochure), 1928.

Harrison, Phyllis, ed. *The Home Children.* Winnipeg: Watson & Dwyer, 1979.

Harvey, Clive. *The Last White Empresses.* London: Carmania Press, 2003.

Hustak, Alan. *Titanic: The Canadian Story.* Montreal: Vehicle Press, 1998.

Jones, David Laurenc. *Tales of the CPR*. Toronto: Fitzhenry & Whiteside, 2003.

Knowles, Valerie. *From Telegraph to Titan: The Life of William C. Van Horne*. Toronto: Dundurn Press, 2004.

Krancke, Theodor (Admiral). *Pocket Battleship: The Story of the Admiral Scheer*. New York: W.W. Norton & Company, 1958.

Lamb, W. Kaye. *Empress to the Orient*. Vancouver: Vancouver Maritime Museum Society, 1991.

Musk, George. *Canadian Pacific: The Story of a Famous Shipping Line*. London: David & Charles, 1981.

Stanley, Jo. *Women at Sea: Some Experiences of Canadian Pacific Stewardesses Sailing Out of Liverpool in the Inter-War Years*. Pamphlet in National Maritime Museum, Greenwich.

Turner, Robert D. *The Pacific Princesses: An Illustrated History of Canadian Pacific Railway's Empress Liners on the Pacific Ocean*. Victoria: Sono Nis Press, 1981.

Wallace B. Chung Collection. "Dining in Style." *www.library.ubc.ca/chung/cp_story/cp_story8.html* (accessed April 23, 2007).

Woollett, W. *Have A Banana!* North Battleford, SK: Turner Warwick Publications, 1989.

INDEX

ALSO BY PETER PIGOTT

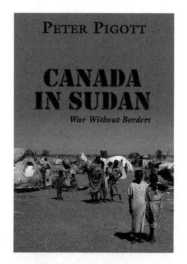

Canada in Sudan: War Without Borders
978-1-55002-849-2
$35.00 / £20.00

An ancient Arab proverb states, "When Allah made the Sudan, he laughed." Had he known the country's future, he would have done better to cry. To most of the world, Sudan means Darfur and the tragedy of atrocities and ethnic cleansing that has occurred there. This book explores this troubled nation, telling the story from ancient times through to the modern era and the work of Canadian archaeologists, aid organizations, and Canadian Forces military observers deployed to Sudan as part of Operation Safari.

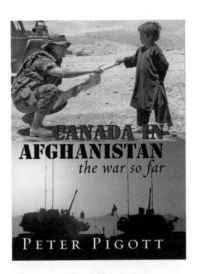

Canada in Afghanistan: The War So Far
978-1-55002-674-0
$35.00 / £18.00

Canada in Afghanistan introduces readers to Afghans and their culture, gives historical background from our involvement since 9/11, and covers operations casualties and the results. Also included is an examination of a new strategic experiment — the provincial reconstruction team and the technological advances used in this war. Cautionary predictions conclude the book. *Canada in Afghanistan* is an introduction to what is happening in the country.

Available at your favourite bookseller.

DUNDURN PRESS
www.dundurn.com

What did you think of this book?
Visit *www.dundurn.com* for reviews, videos, updates, and more!

ALSO BY PETER PIGOTT

Canada in Sudan: War Without Borders

Canada in Afghanistan: The War So Far

Royal Transport: An Inside Look at the History of British Royal Travel

On Canadian Wings: A Century of Flight

Taming the Skies: A Celebration of Canadian Flight

Wings Across Canada: An Illustrated History of Canadian Aviation

Flying Canucks II: Pioneers of Canadian Aviation

Wingwalkers: The Rise and Fall of Canada's Other Airline

Flying Canucks: Famous Canadian Aviators